AROUND THE WORLD
IN 80 PLANTS

An Edible Perennial
Vegetable Adventure
in Temperate Climates

STEPHEN BARSTOW

Permanent Publications

Published by
Permanent Publications
Hyden House Ltd
The Sustainability Centre
East Meon
Hampshire GU32 1HR
United Kingdom
Tel: 0844 846 846 4824 (local rate UK only)
          or +44 (0)1730 823 311
Fax: 01730 823 322
Email: enquiries@permaculture.co.uk
Web: www.permanentpublications.co.uk

Distributed in the USA by
Chelsea Green Publishing Company, PO Box 428, White River Junction, VT 05001
www.chelseagreen.com

Stephen Barstow's website: www.edimentals.com

Photographs © Stephen Barstow, unless stated otherwise

Designed by Two Plus George Limited, wwwTwoPlusGeorge.co.uk

Index by Amit Prasad, 009amit@gmail.com

Printed in the UK by Cambrian Printers, Aberystwyth

All paper from FSC certified mixed sources

The Forest Stewardship Council (FSC) is a non-profit international
organisation established to promote the responsible management of
the world's forests. Products carrying the FSC label are independently
certified to assure consumers that they come from forests that are
managed to meet the social, economic and ecological needs of
present and future generations.

British Library Cataloguing-in-Publication Data
A catalogue record for this book is available from the British Library

ISBN 978 1 85623 141 1

CONTENTS

The author's world record salad with 537 varieties.

ABOUT THE AUTHOR

STEPHEN BARSTOW grew up in the south of England, and spent seven years in the Universities of Exeter, East Anglia in Norwich and Heriot-Watt in Edinburgh, where he was awarded a PhD in 1981 specialising in ocean waves. While a student in Edinburgh, he became interested in organic vegetable growing. A big early inspiration was founder and organic pioneer Lawrence Hills whom he met at HDRA (Henry Doubleday Research Association) in the early 1980s. In 1981, Stephen moved to Trondheim in Norway to work. Both he and his wife were vegetarians, which was virtually unheard of in Norway at that time, and there were only a handful of vegetables available in supermarkets. Growing their own vegetables was therefore a necessity and most of the vegetables Stephen grew in Scotland turned out also to be possible in their new home. He also quickly discovered the Norwegian Useful Plants Society (the over 100-year-old Nyttevekstforeningen, see box, page 210).

Another inspiration in the mid-1980s was Roger Phillips' book *Wild Food*. Contacting Phillips, Stephen was loaned a set of slides from the book which he used in talks on wild edibles in Norway. At the end of the 1980s, he began to collect some of the local wild edibles and planted them in a bed in his garden. About the same time, he obtained a copy of *Sturtevant's Edible Plants of the World* through the Abundant Seed Foundation in the USA. It has notes on some 3,000 different edible species worldwide (N.B. Some are no longer recommended as edible, so don't use this work blindly!). To his surprise, many of the species were perennial plants commonly cultivated in Norwegian gardens.

With assistance from various seed exchange clubs, Stephen's collection of edible plants grew rapidly. Inspired first by Sturtevant and later by Ken Fern and Plants For A Future, Stephen has sown several hundred new species every year in addition to traditional vegetables and the collection peaked at some 3,000 varieties.

Stephen's garden is located on a rocky hillside near the village of Malvik, 15km east of the Norwegian city, Trondheim, and with a beautiful view over Norway's largest fjord, the Trondheimsfjord. Dubbed 'The Edible Garden' when it was presented in a Norwegian television gardening series in 2003, this abundance made it relatively easy for Stephen to set the world record for the greatest number of plant varieties in a salad. This world record attempt took place on 19th August 2001. The final salad had a grand total of 363 distinct plant varieties. However, this was well and truly beaten at the follow-up event on 24th August 2003 when a salad with 537 varieties was put together (see photo opposite).

Stephen has written a number of articles both in the journal of the Norwegian Useful Plants Society, the largest Norwegian gardening magazine, *Hagetidend*, and *Permaculture* magazine. Since 2006, he has been national coordinator of the Norwegian Seed Savers (protecting heritage Norwegian vegetables, including some perennials) and won the 2012 Norwegian Plant Heritage Award.

Over the last few years, Stephen has had a part-time job working for the Norwegian Genetic Resource Centre on collecting old perennial vegetables and herbs from all over Norway, including various Alliums, asparagus, Good King Henry and others.

A Note on the Climate

Stephen's garden is close to 64ºN, in an area of extreme climatic variability. The grass can be green on 1st January and snow might lie for a short while on 1st June. Locals talk about having two seasons – the green and the white winter. However, it is surprisingly mild for the latitude, not far from the Arctic Circle, due to the effect of the North Atlantic drift (continuation of the Gulf Stream). The fjord never freezes in winter and this helps provide a local climate where minimum winter temperatures are seldom much below -20ºC. In fact, even though there is much snow in the hills around, there are long snow-free periods in the garden. This is not necessarily a good thing as a stable snow cover acts as a good insulator for less hardy perennials. The mean monthly temperature ranges from about -3ºC in January to 15ºC in July, so the summers are cool.

CONTACT THE AUTHOR

I would very much appreciate your feedback, comments, seed, plants etc., so please don't hesitate to contact me at:

Email: sbarstow2@gmail.com

Facebook: Stephen Barstow, www.facebook.com/stephen.barstow.7

Facebook groups: Edimentals, Plant Breeding for Permaculture, Friends of *Hablitzia tamnoides* and Friends of Ground Elder

Website/blog: www.edimentals.com

DEDICATION

To my friend Sébastien Verdière and your amazing edible garden at
Château de Valmer: so sad you never made it to Norway,
nor held this book in your hands, bon voyage my friend.

To my dear Mum and Dad

To Alva Barstow, so glad you liked the *ALlium VAlidum* I gave you,
you are my little hope for the future...

DISCLAIMER

We have not included detailed identifications of the type you would find in a field guide as this is mainly a book to inspire perennial vegetable gardening rather than foraging. In any case, many of the plants are found over a wide geographical area and confusion species would vary between region, so this would have been an impossible task to get right. Many of the plants are what I like to call Edimentals (edible ornamentals). If you are purchasing plants, it is preferable to source these from nurseries specialising in edibles as there will be more focus on getting the identification right than for an ornamental nursery. Nevertheless, we take no responsibility for readers misidentifying plants. It is also always advisable to try just a small amount of new plants the first time, as you may be allergic to the plant in question.

ACKNOWLEDGEMENTS

When I look back over the years, there are many people who have helped me along the way. Wandering around my edible garden, many of the plants remind me of people in one way or another. It may have been best not to try to name people here as I am bound to have forgotten people, so very sorry if you're in that category. There follows a short list...

Thanks are due to Robin Allen (a big gardening inspiration in the early days), Telsing Andrews (sister-in-arms, thanks for the interview), Magnar Aspaker (for the Norrland onion), Per Arvid Åsen (Scandinavian monastery plants), Sergey Banketov (for the wild Caucasian Hablitzia and much more), Paul Barney (of Edulis nursery, intrepid edibles explorer), Trevor Barstow (for hating Brussels Sprouts), Jonathan Bates (who discovered Hablitzia in a parallel universe), Alexandra Berkutenko (for giving access to plant material from the Magadan and the Russian Far East, in particular *Aster scaber*), Joost Bogemans (shame about your DisASTER whilst commercialising halophytes), Mats and Marie-Louise Borrefors (my friends at Frostviken Keramikk, for the salad bowls), Emma Cooper (fully fledged ethnobotanist with a wonderful blog), Martin Crawford (forest garden and unusual edible inspiration, Agroforestry Research Trust and newsletter), Lieven David (Belgian Oerprei and much more), Mark McDonough (The Onion Man), Kjell Dragland (the first Norwegian Hablitzia nursery), Stephen Facciola (I wore out your *Cornucopia II*), Ken Fern (hero of Plants For A Future, I wore out your database), Geir Flatabø (his knowledge of the plant world and edimental garden in Ulvik, Norway), Ove Fosså (Vossakvann and Slow Food Norway), Alys Fowler (thanks for coming to Norway and for the great write-up in *The Thrifty Forager*), Reinhard Fritsch (Allium expert at Gatersleben), Marie Gaden (so many of my plants came from Marie), Paolo Gaiardelli (Italian-Icelandic perennial vegetable breeding), Melana Hiatt (you helped so much with sourcing American species in the days of the Wild Forager and Edible Wild email groups), Lawrence Hills (HDRA hero), Stewart Hinsley (all things Malva), Søren Holt (part of the *Allium victorialis* and other stories), Chris Homanics (a man to watch), Molly Hougaard (peas and Hablitzia in Denmark), Lena Israelsson (who perhaps subconsciously sowed the seed that became this book, through her own book, *Jordens Täppor*, introduced me to a number of exciting edibles like Hablitzia and *Allium nutans*), Graham Jenkins-Belohorska (perennial kale breeder), Alvilde Johansen (generous local gardener), Ossi Kakko (who introduced me to Good King Henry as a grain plant), Frank van Keirsbilck (and his wonderful edible garden, Andes in Flanders!), Kirsty McKinnon (coordinated the Norwegian organic garden network for many years), Jan Knuiman (*Aster tripolium* and much more), Leena Lindén (for all your work on Hablitzia in Finland), Judith van Koesveld (Victory Onion pesto from the Lofoten Islands), Jan Erik Kofoed (hero foraging teacher in my area, I learnt so much from you), Helmut Lieth (halophytes), Leda Meredith (an old-timer from Melana's table and queen of New York foraging), Kat Morgenstern (of Sacred Earth fame for all the wonderful advice, knowledge and encouragement), Brynhild Mørkved (Tromsø ethnobotanist who discovered *Allium victorialis* and Hablitzia in Norway), Aiah Noack (Edimentals collaborator), Anemette Olesen (her books inspired my interest in unusual edibles), Arne Odland (sowed a seed in me after I gave my first Round the World talk to the local group of the Norwegian Botanical Society in Trondheim in 2006, encouraging me to convert the talk into a book; it took a long time!), Inger-Lise Østmoe (Fru Matsprell), Li An Phoa (searched for and found Hablitzia in the Caucasus, Spring College), Juerg Plodeck (Species Hemerocallis-man), Saideh Salamati (eats Tromsø Palm!), Misoni Sandvik (foraging stories from her childhood in Korea), Lorna Smith (and the Hoary Mullein in Norwich which started all this), Owen Smith (too far ahead of his time with unusual edible plant company Future Foods from 1989 and all things rhizospheric), Ronny Staquet (Belgian/French Edimentals/Decomestibles), Eileen Stoupe (for sharing), Samuel Thayer (my favourite foraging author), Lila Towle (hero of Danish Seed Savers), Åke Truedsson (Sweden's Allium guru), Justin West (searched for and found Hablitzia in the Caucasus) as did Tycho and Karoline Rosehip as we go to press in September 2014, Ovin Udø (for the 100 year old 'Catawissa' onion from Udøy), and to Robin and Hazel Barstow for posing for the embarrassing pictures. Finally, thanks to whoever has been arranging all the cosmic resonating that's been going on over the last few years above and far beyond mere chance, in particular a memorable day with lactoRita, TeraMeg from Woodstock, VT and Vrrrooonica, together with miracle man Tom Harald Eckell at the Århus andelsgård (CSA) near Skien.

Thanks also to Åsmund Asdal and the Norwegian Genetic Resource Centre, and Svein Solberg and Nordgen for financial support helping with researching the Scandinavian perennial vegetables.

Put a seed into the ground
Wait for the sun to come around
Nurture it with love and care
Give it sun and rain and air

Micky Jones et al., 1972

FOREWORD

by Alys Fowler

I have been patiently waiting for this book and then impatiently pestering for it, drumming my fingers loudly. And then one day it appears. Like everything that you have to wait for in life, it's better for it.

This book speaks of its maker ... It's a wonderfully detailed, often eccentric look at all the plants you've ever wondered were truly edible. Stephen is an extraordinarily clever man with a truly academic approach to knowledge, thus every detail you could wish for is in here. I've been poring over my copy and have made a list of must-try plants, planning how I can rearrange my garden this winter so I can fit in more of these.

There are several reasons why Stephen's work is so important. Firstly, the climate in which Stephen grows is not easy. True, he has a fjord to keep the worst of the freezing temperatures away, but he has a very short growing season. His garden is also on bedrock often just inches below the soil surface. He's a committed permaculturist so you won't find electric strimmers or extra heat for the greenhouse – all his rainwater is recycled and I have a fantastic picture of a year's worth of Norwegian newspapers suppressing weeds.

All of which amounts to this: if he can grow it, so can you.

This tome is a treasure trove of truly useful perennial plants for making healthy, ecologically balanced, edible gardens. Our climate is increasingly unpredictable and many traditionally grown crops are not faring well in such conditions. We need diversity in our crops, we need people like Stephen who explore the boundaries of what's edible and worthwhile to grow, and we need people like you to get inspired and start growing them too. Anyone who reads this book and acts on it is an early adopter of a brave new growing world. Get sowing, write about it, write to Stephen, join social media groups and tell the world that we have found new things to eat and the future tastes fine!

ALYS FOWLER
Garden author and broadcaster

THE PURPOSE OF THIS BOOK

With this book I want to share with you my experiences of some 30 years of trialling a large selection of largely perennial vegetables here in Malvik, Norway. Rather than giving short descriptions of many of the thousands of species and varieties that I've tried, I've settled on giving a more detailed description of around 80 of my favourites, most of which I will use in a normal year and most of which have thrived in my relatively cold climate. The seed of this book was a talk I gave to the local groups of the Norwegian Botanical Society and the Norwegian Useful Plants Society back in 2006-2007. The talk, and now this book, takes the reader on a gastro-botanical journey around the world in search of perennial vegetables and the stories they tell. The journey will take us underground gardening in Tokyo, beach gardening in the UK, and roof gardening in the Norwegian mountains, and will involve stories of the wild foraging traditions of the Sámi people of northern Norway, the rich indigenous food traditions of the Mediterranean peoples, the high altitude ethnobotany of the Rolwaling Sherpas in the Himalayas, wild gathered Sansai and Sannamul or mountain vegetables in Japan and Korea respectively, and a wild aquatic plant that sustained Native American tribes with a myriad of food and other products.

The book is divided into six chapters or legs of this journey, starting fittingly on the streets of London, through western and central Europe, the Mediterranean countries, West Asia, the Caucasus, the Himalayas, Siberia, East Asia, a short stop in Australasia, South America, North America and finally via Greenland to Scandinavia. A number of cosmopolitan species could have been included in any of the chapters and I have in such cases chosen the place or country I most associate with the species or the country with the most interesting story about the plant in question. Thus, for example, the common dandelion becomes French as it is mainly in that country that it is cultivated commercially and sold on markets.

I have also chosen to restrict this book to plants which provide leafy greens, excluding root crops although secondary uses are also mentioned. These are mainly herbaceous plants (i.e. they die right back to the ground in winter) but include a couple of herbaceous climbers and one small deciduous tree. Most of the plants presented will tolerate some shade and about 10% are real woodlanders accepting quite deep shade. Thus, I introduce at the same time a selection of the best perennials suitable in a forest garden system (the table on page 265 gives a look-up summary).

Almost all of the plants in this book have been wild gathered by native peoples even up to recent times. With a few exceptions, such as globe artichoke/cardoon and asparagus, the plants themselves are little improved compared to the wild species. I was therefore surprised to discover that several of these wild plants actually give higher yield than any of my traditional vegetables! I was originally inspired on this quest for perennial vegetables of the world by local foraging traditions where I live, or perhaps lack of traditions, for it is rather ironic that Norway should have a Useful Plant Society (page 210) when traditions here are not particularly rich. I was oblivious to the fact at the beginning that when I started moving some of the best local wild edibles into my garden for convenience, I was doing the same as native people had done for millennia, the first stage of domestication! In fact many of the plants in this book have been cultivated on a small scale in home gardens.

I should thank Alys Fowler, who pointed out during a memorable visit here whilst researching her book *The Thrifty Forager* that when I collected food for dinner in my garden it really wasn't that far removed from foraging. With a large collection of wild gathered plants from throughout the temperate world I could be a Japanese forager one night, a forager in an Italian mountain village the next and maybe my next move should be to invite Japanese, Native American, Nepalese and Italian foragers to an international forage at my place! Now that would be interesting...

In reality, there are a whole range of interactions between people and edible plants from wild gathered to advanced garden cultivars far removed from the wild species. Native peoples would, for example, often manage plants in their wild environment to maintain the plants and increase their yield. This might involve in situ weeding, modifying the habitat through removing trees and shrubs, protecting plants against grazing, and even active planting. This practice is sometimes known as incipient horticulture and target species were most often perennials and plants could be kept living and producing for generations. I realise now that I have been doing all of these things in the semi-wild part of my garden.

Other wild plants were already found in garden environments on disturbed soil; these are what we normally call weeds! But most weeds are edible as they don't need to produce an arsenal of chemicals to protect themselves against grazing animals and some are also perennial. I had for a long time harvested or foraged weeds from my traditional vegetable beds, plants such as common chickweed, *Stellaria media*, which would grow quickly in spring and smother my potato beds and be ready to pick before the potatoes had really started growing. I also let common sow-thistle, *Sonchus oleraceus*, seed itself on the edge of my vegetable beds where they don't really compete, inspired by the Maori of New Zealand who do the same in their vegetable gardens (see page 164). Harvesting weeds then increases total yield on a piece of land, no wonder that it has been practised in many cultures around the globe. In the southwest US and Central America edible weeds are valuable and are known as Quelites. In Japan, we will later see that perennial

Hosta is tolerated by rice farmers as a weed as it has its own value on the market (see page 144). Rivera et al. (2006) use the generic term Cryptocrop for these encouraged or useful weeds.

This book does not discuss the medicinal properties of the plants covered, only in the important preventative medicinal sense. I am convinced from my extensive reading researching this book that the healthiest diet is one rich in a diverse mix of leafy greens incorporating wild and semi-domesticated plants as this provides both more nutritious food and a wider range of protective phytochemicals such as antioxidants. Modern vegetable cultivars have after all largely been selected for other characteristics than nutrition and antioxidant activity, such as yield, transportability and (sweeter, less bitter) flavour.

The authorities here have a campaign to increase vegetables and fruit in the diet *Fem om dagen* or 5-a-day. The Barstow diet/lifestyle recommends 80-a-day (this always gets a laugh at my talks). In addition, if at all possible, do whatever you do manually (digging, biking, walking, mowing...) and you will be set up for a long healthy life. Well, I must be honest that I don't really often manage 80 varieties, the norm in summer is about 20, less in winter! Just aim for as many as possible... This diet has largely been inspired by Mediterranean wild gathered food traditions related in more detail in Chapter 2. It was in Crete, where people could often in the past recognise maybe 100 wild edibles, that the protective nature of a species rich vegetable based diet was first recognised and numerous studies over the last 15 years or so have thoroughly documented similar traditions throughout the Mediterranean, notably in Italy. These multi-species dishes originally inspired my species-rich mixed salads (see page v). It also turns out, at first sight somewhat surprisingly, that there are many common species in these Mediterranean dishes also found growing wild in northern Europe. This is due to the fact that many of the species used are cosmopolitan weeds, having adapted over time to different climates. Therefore, it is possible to reconstruct these Mediterranean-style dishes elsewhere. For example, on page 62, I describe a 56-species Sicilian *calzone* that I made at home. Delicious, fun and highly nutritious. One bite of one of these *calzones* and you will eat a wider range of vegetables than most people nowadays will consume in a lifetime. However, I don't think it is that important to use the same species as used in the Mediterranean, just use what you have at hand.

Although I could have incorporated information with available data on nutrient and antioxidant content of the species included in this book, the data is often not really comparable as levels may vary with harvesting time, weather, growing conditions etc. perhaps giving the wrong conclusions, and there is little data on many of the species included. If you eat quantities of leafy greens from a wide mix of species, you will not need to worry about this.

My choice of species to include in this book has of course largely been determined by what grows well for me here in Norway. If you have a very different climate to me you may well find that some of my favourites do not grow well where you are. If you nevertheless would like to increase your chances of succeeding, then try to source seed/plants from different sources, as there is often a large genetic variation within a given species across its wild range. For example, when I introduced the Caucasian spinach, *Hablitzia tamnoides* (Chapter 4), the seed I provided was from plants which had adapted to Scandinavian conditions with cold winters and mild summers over 100 years. Initial trials of the plant in warmer climates met with limited success, but seed from a wild sourced plant seem to grow better in warmer climes. So please also share your experiences!

As this is primarily a gardening rather than a foraging book, it does not contain detailed descriptions allowing you to identify the plant in question in a wild setting as would be essential for a foraging guide. This would have been a major undertaking as some plants have a very wide geographic range and different confusion species might be present in different areas. It is important to realise that it is not unusual to end up with the wrong plant when starting from seed, particularly if you trade over the internet or obtain seed from seed exchanges as I have largely done, but this also sometimes happens when sourcing from commercial sources. In particular, Allium (onion) species are very often wrong, and even plants in botanical gardens are actually more often wrong than correct! It is probably best to try to source seed and plants from nurseries and organisations specialising in edible plants. Many of the plants in this book are mainly available as ornamentals at present and general nurseries will not be so concerned with selling you the wrong thing as an edible plant nursery would.

I have introduced the term Edimentals (short for edible ornamentals) because these I believe are particularly valuable in a garden as they double as food and ornament. Visiting botanical gardens and other gardens, I've often enjoyed spotting the edimentals in the ornamental borders. There are more than you would perhaps expect. This is not so surprising however, when you realise that an estimated 30% of all wild species have actually been used for food.

This is also not a cookbook, but I have included a number of local traditional recipes and I also describe typical ways of preparing these plants for the table. I personally rarely use recipes anymore and I just improvise, jazz cooking if you like. It's much more fun and dinner's never boring!

In each of the species accounts which follow, I give basic botanical details about each plant including its size, habit, habitat and where it is found in the wild. Other closely related species are discussed plus details of how the plant has been used across its wild range are also given, as is my own personal experience. Finally, details of how to propagate and cultivate the plant in question are given and its availability in the trade is also discussed.

I sincerely hope that this account inspires you to try some of my recommendations and perhaps also some of your own. It's been a lot of fun.

About Perennial or Permavegetables

Apart from complementing traditional vegetables, there are many merits to perennial vegetables as follows:

Advantages

- Low maintenance, more or less looking after themselves, requiring little more than a compost mulch once in a while.
- You don't have to sow and plant every year.
- They lock up more CO_2.
- Many can be grown on marginal land and odd spots in the garden where you wouldn't dream of growing traditional vegetables.
- Many thrive in shady conditions.
- Pests are absent or much less of a problem than in traditional vegetables during the harvest season (spring).
- Watering is also not normally required as soil moisture is often high in the spring when growth is at its maximum; lower energy intensive.
- Nutrient and antioxidant levels are likely to be higher than in traditional vegetables.
- Yields in some species are surprisingly high when you consider these are unimproved wild selections; there is therefore a lot of potential for breeding improved selections.
- Many can double as ornamentals in summer.
- Air drying for preservation is much easier at this time of year as harvest is followed by the driest, warmest weather of the year; preservation by lactofermentation is also easier in warmer weather.
- One can also often harvest repeatedly (cut-and-come-again), although more research is needed to develop optimal cultivation/intercropping strategies (if there is such a thing in polyculture!).
- Perennials are much more robust against the increasing vagaries of the changing climate and bind more CO_2 than traditional vegetables.

- Roots can be forced in winter for fresh out-of-season greens.

- Perennials are probably more productive in marginal areas as they start assimilating solar energy from early spring.

- Some perennial traditional wild crop relatives may have disease resistance (e.g. perennial cabbages may be more resistant to clubroot).

- If you have limited space, it makes more sense growing perennials as vegetables tend to be more expensive in spring.

There are of course also some disadvantages

- The land is permanently occupied and only one harvest a year is usually possible.

- Perennials are mostly productive in the springtime.

- Perennial weeds may reduce yields, but with knowledge weeds can also be a resource.

- Perennials don't last forever and some will need replanting every few years to maintain yields.

- Viruses can be a problem (as is the case with potatoes, garlic, shallots and rhubarb).

- Improved varieties are generally not available (here we can all contribute; join the Facebook group Plant Breeding for Permaculture).

Imagine a world without ready access to supermarkets offering more or less any vegetable at any time of the year. Actually, it doesn't take much imagination. Here in Norway, I can remember that only 25 years ago there were only a handful of vegetables available in supermarkets in winter and the way things are going (climate change, peak oil etc.), in another 20 years seasonal vegetables should once again dominate our consumption. People have in the meantime become more accepting of weird and wonderful vegetables. Therefore, we should be looking at how to diversify locally produced vegetables, so that we can maintain a wide variety of local produce. One group of vegetables that has so far been little exploited are the perennial mainly spring-cropping species. Ken Fern, Plants For A Future and forest gardeners such as Martin Crawford and the late Robert Hart, as well as Eric Toensmeier in the US have done much to show the wide range of plants that could be used. This is my small contribution.

STEPHEN BARSTOW
Malvik, January 2014

chapter 1

WESTERN AND CENTRAL EUROPE

Starting on the streets of London, my selection of 12 perennial vegetables associated with western and central Europe north of the Alps and Pyrenees is a mixed bag taking us to some unlikely places. Three of these plants could actually today be wild-foraged more or less anywhere in the temperate world as they have all been spread from their original wild range in Europe. They are watercress, dandelion and stinging nettle. People have always taken their favourite plants with them on their travels, going back to the Romans and beyond. Primitive and perennial cabbages were no doubt taken northwards as the Roman Empire expanded. This probably also applied to watercress, Good King Henry and Bath asparagus, all common wild-foraged plants in Italy up to the present day. However, there is evidence of some of the wild gathered plant traditions of today's Italy (Chapter 2) having originated in Celtic traditions north of the Alps (Paoletti et al., 1995). Right up to the present day, the cultivation of perennial brassicas has survived in isolated areas throughout northwest Europe, including France, Belgium, Germany, Portugal and the UK. Most were on the edge of extinction! I will introduce you to the Hampshire Perennial Vegetable Triangle, a small area in which two of the best-known British perennial vegetables were domesticated and eventually commercialised. These are sea kale and watercress. In particular, the former should today be a national treasure, perhaps the most British of all vegetables, now ironically being grown commercially on the other side of the English Channel. I will also take you on a visit to the Jurassic clifftop vegetable gardens of Dorset where several well-known and less well-known perennial vegetables grow side by side. Finally, one of the best known and widespread wild onions in Europe, ramsons, is celebrated in a 10-year-old festival in a small German town. However, we kick off the book with the cry of 'crest marine' in London.

Crithmum maritimum

FAMILY: Apiaceae
ENGLISH: Rock Samphire
FRENCH: *Criste Marine*
GERMAN: *Meerfenchel*
ITALIAN: *Finocchio Marino, Bacicci*
SPANISH: *Hinojo Marino*

The rock samphire could perhaps rather have been called death samphire having possibly killed more people than most poisonous plants. It was formerly so sought after as a vegetable that people would risk their lives scaling the precipitous cliffs it inhabits to harvest it. On the streets of London, the cry of 'crest marine!', its popular name, would have been commonplace. Shakespeare described this 'dreadful trade' in King Lear in the early 17th century:

> 'Come on, sir; here's the place: stand still. How fearful
> And dizzy 'tis to cast one's eyes so low!
> The crows and choughs that wing the midway air
> Show scarce so gross as beetles: half way down
> Hangs one that gathers samphire, dreadful trade!
> Methinks he seems no bigger than his head:
> The fishermen that walk upon the beach
> Appear like mice.'

This was inspired by the samphire harvest at Dover and today this place is known as Shakespeare Cliff. Marginally safer is the harvesting technique developed by Welsh naturalist John Price (school friend of Charles Darwin). He is quoted as saying, 'Here true samphire grows, which we used to get by shooting it down'! Further, diarist Samuel Pepys is known to have been given a barrel of samphire in 1660. The popularity of this vegetable declined as it became scarcer and was almost unknown from the late 19th century.

Rock samphire's range is from the UK and Helgoland in Germany in the north, southwards along the Atlantic coastlines of Europe, throughout the Mediterranean and also on the Black Sea coasts of Crimea and the Caucasus. In the UK, it is rare north of Suffolk on the east coast and is rare in Scotland on the west. Here in

1 & 2: Wild rock samphire is nowadays protected from commercial harvesting; Health and Safety legislation would probably have forbidden its harvest anyway! Here growing on top of the chalk cliffs on the Dorset Jurassic coast.

Norway, it was unknown until around the year 2000 when it started appearing along the southern coasts and this has been seen as a strong indication of climate change. This is because its occurrence seems to be linked to coastlines with January mean temperatures above 4°C. Apart from cliffs it's nowadays quite a common plant growing on sea defence walls. In Mediterranean countries, it has also colonised old castles and ruins. *Crithmum* is a so-called monotypic genus in the carrot family (i.e. there is only one species), and actually grows alongside wild carrot on English chalk cliffs. It is a low growing perennial, woody at the base.

3: Brittany's Salicorne au Vinaigre, *still harvested commercially on the mudflats; nowadays increasingly also cultivated with seawater irrigation in Mexico and other countries; behind the jar is my pot grown* Salicornia quinqueflora, *an interesting Australasian tender perennial species.*

This plant was mostly used in the past to make a popular pickle. A 17th century text said, '...of all the sauces, there is none so pleasant, none so familiar and agreeable to Man's body as samphire.' The best time to gather the leaves, stripping them from the coarse stems, is in the spring before flowering. The seeds are also sometimes pickled or used as a spice later in the year.

Nowadays, the samphire that is sometimes available commercially is not usually *Crithmum*, but rather various annual Salicornia or glasswort species. In the past, Salicornia, *Inula crithmoides* (golden samphire) and *Suaeda maritima* (sea blite) were substituted for real samphire. In the 19th century this 'cheating' was looked down upon, as the real thing was far superior as Saul Dixon (1855) relates: 'The pickled Salicornias taste of nothing but the vinegar and the spices...'

In Mediterranean countries, *Crithmum* has also traditionally been an important wild gathered plant back to ancient times and is still collected locally today.

Hedrick (1919) records that the first reference to *Crithmum* being cultivated was in Quintyne's *The Complete Gardener* from 1693. Thereafter there are few references to its cultivation in the 18th century and for the first time in the US in 1821. In the 19th century, growing your own samphire was suggested as the only way to be sure of getting the real thing. However, this didn't really take off in a big way. In a letter in the *Transactions of the Horticultural Society of London* in 1822, John Braddick tells of his positive experience with growing rock samphire in London. He had paid for the collection of a plant from Portland together with 'a ton of the soil and white chips of the white rock in which it grows.' (N.B. digging up plants is illegal today.) He made sure that the planting place was free draining down to five feet! He writes, 'It has continued to flourish with me for some years and has never failed to produce for the use of my family an ample supply of young shoots, which are cut twice in a season.' His advice fortunately doesn't have to be followed literally, but good drainage and a warm location as in a south facing wall is advisable, particularly for inland gardens with mid-winter average temperatures near or below 4°C. It may also be necessary to protect the plants in cold weather ... and make sure you collect some seed just in case.

I'd never successfully grown this plant; even in summer it just seems to stagnate as it's too cold and I have nothing like a southward facing sea wall to satisfy it. However, in 2012 I grew it successfully inside and was able to harvest it at Christmastime. I adapted a recipe I found on the Celtnet Recipes website for 'rock samphire hash' (see box).

At present both plants and seed are available in Europe, but are less commonly offered in the US. Like other umbellifers, seed quickly loses its viability, so source fresh seed if possible. I've several times found seed in winter in various parts of the plant's range. Division can also propagate it and root cuttings are probably also possible. In the south of its range, it is recommended to sow seed in autumn. Germination is then relatively quick and the seedlings will need to stand over winter and may need protecting, as they are sensitive to sub-zero temperatures. In colder areas, sowing in late winter outside is the best strategy.

Plants should be cut back hard to maintain a compact growth form and plentiful new leaves. Where rock samphire thrives, it will self-sow.

In recent years, this plant is one of the halophytic (salt-tolerant) plants being studied for biosaline agriculture

Improvised Malvik Rock Samphire Hash

Combine rock samphire, olives, cucumber and a few capers. Mix a little vegetable stock (I used bean cooking water), a little vinegar, garlic and chilli, lemon zest and juice with black pepper and nutmeg and bring to the boil. Add the samphire mix and simmer for half an hour. Whisk up an egg yolk and gradually add with slivers of butter, stirring until the mixture has thickened.

4 & 5: Rock samphire in the Chelsea Physic Garden, London (left) and in a naturalistic setting in Kew Gardens, London (right).

(see the account of *Aster tripolium* in Chapter 6). It is seen as a potential future oil seed crop. Incidentally, Salicornia also has oil rich seeds and is already cultivated for oil in Mexico.

A comeback for this neglected aromatic vegetable is long overdue!

Crambe maritima

FAMILY: Brassicaceae
ENGLISH: Sea Kale
FINNISH: *Merikaali*
FRENCH: *Chou Marin*
GERMAN: *Meerkohl*
NORWEGIAN / SWEDISH / DANISH:
   Strandkål
PORTUGUESE: *Couve-marinha*
RUSSIAN: *Katran Primorskoi*
SPANISH: *Col Marina*

As people have moved around the world, they have always taken their favourite vegetables with them. The Romans certainly did, introducing various favourites to Britain, as did Europeans who colonised North America and Australasia, Indians and Pakistanis to the UK, and modern day migrant workers in western countries. Sea kale is debatably the most British of all vegetables and I took it with me to Norway when I migrated here in the early 1980s, along with broad and runner beans.

I remember buying it after seeing an advert for sea kale thongs in *The Garden* (Journal of the Royal Horticultural Society) in the early 1980s. Thongs are just a fancy name for sea kale root cuttings. I had been looking out for these as I had read about sea kale in John Seymour's *Self-Sufficient Gardener*. I prepared a special beach bed, a sloping area above my pond, adding seaweed and shell sand to the earth and a mulch of gravel on top. Almost 30 years on and I still have those plants in my garden and I still harvest the spring shoots every spring, the most perennial of my perennial vegetables!

Sea kale is a halophyte or salt tolerant plant (see box on page 236), found on both sandy and shingly seashores. It has also colonised the gaps between the basalt blocks on Dutch sea walls. It has a so-called disjunct geographic distribution being found both on coasts of northwest Europe as well as the Black Sea coasts of Crimea, the Sea of Azov and the Western Caucasus. It is commonest in the UK along the south coast from Suffolk to Cornwall and also in North Wales and northwest England. It is scarce in Scotland and Northern Ireland. Otherwise it can be found in northern France, and increasingly in the Netherlands and southern Scandinavia. It has also naturalised in a few places on the west coast of the US.

The gathering of wild sea kale along the coasts of the UK is no doubt a very old tradition and is documented from the 17th century. The well-known English diarist and gardener John Evelyn (1699) wrote '...our sea-keel (the ancient Crambe) ... growing on our Coast, are very delicate...' Growing on unstable beaches, some plants would naturally have been buried during winter storms and people would have discovered that the resultant blanched spring shoots had a better, less bitter taste. This led local people to the idea of managing the plants in situ by heaping sand,

6: Sea kale in typical beach habitat; people would heap shingle over the plants to blanch the young shoots.

7: A sign in the Chelsea Physic Garden in London, next to traditional sea kale forcing pots, commemorates William Curtis as the most important catalyst for the popularisation of sea kale as a vegetable in England.

shingle or seaweed over the crowns in the spring, before growth started. Management of wild gathered plants is well known elsewhere in the world and is a primitive form of gardening, the edible product being enhanced by local temporary habitat modification. Perhaps this natural sea kale blanching gave the idea for blanching other strong tasting vegetables?

Domestication of sea kale seems largely to have been due to the efforts of the botanist William Curtis, who was Praefectus Horti at the Chelsea Physic Garden in London in the 1770s. It is still grown there (see photo 7). He wrote a pamphlet, 'Directions for the culture of the Crambe maritima or Sea Kale, for the use of the Table' in 1799 to bolster his efforts in introducing it as a market vegetable. Some years prior to this, in the mid 18th century, well-known English naturalist/ecologist Gilbert White was growing sea kale. His garden was in Selborne in Hampshire, only five miles from Curtis's home in Alton. In 1753, it was to be found on the market in Chichester, apparently cultivated. White and Curtis lived incidentally only 15 miles from Alresford where that other great British vegetable, watercress, was also soon to be commercialised. Alresford, Selborne and Alton should be celebrated as the Hampshire perennial vegetable triangle or the UK hotspot of perennial vegetable domestication.

Curtis's work provided the initial stimulus for the popularity of this vegetable over most of the 19th century, both wild collected and cultivated. However, so much was gathered on the English coasts to meet the demand from London markets that it became a rare plant in the wild. It is nowadays protected in the UK and elsewhere, so there's even more reason to cultivate it.

It took only a few years for word to spread to North America. The *American Gardener's Calendar* was the most comprehensive gardening book in the United States in the first part of the 19th century. US President Thomas Jefferson is said to have been inspired to try sea kale when he read about it in *The Calendar*. It became one of Jefferson's favourite vegetables.

A German translation of Curtis's paper on sea kale appeared in 1801, but it never seems to have taken off in a similar way in Europe. Vilmorin-Andrieux (1920) in France says that sea kale had followed the British around the world and although some people grew it in France, there was usually some English connection. He wrote: 'It has gone to America and the Antipodes, but has not crossed the Channel.' So, what happened to the vegetable that should be a national treasure in England? Today, roles are reversed and it is grown commercially, albeit on a small scale, on the Continent but not as far as I'm aware in the UK. Elsewhere, it seems also to have been domesticated in its Black Sea range, but little information seems to exist apart from a record of it being grown as a vegetable in the Caucasus in the 1930s.

For the best information about the cultivation of sea kale, your best bet is actually to consult gardening books from the 19th century as most devote several pages to this popular, at that time, vegetable.

When sea kale is in seed it is easy to tell from most other brassicas, as the seedpods are spherical, each hard pod containing one seed. The pods are purpose designed to float on the sea, dispersing by wave and current action along the coast in winter storms. The best way to germinate seeds is to observe what happens in nature. No, I'm not going to ask you to collect seawater and float your seeds for several days before sowing ... Some authors advocate shelling the seeds (a laborious process if you want many plants), others (such as Vilmorin-Andrieux, 1920), explicitly state that you should sow them in their pods. If possible, I would suggest sowing them as fresh as possible in autumn or as early in the winter as possible and exposing them to winter weather in a cold frame. The chances are higher that they will germinate in the spring the earlier one sows the seed and the more rough winter weather they experience. They will probably germinate unevenly over time and some may not germinate before the following year, so don't give up if you get no germination, this is a vegetable you may well have for the rest of your life! Unlike other brassicas, sea kale seed loses its viability quite quickly, so make sure your seed is fresh.

If you want more plants, you may wish to take root cuttings or thongs yourself. It is usually recommended that these are taken in the autumn and that they are stored over winter in a cool place in wet sand. Thongs are normally the straight side roots coming off the main root and are typically about 1cm in diameter and between five and 10cm long.

Sea kale will grow best on well-drained sandy soil in full sun. Dig in half-rotten organic manure or ideally seaweed before planting. In the 19th century it was recommended to plant three plants in each station and about two feet apart and stagger the rows for maximum yield. As sea kale grows quite slowly, the spaces between the young plants were used to grow other quicker-growing plants such as cauliflowers, spring cabbages and lettuce. They were sometimes also intercropped with asparagus, another seaside perennial vegetable with similar cultural and fertiliser requirements. Another possibility is to interplant with salt-loving *Aster tripolium* (see Chapter 6) which will also add colour to the bed. In the long term it's best to be patient and don't be tempted to start harvesting too early. Starting from seed, in warmer climates you can start harvesting at 2-3 years old and at 1-2 years old from thongs or plants. I don't normally cut off the flowers as it's an attractive plant, but, for maximum yield, it would be best to remove them as they appear making sure you eat the tasty, milder sea kale 'broccolis'! This way, the plant doesn't waste energy in producing seed. Incidentally, sea kale is self-incompatible (i.e. it needs to cross-pollinate) and you will therefore need at least two different plants to produce seed.

Due to sea kale's rather strong taste, it is usually blanched and this is most easily accomplished using a large clay or plastic pot. In the 19th century, the special clay kale pots were for the rich as they were (and are still) rather expensive. It was claimed by some that simple earthing up of the plants led to a more delicately flavoured crop than those forced in the warmer conditions under the pots.

8: The sweetly scented sea kale flowers add beauty to the edible garden in mid-summer.

9: The grey-green creeping leaves of sea kale are also attractive, here used as an edging plant on a border at RHS Garden Wisley in the UK.

Whether this was just a kick at those who could afford the extravagance of a designer pot I don't know, but there could well be something in it...

I had a chuckle though when I read the following in a book by Edmund Saul Dixon (using a pseudonym!) in 1855:

> 'A caution should be given to avoid a mode of culture highly approved by many who grow to sell, but do not themselves eat, sea kale. Instead of protecting and blanching the shoots by a covering of sweet earth, they overwhelm their beds with a barrowful of leaves collected in autumn (oak leaves are most in vogue), and just shovel them on one side when the crop is fit for the knife. This plan has not a single advantage over the earthing system, except indulging the laziness of the cultivator; for any decrepit old woman could sprinkle a few apronfuls of leaves over her garden; but the other mode requires an able-bodied man to execute it properly...'

I won't ever be able to blanch with leaves again without reflecting on this passage.

In the 19th century they would also sometimes add a deep layer of fresh manure between the blanching pots as a hot bed, the heat from the rotting manure giving an even earlier crop. Some big estates would even force sea kale for Christmas as a special treat. Roots could be dug up in the autumn and forced like chicory under cover (you could also plant your sea kale closer together than recommended and use the thinnings for forcing). It was recommended to take a piece of the crown when cutting the blanched sea kale. The same is recommended for dandelion sold at markets (see photo 70 on page 46) because the leaves don't then wilt so quickly.

My experience is that sea kale is hardy down to about -15 to -20°C without winter protection or snow cover. Earthing up in the autumn for spring blanching can therefore serve a double purpose in areas in the marginal sea kale survival zone. I thought I had finally lost my oldest plant after a recent very cold winter but shoots did finally emerge in June from deeper thongs that hadn't died!

Sea kale has resistance to many diseases and pests of the cabbage tribe. Personally, I've never seen slug damage to the spring shoots which some report. They only attack my plants late in the season when the leaves have completed their mission. If you do have problems with spring slug damage and have access to fresh seaweed, you could mulch your plants with it, benefitting the sea kale and the salt deterring the slugs.

France and the Netherlands have taken the lead in commercial production of sea kale. Research carried out in France, where forced sea kale has been available on a small scale, is reported by Péron (1990). Similar techniques to that used for commercial production of Witloof chicory have been developed and modern micro-propagation techniques have been used for initial rapid increase of cultivars. In the Netherlands, we will discuss the market success of salt tolerant *Aster tripolium* in

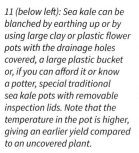

10 (left): The spring 'purple brain' leaves.

11 (below left): Sea kale can be blanched by earthing up or by using large clay or plastic flower pots with the drainage holes covered, a large plastic bucket or, if you can afford it or know a potter, special traditional sea kale pots with removable inspection lids. Note that the temperature in the pot is higher, giving an earlier yield compared to an uncovered plant.

12 (right): Freshly harvested blanched sea kale (right), the flowers resemble small broccolis and are also delicious, with unblanched sea kale (top right) and the light green cultivar 'Lilywhite' (top left). Also shown are leaves of Aster tripolium (see Chapter 6) and annual edible Atriplex prostrata (left) which germinated in the seaweed mulch.

Chapter 6 and this has inspired attempts at farming other salt tolerant vegetables. Since 2008, sea kale has been grown commercially on the island Texel in the Wadden Sea and has so far been well received by the market. *Crambe maritima* is a genetically variable species and little research has so far been carried out into selecting better varieties.

Seed, thongs and plants are relatively easy to source in the UK at present. The RHS Plant Finder listed 30 nurseries offering the plant in 2014 and three nurseries offered the light green leaved cultivar 'Lilywhite', a variety that has been around since at least the early 1900s. Seed, including 'Lilywhite', can also be purchased from various seed companies, although be aware that cultivars will not necessarily come true from seed. Thongs are also currently available from one seed company in the UK. They are offering a new variety, 'Angers', which is described as 'highly productive giving more succulent stems which blanch more readily than other varieties.' Other old varieties, 'Feltham White', 'Ivory White' and 'Pink Tipped' seem sadly to have been lost. In North America, seed is also sometimes available.

Sea kale can be used in the kitchen in many different ways, from simply steaming and serving with melted butter, to boiled and fried with chilli and garlic, and in oriental stir-fry dishes. According to the book *The Kitchen Garden* (Saul Dixon, 1855) the following was the usual non-aristocratic way to serve it: '...pile it on sippets of toasted bread previously soaked in kale-water, and pour over it some white sauce, or melted butter...'

Join me in enjoying this aristocrat of the vegetable kingdom!

Nasturtium officinale (syn. *Rorippa nasturtium-aquaticum*)

FAMILY: Brassicaceae
CHINESE: *Dou Ban Cai, Sai-Yeung Choi*
ENGLISH: Watercress
FRENCH: *Cresson de Fontaine, Cresson d'Eau*
GERMAN: *Brunnenkresse*
ITALIAN: *Cressione Aquatico*
JAPANESE: *Kureson, Mizu Garashi, Oranda Garashi*
RUSSIAN: *Kreson, Kress Vodianoi*
SPANISH: *Berro*

I grew up in Eastleigh in Hampshire, UK, only about 12 miles from the centre of watercress production in Alresford. My mum bought bunches of watercress at the greengrocers and we ate it either in watercress and cheddar cheese sandwiches or in mixed salads. Surprisingly perhaps, I actually enjoyed the peppery taste as a kid. Mum told me that she was well aware that watercress was both nutritious and healthy. The harvested plant doesn't have a long shelf life and much of the crop was sold locally and via the Watercress railway line to Covent Garden in London.

Nasturtium officinale is a truly wild plant in southern and central Europe, North Africa and West Asia. However, it has been introduced as a vegetable and has naturalised on a large scale worldwide, including China, Japan, the Philippines, South Africa, Australasia and North America. It has spread in the US on such a scale that it is now on the noxious weed list of 46 states. Steve Brill, well-known US forager, jokes that its spread is due to all those people sloppily eating their watercress sandwiches on river banks, pieces falling into rivers and rooting! For this semi-aquatic perennial grows typically in slow-moving streams and in ditches, often preferring alkaline conditions such as in the chalk streams and rivers of Hampshire where its UK cultivation started.

Watercress has since ancient times been one of the most popular wild-foraged greens in Europe, its popularity eventually leading to its domestication. However, there is a small but real danger of contracting liver fluke from the wild plant. Therefore, it is safest to use wild watercress cooked rather than in salads. Nevertheless, the wild plant is widely reported as being used in salads and it is actually pretty safe if one only picks the shoot tips well above water level where the larvae are found as they apparently cannot climb.

In Spain, a recent study ranked watercress the most popular traditionally foraged vegetable (Tardio et al., 2006). Similarly, it has been commonly used throughout Italy. We can get some kitchen inspiration from traditional Italian recipes such as

13: Watercress in its natural habitat along the River Itchen at Allbrook, Hampshire, where I was born!

mixed salads (e.g. with dandelion and chicory), simply boiled and fried in olive oil with chilli or try watercress pesto (simply replace the basil in a standard pesto recipe with watercress leaves and serve over pasta). In France, *potage cressonnière* is a popular thick watercress and potato soup.

In the Far East, watercress has also become quite popular and it is almost always cooked, excellent in stir-fries and used in wonton soups. In Japan, watercress was introduced by foreigners around the 1870s and became known as 'Dutch mustard'. It is nowadays known as *kureson* after the French *cresson*. It has also been popular in Japan in a European-style soup or as an *ohitashi* dressed salad (the greens are boiled, chilled and then flavoured with a soy sauce, *dashi* and *katsuobushi* dressing).

In North America, well known foraging writer Euell Gibbons devotes a whole chapter to watercress in his 1962 book *Stalking the Wild Asparagus* under the title 'The Nose Twister King of Wild Salad Plants'! The nose twister bit alludes to the Latin meaning of Nasturtium from nasus (nose) and tortus (twisted). By the time Gibbons was foraging in the US, watercress was already found naturalised in every US state and his encouragement to the reader to plant it in the local stream certainly did nothing to slow its spread. He considers this plant as a welcome introduction and says it is the salad plant with the longest season of any wild collected plant (harvestable in all but one month of the year, January). Many Native American tribes had also learnt to appreciate it as a valuable vegetable, eating it as a salad and cooked.

Watercress cultivation can be traced back on a small scale to the *cressonnières* in France mentioned in documents from the 12th and 14th centuries, although it is likely that it was also cultivated in ancient times in the Mediterranean region. What we would recognise today as commercial cultivation originates in the late 18th century in Germany from where that great vegetable innovator Napoleon (see also *Bunias orientalis*, page 99) imported the technology to France (near Versailles) in the early 19th century. The first watercress cultivation known from the UK, at Gravesend in Kent, is from about the same time. Its cultivation has since spread on a small scale to many countries around the globe, including the US, southeast Asia, many African countries, New Zealand and Australia. The town Huntsville, Alabama in the US touted itself as the watercress capital of the world in the first part of the 20th century, but production is much reduced today.

In the UK, watercress is today grown on special spring-fed beds, through which the water flows at a controlled rate and depth with a nearly constant temperature throughout the year of a little over 10°C. Due to the susceptibility of this plant to viruses, plants are nowadays, at least in temperate countries, almost always grown commercially from seed as annuals. In some parts of the world such as Africa, it is however still largely propagated vegetatively. Although mechanical harvesters have been developed this is still largely a crop involving much manual labour. A few farms

14-17: The centre of the watercress universe in the Hampshire village Old Alresford.

have also grown watercress organically since the mid-1990s. There aren't many cultivars and the most common variety is 'Dark Green American'. In the past, a naturally occurring hybrid between the two closely related species *Nasturtium officinale* and *N. microphyllum* (One-rowed watercress), known as brown cress (as it inherited the brownish winter leaves of *N. microphyllum*), was cultivated. However, this sterile clone had to be vegetatively propagated and the build-up of viruses led to its demise. Selections of late-flowering strains have been made locally by farmers to extend the season as long as possible into the summer. A variety 'Aqua' is currently sold by several UK seed companies and is described as crisp textured with a pungent flavour.

In a garden, it is not necessary to have running water for successful cultivation of watercress and it will also grow well in ordinary garden soil as long as the soil is kept damp. Some people make special trenched beds using a layer of clay or plastic to keep the soil damp. In Japan, watercress is often grown on balconies in special hydroponic boxes specially designed for the purpose. It is, however, important to bear in mind that it is a cold season crop and long summer days above 12 hours stimulate the plant to flower. Watercress is also not very hardy and therefore not easy to overwinter in cold gardens. Under commercial production, fields can be flooded to protect the plants during cold periods.

Both plants and seed are available from nurseries and seed merchants and if you are lucky enough to be able to buy packets of watercress in your area, it's worth knowing that it is easy to root the stems! Watercress tolerates quite shady conditions. It is most often sold nowadays in packets of mixed salad greens together with rocket and

18: Brooklime, Veronica beccabunga, *is very hardy and is one of the possible watercress surrogates you might want to try if you can't grow the real thing.*

baby spinach. In marginal areas temperature-wise, try growing your watercress under cover in a cold greenhouse or use cloche protection or similar. *Nasturtium microphyllum* is also reputedly hardier. If you're in a watercress-unfriendly area, you could try one of the alternatives with a similar taste, such as land cress (*Barbarea verna*), wintercress (*Barbarea vulgaris*, see Chapter 6) and brooklime (*Veronica beccabunga*). It would be nice if the old hybrid brown cress had been available to the home gardener, but I've never seen it offered. Where watercress thrives, it grows quickly and can be cut several times during the long growing season. A perennial bed can reputedly be maintained for 10 years or more.

In recent years, watercress has been marketed as a superfood following studies claiming that it is full of antioxidants and other goodies and protects against some forms of cancer. Well, I reckon my mother already knew that in the 1950s!

Brassica oleracea (var. *ramosa, viridis* and *acephala*)

FAMILY: Brassicaceae
ENGLISH: Kale
FRENCH: *Chou d'Aigrette*
GERMAN: *Grünkohl*
SPANISH: *La Col Verde*

When I was a kid, we would often spend our holidays in a campsite at a place called Durdle Door, near Lulworth Cove in Dorset. The 'Door' is a natural arch on what is now known as the Jurassic Coast. I was unaware until a few years ago that on top of the cliffs one can see a selection of fossil vegetables. These have been considered to be the wild progenitors of three of our commonest vegetables, wild cabbage (*Brassica oleracea* var. *oleracea*), wild carrot (*Daucus carota* ssp. *carota*) and sea beet (*Beta vulgaris* ssp. *maritima*). I also found another formerly cultivated vegetable already discussed in this chapter, rock samphire (*Crithmum maritimum*) cohabiting with the others. Apart from wild carrot, the other three are all perennial species.

It has long been debated whether the wild cabbage found along the Atlantic coastlines of Europe from Britain, France to the Iberian peninsula and Mediterranean is actually the species originally domesticated from and resulting in the myriad of forms available today from heading cabbages to kales to kohlrabis. Genetically, the Atlantic material is closest to our present cultivated forms, compared to other candidate species in the northern Mediterranean area. However, the latest research (Maggioni et al., 2010) points to the Atlantic populations having rather 'gone wild'

19: Wild cabbage atop the Jurassic cliffs at Durdle Door, Dorset.

than being truly wild. So, it now seems likely that the Romans or Saxons introduced primitive cabbages to Britain, and plants had escaped in the past and established the present day cliff top populations. It is therefore not surprising that these escaped cabbages show similar genetics to present day brassicas. It seems that a number of closely related Mediterranean species were the actual starting point for today's brassicas, all of which were perennials.

Kales are the most primitive of today's cultivated brassicas and it seems that branching bushy kales are closest to *Brassica cretica*, a species from Greece and Turkey, whilst stem kales are related either to *Brassica rupestris* (from Italy and Sicily) or *B. incana* (Italy and the Balkans) (Dixon, 2006). All of these species inhabit cliff top and montane habitats out of reach of grazing animals and often on lime, just like the Atlantic wild cabbage. Relic primitive wild kale populations are also known from the Crimea (*B. rupestris/incana*) and Lebanon (*B. cretica*). Primitive kales have also been cultivated locally around the Aegean up to modern times and these plants resemble our sprouting broccolis. Other species include *Brassica montana* (syn. *B. oleracea* ssp. *robertiana*) and *B. insularis* of the western Mediterranean.

In recent ethnobotanical studies in the Mediterranean countries, Rivera et al. (2006) document that *B. cretica* has been wild gathered for food up to modern times and *B. montana* is still used in the Garfagnana in Italy (Pieroni, 1999). In fact, in one part of this mountain valley, it is a good omen to come across and eat a leaf of this plant as the people in the past worshipped St. Viano, a recluse in the Middle Ages, who is said to have survived eating only wild kale! Popularity of these wild brassicas would have given the original impulse towards their domestication. Pliny the Elder who lived in the 1st century AD is quoted by several authors as referring to the Tritian kale which was propagated by cuttings.

Despite their neglect in the vegetable gardening literature, several forms of perennial kale have survived into the 21st century and thanks to interest in permaculture and perennial vegetables their future seems now more certain. Some amateur breeders are now even putting effort into developing new varieties. They are all easy to propagate from cuttings. There follows an overview of the most common types of perennial cabbages/kale:

Daubenton

This variety has a low bushy spreading form and is the perennial kale which is most readily available

20: Dorset clifftop wild cabbage in my garden.

commercially, various nurseries offering it in France. Its history doesn't seem to be known, although it has been suggested that 18th century naturalist Louis Jean-Marie Daubenton discovered it. It is apparently not a reference to the district of Aubenton in northern France near the Belgium border. Vilmorin-Andrieux describes it as 'chou vivace de Daubenton' in 1856. Fearing Burr (1865) refers to it as 'Daubenton's Creeping Borecole'. It is claimed that this kale was commonly cultivated in the Middle Ages, but I haven't found confirmation of this. A superb variegated form, 'Daubenton panaché', is also available and is a good candidate for the edimental garden, the variegation being yellow on young leaves turning white as the leaves age. I received both of these as cuttings and I was surprised by their vigour, productivity and healthy appearance over most of the season. The variegated plant wasn't that much less vigorous than its green-leaved sister, but has proved more difficult to overwinter. Although they are quoted as reaching 1m when mature, my plants grew the 1m laterally, the stems eventually lying along the ground and rooting in a few places. Thus the Daubentons could easily spread to cover a large area with time if given bare earth in which to root. A friend of mine called this one walking kale, an allusion to the walking onion (Allium x proliferum, Chapter 6). It is also claimed that they can live for 40 years. Ken Fern (1997) tells us that he obtained a plant from a friend in 1994 but it had not grown very well for him as it had proven a magnet for caterpillars and slugs. In the US, the Daubenton name seems to have metamorphosed into Dorbenton. However, it has also been claimed that Dorbenton is a self-seeded plant originating from Daubenton. In 2012, I was surprised to be offered seed of Daubenton from the Heritage Seed Library in the UK, but the resultant plants are quite different to my Daubentons which actually did flower this year. As a late flowering purple broccoli was also flowering, I've crossed the two and am excited to see what the offspring will be like! A purple sprouting perennial kale must be the ultimate dream of the permie brassica breeder! Watch this space!

Ehwiger kohl / Eeuwig moes (Eternal cabbage)

This is another low growing bushy form, seemingly closely related to Daubenton. Zeven et al. (1996) show that Eeuwig moes has survived to modern times particularly in the Dutch province of Limburg in the east of the country near the German border, but also locally in Germany and Belgium. Zeven also mentions that relic perennial kales have also survived in the UK, France and Portugal, suggesting that the present patchy distribution could point to a much more widespread distribution in the past. References are given to similar material being grown in England and Ireland as 'Hungry Gap' and as cut-and-come-again in Scotland. There's a strong possibility that both of these have been lost in the UK, the present 'Hungry Gap' being biennial. Material of Ehwiger kohl was collected from home gardens and some 50 plants were analysed for various characteristics, which showed that there were various distinct types.

21 (left): Bushy Daubenton, 'Daubenton panaché' (variegated) and single-stemmed tree collards (at the back) in my garden.

22 (above): **Ehwiger kohl** *or* **Eeuwig moes** *during its first year in my garden.*

Most of the plants were found not to flower. It is considered to taste better and is tenderer than Daubenton. Also in Germany, a blog tells of the wild cabbage on the island Helgoland about 70km off the coast in the North Sea and that the plants there resemble Ehwiger Kohl. Some seed companies offer wild Atlantic cabbage seed and Ken Fern considers it worth growing, reaching 1m tall and 60cm wide, and living up to five years. He comments that the slight bitterness enhances the flavour.

Couve Poda

Perennial kales have also survived in remote regions along the Atlantic coastal zone in Portugal (Dias, 2012). Most commonly known as *Couve Poda* or *Couve de Mil Folhas*, the names *Couve de Pernada*, *Couve de Mil Cabeças*, *Couve Vegetativa* and *Couve de Estaca* have also been recorded. These names refer either to its vegetative propagation, thousand heads or leaves/rosettes or its branching habitat. The aforementioned document has a couple of pictures of these much-branched purple tinged cabbages that are being conserved in Portugal and at Gatersleben in Germany. The sweetish tasting leaves are both used as leafy vegetables in soups or just boiled and served with meat or fish. An interesting illustration from 1586 exists of what is believed to be this kale! Genetic analysis (Zeven et al., 1998) showed that the Portuguese perennial kales were distinct from other kales. These kales also seldom flower.

Tree Collards

This is a very different perennial kale with a single stem branching some way above the ground. It is much taller, non-bushy, with dark leaves, purple leaf petioles and midribs. In modern times, purple tree collards seem to have been more or less exclusively grown in North America, and in particular in California. In the city of Richmond, purple tree collard was appointed the official city vegetable in July 2010. This was inspired by the efforts of the organisation Urban Tilth in encouraging people to grow their own and in recognition that this vegetable is both productive and one of the easiest to grow. A reputedly 3.5m tall tree collard found in an abandoned school garden was the source of some 100 new 'trees' propagated from cuttings and spread in the community. There are two theories as to where this type of kale originates. In California, it is believed that it arrived with Afro-Americans during the World War II period, originating in Africa, a not improbable scenario (see the discussion below about perennial brassicas in Africa). However, there are also stories of it originating in England (the Cottager's kale, see below, is a similar plant known there). Whilst it is said not normally to flower in California, plants that have been spread in recent years in Europe seem to flower annually, possibly due to the colder weather stressing the plants into survival mode.

Ken Fern (1996) was sent this one too, presumably not from California as he says it came from an area of North America with much colder winters than most of Britain. His description of his plant having dark green leaves resembling Savoy cabbages might suggest that there is more than one clone doing the rounds. My plant also seems hardier than I had feared, surviving temperatures down to -20ºC. Fern was told that after a few years it was advisable to 'coppice' the tree cabbage to encourage new growth, but that this treatment sometimes kills the plant. Therefore, it's advisable to root cuttings before attempting this. Whereas Daubenton produces a lot of propagation shoots, tree collards in my experience don't and it is therefore slower to build up stocks.

Cottager's / Crofter's Kale

Cottager's kale is mentioned by Vilmorin-Andrieux in the 19th century as 'a rather variable kind, with green or violet and more or less curled leaves'. Most of the forms of Cottager's have no doubt been lost. However, BBC *Gardener's World* showcased a local perennial Cottager's kale from Taunton Deane in Somerset in July 2010. It is grown in the Victorian walled garden at the National Trust property Knightshayes Court in Devon. The film shows a tallish branching plant with purple leaf petioles that certainly has a resemblance to the American purple tree collard. The gardener at Knightshayes demonstrates how to take cuttings and states that she hadn't seen a single flower on their long row of plants in four years. A bit more information on

23 (above): 'Taunton Deane' perennial kale in the walled garden at Knightshayes Court, Devon.

24 (right): Seed propagated Cottager's kale from the Heritage Seed Library in my garden.

their cultivation can be found in Vilmorin-Andrieux's *The Vegetable Garden*: 'The sprouts of … Cottager's Kales, gathered in spring from the stems cut in winter, are excellent in flavour'. It is likely that this means that the plants were cut back in winter to encourage new spring growth. I visited Knightshayes Court in July 2011 (see the photo above left). The plants were smaller than I had expected, i.e. smaller than tree collards. Nevertheless, it was impressive to see a row of these old kales that had been kept alive vegetatively all these years.

Although the Taunton Deane form of Cottager's kale rarely sets seed it seems that another Cottager's kale that was seed propagated was sold commercially in the UK until fairly recently by Suffolk Herbs (Kings Seeds) as did Marshall's of Wisbech in the 1960s and various other companies back to the 19th century. In Barr's seed catalogue (1927) this kale is described as: 'leaves generally crimped or curled on margin and having greenish or purple stems; the plant is tall and robust, yielding in spring a large crop of delicately flavoured side-shoots.' This still seems to be a good description of this plant. The Heritage Seed Library in the UK kindly sent me some seed in 2011 (see the photo above right).

Woburn Perennial Kale / Everlasting Kale

Sadly this kale is almost certainly no longer with us, despite a glowing report by the Gardener of the Duke of Bedford in the *Transactions of the Horticultural Society* in the early 19th century. It was cultivated in the gardens of Woburn Abbey, owned by the Duke. The plants flowered at about 7ft high after seven years without flowering. Although initially grown as an ornamental, a trial had shown that it tasted as good as the best of the winter greens. Subsequently an area of 150sq yds was planted up with cuttings of the Woburn kale and, once established, it was found to be a winter crop which outyielded other winter greens by a factor of four, despite not manuring the crop. It was concluded that, 'the very superior annual produce of the Woburn perennial kale, the saving of manure, as well of labour in its culture, its hardy nature...are properties which recommend it to a place in every kitchen-garden.' Fearing Burr in *Field and Garden Vegetables of America* (1865) mentions this kale, confirming its arrival in North America, describing it as '...a tall variety of the Purple Borecole, with foliage very finely divided or fringed.' However, yield wise it was said to be exceeded considerably by some of the large heading cabbages and Burr therefore only recommends it for areas with colder winters. It is frequently mentioned in gardening books in the 1800s. There are reports wishing it back into cultivation up to at least the 1940s and I'll extend that to the 2010s, but it is no doubt just wishful thinking.

Nine Star Perennial Broccoli

Seed of this early 1900s introduction is readily available today (early references to Curtis's Nine Star Perennial broccoli are presumably to the original selection). This is a distinctive tall broccoli/cauliflower that can continue to produce multiple small white heads for up to five years. It dies when it sets seed and it is therefore important to harvest all the flower shoots. Robert Hart (1991) grew this in his forest garden but says that '...it is too greedy and demanding to find a place in a co-operative community'; see also Whitefield (1996). The leaves are also quite tasty.

Others noted as perennial include the UK heirloom 'Ragged Jack' kale (e.g. Phillips, 1993 notes it as perennial). However, this is usually grown as an annual and as far as I know it doesn't perennialise. It is probable that it evolved from originally being perennial. It has also been suggested that Woburn kale at some time got confused with 'Ragged Jack' and different plants shared this name for some time.

About one hundred years ago, Jersey kale or Walking Stick kale was to be found on almost every farm and garden in Jersey, grown mainly as cattle fodder, but also widely eaten in soup by the locals. Plants could reputedly reach 5m tall in the mild

25-26: Nine Star Perennial broccoli.

climate of the Channel Islands. They were seed propagated in the late summer and harvested a year later. Although sometimes referred to as perennial, my experience is that it dies after setting seed. Their life cycle is just somewhat longer than other brassicas. Seeds are widely available and this plant is often just grown as a curiosity. The leaves are certainly edible, but not the best tasting brassica (see Hew and Rumball, 2000, for a good account of the Walking Stick kale).

African Perennial Kales

I have noted above the possible origin of tree collards in Africa and it's therefore interesting to look for evidence of the cultivation of perennial brassicas there. The best sources are the PROTA (Plant Resources of Tropical Africa) project and Mvere and van der Werff (2004) which is available online from the PROTA website. Here we can read that tall forms of *Brassica oleracea* grown for repeated leaf pickings are popular everywhere in East and southern Africa, but are less common in central Africa and rare in West Africa. In East Africa, leafy kales are in fact the most important traditional vegetable. The main type is *sukuma wiki*, and there are both vegetatively propagated and seed-propagated cultivars of this.

In the south there are two vegetatively propagated forms recognised and I quote from PROTA:

Rugare: Rarely seed propagated (flowers only at high altitudes and after some degree of vernalisation); plants 2-3m tall, for repeated leaf pickings, white flowering; many small shoots developing at the base and lower internodes (hence also called thousand-headed cabbage); long life and harvest season; pale blue-green and somewhat curly leaves, but clones available with different leaf colour.

Viscose: A selection from 'Rugare' that has gained popularity for commercial production with repeated leaf pickings because of its improved hardiness in the field; rarely seed propagated (segregates into different types); leaves darker green and more pronouncedly curled than 'Rugare', some clones in between 'Rugare' and 'Viscose'.

Pictures I've seen of *sukuma wiki* from Kenya look similar to Jersey kale with a long stalk and green leaf petioles and leaves.

South American Tree Kale

On a trip to Ecuador, Jeremy Cherfas wrote in his Agricultural Biodiversity Weblog of finding two varieties of non-flowering perennial tree kale in the garden of an agrotourist lodge near Cotacachi. One of the two had wonderful purple curly leaves. Cuttings were taken and shoots from the young plants were eaten. In a reply to the blog, ethnobotanist Eve Emshwiller could tell of a perennial kale she found growing commonly in Cuyo-Cuyo in southern Peru, called locally 'The Flag of Cuyo-Cuyo'. No one knows anything of their origin and there is no further information on how common they are.

Modern Perennial Kales

Some amateurs have recently set out to try to cross some of these perennial kales, myself included as I noted above. The Homegrown Goodness forum and the Facebook group Plant Breeding for Permaculture are the best places to follow progress. A red Daubenton type has been one suggested objective. However, the fact that several of these are shy flowerers adds to the challenge. Tim Peters in the US has developed the hardy 'Western Front kale', and about 50% of the seed propagated plants show signs of becoming perennial. Similarly, 'Pentland Brig', which was released in about 1980 from a cross of 'Hungry Gap' and 'Scots curly kale', also has perennial blood, although it is uncertain whether it is the modern or old perennial 'Hungry Gap' which was used.

All of these perennial kales can suffer from similar cultivation problems as the annual/biennial types, although some are reported to show more resistance to slugs and insects. My experience is that they do indeed seem to be quite resistant early in the season, but can nevertheless be severely attacked later when growth has slowed down. Unlike many perennial vegetables, kales have green leaves in winter and this is very tempting for pigeons and deer, so consider protecting your plants.

Most of these perennial kales seem so far only to be available through 'word of mouth' in both Europe and North America, but it is likely that they will become more widely available in the years to come.

Beta vulgaris ssp. maritima (syn. Beta maritima)

FAMILY: Chenopodiaceae
ENGLISH: Sea Beet
FRENCH: *Betterave Maritime*
GERMAN: *Wilde Runkelrübe*
ITALIAN: *Bietola Comune*
RUSSIAN: *Svekla Primorskaia*
SPANISH: *Remolacha Maritima*

This is the last of our primeval perennial vegetables from cliff tops, and is just the thing for the forest-free coastal permaculture garden. Sea beet is a common plant of many coastal habitats in Europe and North Africa, including the Canary and Cape Verde Islands. Whereas it is mainly perennial in the north of its range, the Mediterranean populations are mainly annual or biennial. It has over the last 20 years spread northwards in Scandinavia, first discovered in Norway in 1991, rapidly extending its range in the ensuing years. In the UK, its current range is similar to that of *Crithmum*, largely limited by its lack of winter hardiness. Sea beet has also naturalised in a few places near the coast in North America. Plants on the Atlantic coasts of Europe can reach over 1m when in flower, the glossy dark green leaves affording protection against winter sea spray.

As with cabbages, it is astonishing what a diverse range of vegetables has been created starting with the wild sea beets of Europe; just consider the range of beetroot forms and colours, the multi-coloured Swiss chards, sugar beet and mangelwurzels; all have the same common seashore ancestor, *Beta maritima*.

The story of the domestication of the beetroot tribe started in ancient times probably in the eastern Mediterranean. Leaves of the wild beets (*Beta maritima* and other species) have been wild gathered in the Mediterranean countries right up to present (see also Chapter 2). Leaves are mostly cooked by boiling like spinach, frying, or occasionally eaten raw although many people find that raw leaves have an unpleasant taste in the mouth (as do beetroot tops and Swiss chard). In Cyprus, Della et al. (2006) document its use in *pittes* (pies), boiled alone or boiled with legumes. Pieroni (1999) has it as an ingredient in the multi-species *minestrella* soup and Lenti and Venza (2007) note various ways that sea beet was traditionally used in the kitchen.

27: Clifftop sea beet in July at Durdle Door, Dorset.

Some good recipes and mouth-watering pictures can be found in Roger Phillips' *Wild Food* from 1983, including sea beet quiche and sea beet stuffed pancakes. Mabey (1972) claims that he hasn't met anyone who has eaten both wild and cultivated beet leaves who doesn't agree that the wild plants have better flavour.

28: Sea beet roots from a five-year-old pot-grown plant.

The first domesticated plants were leaf beets or chards and both the Romans and Greeks cultivated these. The origin of beets with swollen taproots is uncertain, but can be traced back to the Middle Ages, fodder beets or *mangelwurzels* appear in the 18th century and sugar beets not until the early 19th century. Nowadays, the sugar beet has become the most economically important derivative of that modest coastal plant, thanks to modern man's addiction to all things sweet, supplying today some 30% of world sugar demand. Due to the leaf spot fungus, *Cercospora*, which causes devastating disease of beets including sugar beet, scientists have in recent years collected material from resistant wild sea beets along the coasts of Europe, including the perennial form from northern Europe, in successful attempts to breed resistance into commercial stocks.

Perennial sea beet is not difficult to cultivate if your climate suits it. The main limiting

29-30 (above and left): Beetroot 'Bull's Blood' and Hungarian fodder beet (Roszsaszinu Beta) are used for their tasty leaves.

31 (left): Row of luxuriant sea beet in the vegetable garden at the Utrecht University Botanical Garden at Fort Hoofddijk, Holland.

factor is its lack of winter hardiness. If you are able to overwinter biennial Swiss chard (leaf beet), then you should also be able to grow sea beet as a perennial. Plants I've seen under cultivation in Holland seem to produce usable quantities of leaves and other reports indicate the same. As with other coastal plants, soil with good drainage is recommended and seaweed is an excellent fertiliser. Seed can be sown in spring at the same time as you would start other beets. A sunny position is best, as they dislike shady conditions. A few seed companies offer seed. Alternatively, if you are in northern Europe, suggest to your family an autumn trip to the beach and select some seed from good-looking plants.

Sadly, there are so far no cultivars available of perennial beets. A number of beetroots are also grown for their attractive edible leaves. Varieties like dark purple leaved 'Bull's Blood' and 'McGregor's Favourite' are sometimes used as edimentals in ornamental borders. 'Green Top Bunching' and 'Lutz Green Leaf' and the Hungarian fodder beet 'Roszsaszinu Beta' are also all grown for their tasty leaves. Why not set your sights on developing a perennial red-leaved leaf beet? You could try crossing 'Bull's Blood' with wild sea beet (all beets should cross easily). I also suspect that some selection work on sea beet has already been carried out by the developing saline crop industry (see discussion under *Aster tripolium*, Chapter 6). Commercial sea beet seed is now being offered by at least one company.

Ornithogalum pyrenaicum

FAMILY: Liliaceae
ENGLISH: Spiked Star of Bethlehem, Bath Asparagus, Prussian Asparagus
FRENCH: *Aspergette, Ornithogale des Pyrénées*
GERMAN: *Pyrenäen-Milchster*
ITALIAN: *Latte di Gallina a Fiori Giallastri, Ornitogalo dei Pirenei, Ornitogalo Selvatico*
SPANISH: *Ornithogalum de los Pirineos*

Ornithogalum pyrenaicum, the Spiked Star of Bethlehem, is a pseudo-asparagus, used mainly in southern Europe, with an excellent mild flavour. It is hardy enough to overwinter in my northern garden and the up to 1m spikes of white star-shaped flowers make it also one of the finer edimentals for temperate gardens. The flower spikes are a decent size and are harvested just before the flowers emerge (the dense inflorescence only starts to elongate as the flowers open). Note that once the shoots are removed, the plant doesn't flower again the same year, so it is best to have several plants and not harvest all the plants each year (unless you are very hungry)!

32 (above): Clouts Wood is a nature reserve and Site of Special Scientific Interest due to the large populations of Bath asparagus that grow here.

33-34 (far left and left): Bath asparagus is a hardy, beautiful ornamental, but if you eat the flower shoots, it does not produce more.

35: Bath and common asparagus from my garden

36: Bath asparagus risotto is easy to make.

This species is found in the wild as far north as England, where it is rare, although most plentiful in the countryside around the city of Bath. There is an old tradition in this area to gather the flower spikes in the springtime and they were even sold on markets, hence the common name Bath asparagus (Mabey, 1997). It doesn't seem unlikely that this plant and/or knowledge of its edibility go back to the time of the Romans. They may have introduced it for food, the plant later naturalising (the Roman heritage of Bath is well known). In July 2011, I visited a nature reserve called Clouts Wood that is located just south of Swindon in Wiltshire, and about 40km from Bath. Here you can walk amidst large populations of this wonderful plant! I found it growing together with other edibles such as stinging nettle, lesser celandine, ramsons and cuckoo flower.

Otherwise, this plant's distribution stretches from France, the Iberian Peninsula and the Canary Islands, Morocco, Italy, Croatia, Serbia, Greece, Turkey and east to the Crimea and the Caucasus. It grows both in deciduous woods and more open locations such as roadsides and meadows, and even as a weed on arable land in the east of its range. It can tolerate quite dry conditions in summer coming into growth in January in mild winters in the UK.

The use of *Ornithogalum pyrenaicum* as a wild gathered edible has survived in mountain villages in northern Italy where it is prepared by boiling and sautéing (in western Friuli and the Piedmont; Dreon and Paoletti, 2009). It is also a component of the multi-species spring dish *pistic* (Paoletti, 1995; see Chapter 2). Guarrera and Lucia (2007) also document the bulbs being eaten in southern Italy. In France, the fact that this plant was wild gathered is reflected in local names such as *asperge de bois* and *aspergette.*

There are at least three other similar species used in a similar way in the Mediterranean, *Ornithogalum narbonense* (mainly in eastern parts) and *O. pyramidale* and *O. creticum* (Dogan et al., 2004; Rivera et al., 2006). King's Spear or asphodel (*Asphodeline lutea*) is another garden-worthy closely related plant with spikes of yellow flowers, and is one of the commonest wild gathered plants in the eastern Mediterranean. As with other of the *Ornithogalum* species, the flower buds and stems are often cooked with eggs.

37 & 38 (left): Ornithogalum narbonense *(top) and* Ornithogalum pyramidale *(bottom) flower shoots are two other ornamental species that can be used in the same way as* O. pyrenaicum.

39 (above): Asphodeline lutea *is a common ornamental in European gardens, but it is little known that it is a common wild gathered food plant in the Mediterranean from Italy to Palestine.*

Bulbs and plants are available from a few nurseries in the UK as are seeds, but be aware that, from seed, it will take a few years before the plants are large enough to harvest. Bulbs can be planted as deep as 10cm to give extra winter protection. Mine are all from seed and I also planted seedlings of *Ornithogalum pyrenaicum* var. *flavescens* which has pale yellow flowers, a couple of years ago. Seed doesn't apparently need cold stratification to germinate although it won't hurt. Plants often grow in clayey soils in the wild, but drainage needs to be good. However, on the edge of its range, sandy soils might be better. I have lost plants on clay but my best clump has grown well on sand.

Urtica dioica

FAMILY: Urticaceae
CHINESE: *Yi Zhu Qian Ma*
ENGLISH: Stinging Nettle
FINNISH: *Nokkonen*
FRENCH: *La Grande Ortie*
GERMAN: *Große Brennnessel*
ICELANDIC: *Sérbýlisnetla*
ITALIAN: *Ortiche*
JAPANESE: *Seiyou Irakusa*
NEPALESE: *Sisnu*
NORWEGIAN: *Stornesle*
RUSSIAN: *Krapiva Dvudomnaja*
SWEDISH: *Brännässla*
TIBETAN: *Satu*

A nettle bed is an absolute must in the permagarden if you have the space, although most of us will have a ready-made wild source in the neighbourhood wherever we might be in the world. I was fortunate to inherit a large patch in my garden and I've been harvesting nettles as a spring vegetable from this patch for almost 30 years. A second cut is then made in mid-summer to make my most important quick fix organic fertiliser (nettle water). The subsequent new growth can then be used for more nettle greens if you wish.

This is a permanent vegetable, preferring nutrient rich moist habitats, in particular near habitation where

40: The first spring nettle shoots with last year's dead stems.

41: Nettles often grow in large 'colonies', the plants spreading easily in good soil by lateral shoots. You can therefore often pick quantities of nettles from a small area.

human and animal manure has been dumped in the past, in open woods and fields with grazing animals and it thrives also where drifted seaweed accumulates at the highest tideline.

Nettle seeds also hitch a ride with the seaweed and are therefore a common, useful, but easily removed weed on my vegetable beds.

Nettle has, apart from its food value, a myriad of other uses from the stems yielding a strong fibre, as a medicinal, dye plant, an ingredient in anti-dandruff shampoos, compost

42: Children (and some adults) are always impressed when I throw myself courageously into the stingless stinging nettle patch and start grazing! Urtica galeopsifolia *is one 'almost' stingless species found in central Europe.*

activator etc. Its value for wildlife is yet another reason for having it in your garden. It acts as a ready-made bird feeder where my patch has pride of place outside my living room, attracting several species feeding on the seeds in winter and on insects in summer. It is also host plant for various butterflies and moths.

Urtica dioica's original range was throughout Europe from the Arctic to the Mediterranean and east to western Siberia. It has, however, followed the migrations of Europeans and can nowadays be found naturalised on all continents. There are a number of varieties and closely related species, such as *Urtica angustifolia* in eastern Asia, very tall *U. gracilis* (slender nettle) in North America and *U. pubescens* in the Caucasus.

You might want to try one of the stingless stinging nettles in your garden. The Fen nettle, *Urtica galeopsifolia*, is one of these, found in Central Europe and in the Fens in England. Here in Norway, we have two, *Urtica dioica* ssp. *sondenii* found mainly in mountain woodland and *U. dioica* var. *holosericea* found in the south of the country. They are, however, not totally free of stinging hairs, so the head-in-the-nettles stunt isn't totally safe (see photo 42 on the previous page) ... The leaves of fen nettle are narrower than in the ordinary stinging nettle and the plants are probably not as productive, but you rarely get stung.

There are also numerous other *Urtica* species, used by native populations around the world including *Urtica massaica* (yes, you guessed, from Kenya), *U. simensis* (Ethiopia) and, my candidate for the world's fiercest vegetable, New Zealand's 4m tall tree nettle, *U. ferox*,or *ongaonga*. Beware though; people encountering this plant have been stung to death (five hairs are apparently enough to kill a guinea pig; Crowe, 1990). I've seen it growing in shady woodland in South Island and had the chance to sample it, but was too much of a coward to try, something I've regretted ever since! Mason (1950) advises:

43 (below): The aptly named Urtica ferox *from New Zealand is a giant at up to 4m and has fierce needle-like stinging hairs.*

44 (right): Stinging nettles forming an extensive bed above the shoreline north of the Arctic Circle in the Lofoten Islands in Norway.

'**If** you can clip off the leaves ... they are good ... if cooked.' More commonly harvested in New Zealand is native *Urtica incisa*, the scrub nettle.

I always look forward to the first nettle shoots of spring, one of the first fresh vegetables of the year. The plants grow quickly and one can continue using the entire shoots until the plants are some 20cm high. As they continue upwards, the lower stem becomes too fibrous to use and the usable bit becomes gradually shorter. Finally only the upper two to four leaves are usable.

To continue, it's best to cut the plants down again to encourage new growth. I know that most people use gloves or, failing that, a plastic bag to harvest nettles. I find gloves too restricting and simply grasp the nettle* quickly and firmly and snap them off. For nettle water, I use my good old trusty scythe, but make sure it's sharp; otherwise the tall stems can whip back and lash you across the face, not a pleasant experience. In other parts of the world, nettles have been harvested using bamboo pincers (Nepal), iron tongs (Tibet) or just a stick to break off the tender tips (Kenya).

Here in Norway, nettles are probably the most well known of wild foods, most commonly used to make nettle soup, following a similar recipe to caraway soup (see page 253). Wartime information given out by the authorities and Holmboe's (1941) book *Free Food from Wild Plants* state that nettles are probably the most valuable of all wild vegetables in the country making 'excellent vegetable dishes which in flavour and food value can compete with the best one can harvest from the vegetable garden.' As a result, nettles were much used during the war and since the 1970s have once again become quite popular. I personally use nettles in all sorts

---

* The English expression 'grasp the nettle' meaning 'facing a problem with determination' derives from the traditional way of harvesting nettles before the age of gloves and plastic.

Wells Bombardier Brewery
Sponsor of eccentric competitions

Wells Bombardier is a well-known English brewery which has sponsored a series of eccentric competitions including The World Dock Pudding Championships in Yorkshire (see the account of bistort in Chapter 6). The World Nettle Eating Championships is the most extreme though! The competition originated in 1986 when two farmers in a pub in Marshwood, a village in Devon, were discussing who had the tallest nettles on their farm. The discussion ended by one of the farmers wagering to eat any nettle that was taller than his. The longest nettle competition was born, becoming the World Nettle Eating Championships. In 2014, the competition was arranged for the 18th time. The rules are such that the contestant who eats raw leaves from the most two-foot nettle lengths in an hour wins. The contestants are not allowed to bring their own nettles (so my plan to use my stingless stinging nettles won't work...) No painkillers are allowed apart from beer, of course. The world record now stands at an incredible 23m of raw nettle.

45: Self-blanching nettle, Urtica dioica 'Good as Gold'.

46: Local nettles (ortiche) for sale on the market in Venice, Italy, in early April.

of dishes, although ramsons and nettle quiche is a favourite (see page 52). Nettle soup is otherwise popular elsewhere in Scandinavia and the Baltic countries and in Russia (green *borsch*). How's your Estonian? Well, you might be encouraged to learn more when you hear that there's a recently published Estonian wild weed book with 17 pages of nettle recipes (Niiberg and Lauringson, 2007).

Raw food enthusiasts can also partake of nettles as the stinging hairs are easily crushed in the washing and tossing process of putting a salad together. There's even a world record in raw nettle eating at 23m of nettle in one hour (see box on page 31). Another strange custom is Nettlemas Night (30th April) in County Cork when girls would pick bunches of nettles and sting boys whom they held in affection (Coitir, 2008). It was also widely believed that three meals with nettles in May would keep one healthy for the rest of the year.

The simplest way of preparing nettles is just to boil quickly for a few minutes in a minimum of water, adding butter before serving. Drying nettles for winter use can also be recommended. The easiest method is to scythe off the stems and simply hang the plants up to dry in an airy place, later stripping off the leaves from the fibrous stems. The dried nettles are also sometimes ground and added to bread.

In Scotland and Ireland, nettles were in former times an important food and were regularly used in soups and porridge, cooked with water, milk, salt and oatmeal (as in St. Columba's broth, a recipe surviving from the 6th century) and Irish *brachan neantog* (Coitir, 2008). I have found that it is also excellent cooked into a thick porridge with your own homegrown quinoa or Good King Henry seeds (page 93). We are not the first to cultivate nettles either, as Sir Walter Scott referred to the forcing of nettles under glass in Scotland as an early spring kale in his 1817 novel *Rob Roy*. In another Celtic outpost, Cornish Yarg cheese is wrapped in pressed nettle leaves. Nettles are also a common ingredient in the northern England speciality, dock pudding (Chapter 6).

In Italy, nettles are also popular. They are an important ingredient in wild and wild/cultivated mixed soups in the Garfagnana, a mountainous region of Tuscany (see Chapter 2). It is also one of the ingredients of *pistic* (Chapter 2). I also enjoy *gnocchi* with stinging nettle pesto (see box opposite).

Gnocchi with Pesto d'Ortica

300g fresh, boiled nettle leaves (to make *pesto d'ortica*)
1kg potatoes
8 sun-dried tomatoes
100g pine nuts
4 tbsp olive oil
400g wholemeal flour
½ tsp of sea salt

Gnocchi *with* pesto d'ortica *could, in a parallel universe, have developed as a Norwegian dish.*

Boil the peeled potatoes and mash well. Mix in the flour, then divide the mixture into thumb-size 'gnocchis', roll them in flour and leave them to sit for an hour or so. Blend together the cooked nettle leaves with the tomatoes, nuts and oil. Drop the *gnocchi* into boiling water with a little salt. They are ready when they rise to the surface. Add the pesto to the *gnocchi*, decorating with a few pine nuts and you could serve with nettle beer!

Moving east to Poland, *Urtica dioica* was earlier commonly used in all sorts of dishes, but this traditional use died out in the middle of the last century. However, as elsewhere in Europe a renaissance in interest in wild foods has led to nettle soup becoming fashionable again in recent years, particularly in urban areas. Nettle leaves were also, up to maybe 50 years ago, used as a crayfish stuffing in Poland, mixed with eggs and pepper.

In Turkey, an ethnobotanical study in Erzurum Province in north eastern Turkey showed that *Urtica dioica* was, along with *Malva neglecta* and *Rumex crispus*, used in all 60 villages surveyed. In the Himalayas, it is also an important and commonly used vegetable. In Sikkim, one survey showed it being consumed by 85% of people. In Nepal, it would be boiled with maize, millet or wheat flour, adding salt and chilli to make a sort of porridge (Manandhar, 2002). In Tibet, *Urtica hyperborea* was cooked into a thick soup and served with boiled potatoes and *tsamba* (a kind of dough made with roasted barley flour and ghee with water). A word of warning, though, legend has it that a famous Tibetan yogi and poet subsisted on nettle tea, leading his skin to turn green!

In western and central Siberia, another species, *Urtica cannabina* (Konopleva or Hemp-leaved nettle) is also used. This species has rather attractive leaves. It is also used in inner Mongolia (Hu, 2005) and the same author notes the use of *Urtica angustifolia* in northern China and *U. laetevirens* and *U. triangularis* in Tibet.

Finally, nettles were even widely used by Native Americans, the plant being boiled, steamed or fried and the Aborigines in Australia also baked the leaves of *Urtica incisa* between heated stones.

So there's a few ideas for you ... next time you're eating your nettles, think of it as a global ritual enjoyed around the world by local people. You have a good chance wherever you are in the world of finding some kind of food and one of these is nettle.

Allium ampeloprasum

FAMILY: Amaryllidaceae
ENGLISH: Wild Leek, Elephant Garlic, Great-Headed Garlic
FRENCH: *Poireau d'Été, Poireau Perpétuel, Ail d'Orient, Ail Faux Poireau*
GERMAN: *Ackerknoblauch*
ITALIAN: *Porraccio*
SPANISH: *Ajo Chilote*

If you like the idea of a perennial leek which also provides pickling onions, then one of the Pearl onion group of *Allium ampeloprasum* could be what you are looking for. Genuine pearl onions, *Allium ampeloprasum* var. *sectivum*, are still cultivated on a small scale in Germany, Belgium and the Netherlands, where they are known as *perlzwiebel*. On a visit to Belgium in 2008, I was introduced to *oerprei* (literally meaning 'ancient leek'), a useful hardy perennial leek still grown locally and enjoying a bit of a renaissance. In mild winter climates, *oerprei* leaves can be harvested all winter as needed.

Allium ampeloprasum is a widespread and variable species found growing wild in all Mediterranean countries including North Africa and east to Iran. It is the most commonly gathered wild onion in this region and is one of the overall most utilised species. It is used in many different ways, including in omelettes (Spain and Italy); sautéed with other greens (Greece); in Corsican *suppa d'erbiglie* (with *Reichardia, Silene* and *Sonchus oleraceus*); with other greens in the Turkish vegetable-filled flatbread, *gözleme*; in vegetable balls (Italy); boiled with beans or simply raw with olives (Cyprus); with bread (Palestine) and just roasted (Italy). It is mainly the bulbs that are harvested although the leaves are also used. The onions are also preserved by pickling.

Not surprisingly, this useful species has been brought into cultivation since ancient times across its range. The common leek (*Allium ampeloprasum* var. *porrum*) is today by far the most important derivative from this wild ancestor. Now biennial, it has been selected for its long straight stems without bulbs or bulbils and is seed propagated. At the other extreme, the second most important form of *Allium ampeloprasum* is elephant or great-headed garlic that has been selected for its enormous bulbs, larger than regular garlic, but much milder. It is most often prepared by baking in the oven.

47: Oerprei *means 'ancient leek', here in the garden of Lieven David in Belgium.*

It produces long up to 2m flower stems, but the flowers rarely form seed and there are no aerial bulbils so that propagation is normally from the small bulblets that form on the main bulb.

In southwest England and the Channel Islands a bulbous form, Babington's leek (*Allium ampeloprasum* var. *babingtonii*) is found growing wild in a few places, particularly near the sea. This local onion was championed by the Henry Doubleday Research Association (HDRA) from the 1980s, latterly through its Heritage Seed Library scheme, and is cultivated nowadays by enthusiasts. It is a feature of Martin Crawford's forest garden in Totnes, Devon, so it can also tolerate some shade. It is particularly useful in milder areas for its winter leaves. Despite its coastal habitats in the wild, it is quite hardy and I've grown it for many years. It dies right back in winter in my garden.

48 (right): Oerprei *looks like a small leek with flowers that are attractive and vary in colour.*

49 (below right): Elephant garlic is grown for its large bulbs, which are usually composed of several large cloves.

50 (below): Common leek is usually considered a biennial, but it will sometimes betray its perennial origins by multiplying after flowering in the second year as shown here.

51-53: Babington's leek: spring leaves, bulbs and flowers with bulbils.

It is likely that Babington's leek is a relic plant, having probably escaped from monastery gardens and naturalised. It has also been cultivated as an ornamental in England and plantsman E.A. Bowles actually introduced it as an 'edimental' for the back of the border in his book *My Garden in Summer* as long ago as 1914. Unlike elephant garlic, this form has bulbils amongst the flowers and these can be used for propagation.

There are a number of other forms of interest. *Kurrat* is believed to be the leek of the ancient Egyptians, selected for the leaves and still cultivated there. Musselmann (1997) describes a visit to the Delta area near Alexandria. It was seed propagated and the leaves harvested successively at 10-15 day intervals. It is used both raw in salads and in *taameya*, Egyptian *falafel*, which uses broad beans (*Vicia faba*) as its base.

Egyptian *Falafel*

1kg fresh or dried broad (fava) beans
A handful finely chopped *Allium ampeloprasum* onions
3 cloves garlic, minced
1 cup chopped home grown parsley and cilantro
1 tsp ground roasted cumin
1 tsp ground roasted coriander
Pinch of ground dried or finely chopped fresh chilli
Pinch of salt
Pinch of ground black pepper

Shell the fresh broad beans or soak and cook the dried beans. Remove the skins if you prefer a less fibrous *falafel*. Mince all the ingredients together as fine as you like. Refrigerate for an hour or beat in an egg if you don't have time to wait. Heat some olive oil in a pan, form the mixture into small patties and fry until brown.

*54 & 55: National Trust property Knightshayes Court in Devon has a nice collection of
Allium ampeloprasum cultivars in their walled vegetable garden (above). Here I found
a low-growing old Italian form with attractive purple flowers and a tall variety noted
just as being 'related to Babington's leek' (right).*

Broad beans are one of the easiest and most adaptable vegetables and can be grown
from the Mediterranean to northern Norway, so genuine *taameya* could be made at
home anywhere, using the *Allium ampeloprasum* cultivar of your choice.

There are other similar forms in West Asia, including *Tarreh Irani* (*Taree Irani*) or
Persian chives (*Allium ampeloprasum* ssp. *persicum*), quite a common leaf vegetable
in Iran and the Afghan *gandana* is probably also closely related. I had high hopes
of being able to grow *kurrat* at home in Norway when I read an article about this
neglected vegetable in a Swedish vegetable book, claiming that it was hardy,
excellent and perennial. Unfortunately, it seems that this was a case of mistaken
identity and the plants I have seen have turned out to be Siberian *Allium ramosum*
(Chapter 4).

Allium ampeloprasum has been introduced into North America and it is found spread
across the continent. A good dark-red flowered form called the Yorktown onion is
now protected in Virginia and could be worth seeking out. I saw a similar plant in the
wonderful walled garden at the National Trust property Knightshayes Court in Devon.
This would certainly make an excellent edimental!

Messiaen and Rouamba (2004) otherwise give a good overview of this interesting
species.

Taraxacum officinale

FAMILY: Asteraceae
CHINESE: *Yaoyongpugongying*
ENGLISH: Common Dandelion
FRENCH: *Dent de Lion, Laiteron, Pissenlit*
GERMAN: *Löwenzahn, Kuhblume, Pusteblume*
GREEK: *Agrioradiko*
ITALIAN: *Tarassaco Comune*
JAPANESE: *Seiyou Tanpopo*
RUSSIAN: *Oduvanchik, Oduvanchik Lekarstvennyi*
SPANISH: *Achicoria amarga, Diente de León*

I never dreamed that my seed saving activities would lead me for a short period of time to be in control of future homeland security in the US, Canada, Europe and Japan! I'm dreaming? Illusions of grandeur? Well, read on…

You've heard of peak oil, right? Let me introduce you to peak rubber! The price of rubber is being driven through the ceiling through a combination of factors. This includes increasing demand from developing economies increasing oil prices (synthetic rubbers are derived from crude oil). In addition, there is a serious leaf blight disease affecting the rubber tree (*Hevea brasiliensis*). Peak oil would also lead to falling availability of rubber in the world, unless natural sources could be boosted. Added to this, the wish in the US and other countries to be able to produce rubber at home, rather than relying on production in tropical countries where *Hevea* can be cultivated, led to renewed research into a species which previously found favour during World War II when natural rubber supplies from the tropics last dried up. It is none other than the rubber dandelion (*Taraxacum kok-saghyz*), a species that is from a valley in the Tian-Shan Mountains in Kazakhstan. To the untrained eye it could easily be mistaken for the common garden dandelion, important differences being horned bracts on the flower heads and thicker leaves. It was the well-known Russian botanist and geneticist Nikolai Vavilov who studied 150 different rubber-producing plants in the 1930s and found that *Taraxacum kok-saghyz* was the best and only real candidate for rubber production in temperate climates! This plant is well adapted to areas with cold winters and was apparently cultivated both in Russia and the US during World War II. It can also be grown on land that is unsuitable for other crops.

In the 1990s, research activities increased in response to the worries about future supplies of rubber and the desire for increased homeland security. I had grown rubber dandelion in my garden and it also had a milder taste as a salad plant than the common dandelion. Dandelions produce latex as a protection against insects, gumming up their mouthparts and I had wondered if the higher levels of latex meant that there was less

56: Taraxacum kok-saghyz or closely related species.

need for the plant to taste bitter. This was one of the species I collected seed from and it found its way to my Internet seed-trading list! Soon after this list was posted, I received an enquiry from a German university for seed. I was apparently the only current source for this species that they could find. They told me they would buy as much as I could produce. In the following few years I received similar requests from scientists in the US, Canada and Japan and this has by far been my 'best seller' (I don't normally sell seed, but when you get a good offer it's difficult to refuse); see also Gronover and Prüfer, 2010 for a good review of the subject.

I reckon that pretty well anyone likely to read this account will be familiar with dandelions so I hardly need describe them, although there are admittedly a number of look-alikes such as the hawksbeards (*Crepis* spp.), cat's ears (*Hypochaeris* spp.) and *Hyoseris* spp., but many of these have also been wild-foraged for food. Although native to Europe, Asia and North America, two species, *Taraxacum officinale* and *T. erythrospermum*, have spread as weeds worldwide.

57 & 58: Hyoseris radiata *(top) and* Crepis leontodontoides *(bottom) are two of many dandelion look-alikes that are also wild-foraged, cooked and eaten raw in salads. (Ethnobotanical Garden at Orto Botanico, Firenze).*

59: A photograph of a dandelion field like this could have been taken in many countries around the world, here near my home in Malvik, Norway.

60: Taraxacum pseudoroseum, *a not uncommon ornamental in gardens in northern Norway.*

61: *White-flowered* Taraxacum pamiricum.

62: *Beautiful* Taraxacum albidum.

I remember reading an account on dandelions in one of New York forager Steve Brill's books and he informs the reader that dandelions have actually given up sex! Look at the photo 59 on the previous page: this statement would seem to be ridiculous and, judging by their success, it would seem to be that the opposite is true? What he was inferring was that dandelions produce their abundance of seed asexually, through so-called 'apomixis'. Seed propagated plants are then genetically identical to the plant from which the seed was harvested. This is analogous to bulbil-propagated plants such as Babington's leek. In apomixic dandelions this has resulted in a multitude of species or microspecies, depending on the viewpoint of the taraxacologist (yes, a botanist specialising in this fascinating family). For example, in the online Flora of North America, it states that there are anywhere between 15 and 2,000 species and, in Europe, over 1,200 microspecies have been recognised. Thus, what we describe here as *Taraxacum officinale* is actually a group comprising many of these microspecies. However, as hinted at above, not all dandelion species are celibate, complicating matters even more, no doubt to the delight of the taraxaphile. For example, in Japan, the invasive *T. officinale* has been caught spreading its pollen and crossing with native species and the rubber dandelion discussed earlier also apparently relies on cross-fertilisation.

I connect the vegetable dandelion most with the French, well-known for their love of the dandelion salad, a country where it became so popular in the 19th century that it was domesticated and grown commercially for the market as it still is. I've seen it myself on French and German markets in the springtime and I once delighted in purchasing a packet of dandelion seed in a French supermarket.

Leaving France, let's have a quick trip around the globe and look at the other dandelion eaters of the world. In Poland, the leaves were traditionally first boiled, drained and mixed with milk, whey or boiled potatoes (Luczaj and Szymanski, 2007). Dandelions were traditional wild-foraged fare in most Mediterranean countries, and the uses of at least 11 distinct dandelion species have been documented (Leonti et al., 2006). The spring leaves were most commonly used, most often in salads, but they were also boiled and fried. In Italy, Hadjichambis et al. found that dandelions

63: Pissenlit *'Coeur Plein Ameliore'* came from a seed packet that I purchased in a supermarket in Brittany, France. The flowers nod longingly towards home in the summer.

were the second most common wild gathered plant after chicory (*Cichorium*, see Chapter 2). Some simple ways of preparing the leaves included the following: a salad of fresh leaves with olives and wild onion, served with bread; boiled, drained, fried in olive oil with garlic and chilli; boiled in salted water until tender, cooled and eaten with an olive oil and lemon dressing; in omelettes; in Italian vegetable balls; and in Turkish pancakes. Flower stalks (peduncles) were also sometimes eaten as a snack. Dandelion roots have also been used as an emergency food in the past. Sturtevant in Hedrick (1919) tells of the inhabitants of Minorca subsisting on dandelion roots when a swarm of locusts devastated the vegetation on the island. Incidentally, Gibbons (1962), reported dandelion roots to be better as a vegetable than parsnip and salsify. Thayer (2010) also gives them the thumbs up saying they are a decent vegetable with only a hint of bitterness after boiling, reminiscent of salsify, but only young roots are apparently good.

North American foraging writer John Kallas (see page 44) came up with four ways of making dandelions palatable, which can also be used for several other strong plants (https://backwoodshome.com/articles2/kallas82.html):

1. Dilution (not just dandelion leaves but a mix of leaves with different tastes dampens the overall bitterness).

2. Masking (mix with various fats such as oils, butter, grease – a thin oil film coats your taste buds, resulting in reduced sensitivity to strong tastes).

3. Distraction (adding sugar, vinegar or other flavours also reduces the overall bitter sensation significantly).

4. Leaching (Kallas claims that boiling for 3-5 minutes is enough to reduce the bitterness significantly).

(In a garden, blanching (see below) by excluding light can also be used. I can add that preservation by lactofermentation also reduces the bitterness, although I'm not sure if this is just 'distraction' or a chemical transformation.)

In the Far East, we also find dandelions in the traditional diet. Leaves and inflorescences of *Taraxacum mongolicum* are eaten by the Arhorchin Mongol herdsmen in Inner Mongolia (Khasbagan et al., 2000); *Taraxacum cerataphorum* is used in the Magadan (this is also North America's most common native species, the rock dandelion); dandelions were used by the Arctic Chukchi people both fresh, cooked and fermented (Källman, 1997); four different *Taraxacum* spp. were documented in the top five wild-foraged vegetables in Harbin, Manchuria (Baranov, 1967) and a *Taraxacum* spp. is documented as food in South Korea (Pemberton and Lee, 1996).

Hopping over the Pacific to South America, *Taraxacum officinale* has long established itself (there are no native *Taraxacum* species). Some years ago, I was at a conference in Chile and hired a taxi for the day from Santiago to explore the mountain flora high up in the Andes. I was taken to a ski resort and there I found a fantastic range of native alpines in full flower. I remember walking over a ridge and being taken aback at the sight of the mass flowering of common dandelion along the side of a small mountain stream! Recent ethnobotanical studies in South America have shown that native indigenous peoples in remote areas

Dandelion and Sugar Maple Recipe

Trade or buy seed of sugar maple (*Acer saccharum*) or alternative species, see
www.pfaf.org

- Sow (needs cold treatment or stratification).
- Plant in the garden when germinated and sow dandelion seed if it isn't already growing under the trees.
- Weed and nurture for 15-30 years depending on your climate.
- Tap the tree and ferment into maple sap vinegar.
- The easy bit: pick your dandelion leaves and cook with some maple vinegar, eat as greens.
- This can then be repeated for 100 years or more.

Easy when you know how! Please let me know how you get on.

have adopted this plant in their wild-gathered repertoire; e.g. dandelions are among the top five wild-foraged plants for the Mapuche people in Patagonia (Ladio, 2001), and are used in salads, or added to *puchero*, a traditional meal comprising boiled meat and vegetables. They are also used by the Shuar and Saraguros people of southern Ecuador (Den Eyden et al, 2003).

In North America, numerous Native American tribes prized the young leaves of various dandelion species both cooked and raw, including the now endangered species *Taraxacum californicum*. It has been documented that various tribes cooked the dandelion leaves with maple vinegar (see box above). Dandelion greens have also been used by various Eskimo groups (Eidlitz, 1969). The Inuits in Greenland also ate dandelions, dipped in seal oil (Källman, 1997).

People vary enormously in their perception of bitterness. I believe my taste buds' sensitivity to bitter *was* (see below) at the higher end of the scale as I for many years found dandelions simply too bitter to eat. I read in foraging books that the young spring leaves were scarcely bitter, but became too bitter by the flowering stage. No, not my experience at all! I began frequenting US-based foraging flora on the net and I got the impression that people didn't find the young leaves bitter. I read that

64: Living not far south of the Arctic Circle, we have continuous daylight from April to September and this maybe leads to dandelions being extra bitter. Blanching, as here, using a large flower pot reduces the bitterness significantly. This is the French variety 'Coeur Plein Ameliore' which originated in a seed packet I bought in a supermarket in Brest, France – it is a distinct and much grown variety with many leaves held upright.

dandelions growing in shady conditions were less bitter and wondered if the reason my dandelions were so bitter was because I live so far north and the 24-hour daylight from May to July led to the bitterness being concentrated. I therefore began to blanch some of my dandelions using a large flowerpot and that significantly reduced the bitterness, but they were still bitter.

65: Giant flower stalks could result from the long northern nightless days, here demonstrated by my son Robin many years ago.

I eventually saw the light when I followed a discussion on the ForageAhead email group between two of North America's leading foragers 'Dandelion Dude' Peter Gail and John Kallas. Gail has written several essays and books about dandelions including his *Dandelion Celebration* (1994). He also founded the group 'Defenders of Dandelions' to provide information to those who want to make their neighbours aware just how good dandelions are and stop the chemical warfare. He has also organised the National Dandelion Cookoff in Dover, Ohio, still going strong since 1993. Gail says he ate dandelions every day, fresh in the summer and in dehydrated form in winter, growing his own from transplanted wild roots on raised beds in his garden for ease of access. Gail has been rightly coined the King of the Dandelions! However, it was John Kallas' web essay *Making Dandelions Palatable* that explains how such a bitter weed could be so popular around the world. To start with, Gail admits to thinking he was being poisoned the first time he ate dandelion and Kallas also found them very bitter, but was determined to solve the riddle. He first points out that foraging books downplay the bitterness and thinks that the oft-quoted difference between the first mild leaves in spring and bitter at flowering time is also exaggerated. As a result many people are disappointed and permanently put off when they sample their first dandelion. I was with him here ... He says that as part of his PhD he interviewed old timers in rural Michigan. Dandelions were the most common wild collected food in this group and, no, they weren't bitter, they said. Upon asking how they prepared the dandelions they explained that the fresh leaves were mixed with bacon grease, bacon, eggs, salt and sometimes vinegar. Incidentally, *salade de pissenlit et lardons* (salad of dandelion and bacon) is still prepared in France today. In most cultures as you can see in the round-the-world review above, dandelions are almost never eaten fresh alone.

He also found that some people (about 1 in 25) are hardly able to detect the bitterness in dandelions at all. Perhaps these people are over-represented in the foraging community, as they will not be put off on their first taste. It also seems that through our collective 'overdosing' on sweet and salty food in recent times, our perception of bitterness has changed.

66: 'Dilution' is one technique of masking the bitterness of dandelion leaves, better known as the mixed salad.

67: Dandelions grow well in young woodland or forest gardens.

If after reading this, the bitterness still worries you, dandelions with jagged leaves are reputedly less bitter than flat rounded leaved forms. Dandelions also grow well in shady places under deciduous trees. So, perhaps an idea is to find some good-sized dandelions with jagged leaves and transplant them into your forest garden! Blanching using a large pot or earthing up is probably the easiest way to milder dandelions. During the last world war here in Norway, other methods of blanching dandelions were recommended (Holmboe, 1941). One was to dig up turfs with dandelions and turn them upside down in autumn; the emerging leaves would then be blanched! It was also recommended to bring dandelion roots into the dark in the root cellar (under most older houses here). They could then be forced under dark conditions in a similar way to chicory. Presumably winter forcing dandelions in greenhouses, which was practised in the UK in the 1880s (in an age when winter lettuce varieties were yet to become available), also resulted in less bitter greens, even without the blanching.

Otherwise there are various methods proposed in the literature to reduce the bitter component of dandelions before cooking. Here are a few, take your pick:

- Soak for 2-3 hrs in salty water
- Scald with boiling water several times
- Scald with boiling water and then soak in salt water
- Boil for 30 mins changing water twice
- (For roots:) Wash, cut into 0.5cm bits and soak, changing water a few times, for 1.5 hours

68: Dandelion flower stalks or dandinoodles are one of my favourite vegetables from dandelions, simply cooked in boiling water for five minutes with a knob of butter.

I've recommended Samuel Thayer's foraging books elsewhere in this book. In *Nature's Garden*, there's an excellent account of dandelions. His favourite dandelion vegetable is what he calls dandelion crowns, as named originally by Euell Gibbons (1961). I prefer to call them *dandichokes*, as both these and artichoke hearts are located below the flowers. In the early spring, the very young flowers appear at the surface. The dandichoke is just the self-blanched crown between the top of the root, which is a bit below the surface, and the developing flowers. Although small and difficult to clean, they are very tasty.

I have discovered that the flower stalks of many plants in the *Asteraceae* are surprisingly tasty, milder and sweeter than the rest of the plant. Examples mentioned elsewhere in this book include Scorzonera, cardoons, artichokes and burdock (*Arctium* spp.). Dandelion flower shoots, just before the buds open, are really delicious and not very strong tasting at all, yet amazingly there aren't many that have tried them. I call them *dandinoodles* (see photo 68) ! It amazes me again and again how many wonderful veggies we have right in front of our noses and just don't see!

The father of modern US foraging, Euell Gibbons (1961) tells how he once prepared a complete dandelion meal with the roots as a root vegetable, the crowns as a cooked green, dandelion leaf salad, all washed down with dandelion wine, finishing the meal with dandelion coffee! Dandelion: the complete edible!

You'd be forgiven for wondering why on earth one would ever want to grow dandelions. However, commercial cultivation started in the 19th century in response to increasing demand at the market place. Hedrick (1919) tells us that dandelions were already being cultivated for the Boston Market in the US in 1836, cultivation is first mentioned in the UK in 1846, and Vilmorin-Andrieux has dandelions being cultivated in France from 1868. The upright dense-leaved variety 'Coeur Plein Ameliore'

69 (left): Giant dandelion leaves from cultivars 'UK thick leaved' and (right) the 19th century variety 'Vert de Montmagny Ameliore'.

70 (above): Blanched dandelions in the market in November, Freiburg, southwest Germany. Note that part of the upper root is intact which helps stop the leaves from wilting.

(literally 'Improved Full Heart') has been one of the most popular varieties since at least 1883 as it is productive with many leaves and the erect leaf habit also being an advantage, as they don't so easily get soiled. This is the variety I found for sale in a supermarket in Brest, France some years ago and I have been growing it ever since. By 1885 there were at least four varieties available in France including the legendary and stunning Moss-leaved dandelion or *Pissenlit* 'Mousse' which when blanched makes a salad not unlike curled endive. I had decided that the moss-leaved dandelion most likely had been lost. Nevertheless, I put the following wanted notice under its picture and have used it in my talks over the last years:

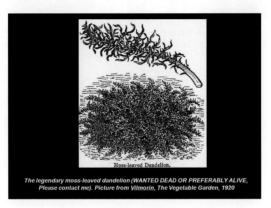

The legendary moss-leaved dandelion (WANTED DEAD OR PREFERABLY ALIVE, Please contact me). Picture from Vilmorin, The Vegetable Garden, 1920

Then, a little miracle happened during spring 2012. I was invited to give a talk at the Danish Seed Savers 25th anniversary in Denmark. As usual I showed this slide, but this time, there was a shout from the back 'I know where you can find it!' It was Søren Holt who you will meet later in the account about Victory onion in Chapter 6. It turned out that a friend was growing *Taraxacum sublaciniosum* 'Delicatesse', a variety that looks very like the moss-leaved dandelion. I still use that slide in my talks, but can now tell people that there was a happy ending.

Another old variety is 'Vert de Montmagny Ameliore' (with large, very long dark green leaves which is also a good blanching variety). Small (1997) mentions a variety 'Mayses' Trieb' specially selected for blanching, although I sadly can't find any recent references to it. Other varieties exist selected for thick leaves and earliness. All cultivated varieties are classified as *Taraxacum officinale*. By the way, don't be taken in as I was when I found what was called Italian dandelion 'Red Rib' on a seed rack. It wasn't until it flowered that I realised it was actually chicory.

Nowadays, dandelion is mostly grown commercially in France and in the US both for medicinal use, as a caffeine-free coffee alternative (easily done at home by cutting up the roots and roasting), and as a vegetable. It is available as a fresh local vegetable around New York in the spring and in winter it is harvested in Florida and Texas. The leaves are harvested fresh with a bit of root attached, as the leaves don't then

71: The dark purple ground-hugging leaves of Taraxacum rubifolium (also sold as T. faroense or incorrectly T. rubrifolium) gives a great splash of colour to a spring salad.

72: Dandelion impersonator Italian dandelion 'Red Rib' is actually a chicory, but it fooled me to start with … the leaf midribs of chicory are hairy whilst dandelion is hairless, but 'Red Rib' is only slightly hairy.

wilt as fast. Canned (i.e. tinned) dandelions are also available in the US. In France, cultivation is nowadays generally on an annual/biennial cycle, sown in the spring with harvest from autumn to spring. For blanching, roots are dug in autumn and forced in the dark. Like forcing chicory, it is recommended with a layer of about 15cm of sand above the root crowns.

Propagation is easy from pieces of root or by seed. This is a relatively easy vegetable as it suffers from few diseases or pests. For the roots it's certainly better to cultivate rather than wildcraft as it is difficult in the wild to tell the age and condition of the roots (young roots are best) and this is much easier to control under cultivation. If you are thinking of growing dandelions, Deppe (2000) advocates selecting good plants locally where you live, as these are already well adapted to your conditions.

I've collected about 10 dandelion species over the last few years, some of which have been used by other gardeners as ornamentals. For example, I found pink-flowered Taraxacum pseudoroseum growing in quite a few gardens in northern Norway, the dark purple leaves of T. rubifolium contrast wonderfully with the yellow flowers and white flowered species like T. albidum and T. pamiricum are relatively easy to find on seed exchanges and internet trading sites (see photos 60-62 on page 40). Japanese T. hideoi and T. denudatum are also sometimes cultivated as ornamentals. I've recently received a fine white flowered form of T. arcticum from Svalbard. I wonder if anyone has ever attempted growing vegetables on Svalbard? The Arctic dandelion would be a good one to grow alongside the Bear Island dandelion (T. cymbifolium). Another pinkish purple flowered alpine dandelion was commonly available in the seed exchanges some years ago, T. carneocoloratum, but it hasn't been seen for some time.

I tell visitors that if they're passing my area in 30 years' time and the roadside verges are full of pink and white dandelions, they know who's to blame…

Sium sisarum var. *sisarum*

FAMILY: Apiaceae
ENGLISH: Skirret
FRENCH: *Chervis*
GERMAN: *Zuckerwurzel*
ITALIAN: *Sisaro*
RUSSIAN: *Svekla Primorskaia*
SPANISH: *Escaravía*

Warning: 'They doe help to provoke urin, and it is thought, to procure bodily lust, in that they are a little windy' and 'The young shoots are pleasant and wholesome food, of a cleansing nature, and light digestion, provoking urine, to which they give a fœtid stinking smell,' (so wrote 17th century English herbalist John Parkinson). Happy with this? Please read on...

Skirret is one of the better-known unusual vegetables that had its heyday in Europe in the 16th and 17th centuries, before the potato established itself. It can be traced back to 1548 in Britain. In France, Olivier de Serres (1651), who was incidentally one of the first to advocate planting several varieties to mitigate the risk of crop failure and also crop rotation, states that it was commonly grown in France in his day. Worlidge (1682) in his *Art of Gardening* describes it as having 'the sweetest, whitest and most pleasant of roots'. Skirret reached North America in the late 18th century, but never really became popular there. I can't find evidence for it being widely used in the Far East as sometimes claimed. The cultivated form has many swollen tubers, about the width of a finger and somewhat longer, arranged in clusters as in dahlias or Yacon. The wild form, *Sium sisarum* var. *lancifolium*, doesn't have usable roots, and the origin of the cultivated form *Sium sisarum* var. *sisarum* is unknown. The name Skirret is a corruption of the name in Germany, Holland and Scandinavia. For example, here in Norway, it is called *sukkerot* (sugar root). The native range of the wild species seems to be from Eastern Europe to central and southeast Russia, naturalised in a few other places such as northern Italy.

Plants are available currently from a few herb nurseries in the UK and seed is also readily available. Vegetative propagation is the best method of multiplying skirret. Seed germinates irregularly and it may be an advantage to sow in the autumn, although spring sowing is also possible. The young seedlings can be transplanted, so you don't need to sow in situ. Division is usually carried out in the spring as the plant starts into growth. Aim for about 20cm between your plants.

This is a book about leafy greens and the reason I include it is that nowadays I grow skirret mainly for its aromatic spring shoots. Shoots have been

73: Skirret flowers are typically umbelliferous.

74: Row of skirret (Chervis) in the fantastic vegetable garden created by my late friend Sébastien Verdière at Chateau Valmer.

75: Partly blanched skirret shoots grown in low light conditions in the author's cellar.

gathered traditionally from wild skirret (*Sium sisarum* ssp. *lancifolium*) in Turkey (see Baser, 1997). The potential for skirret to be exploited for blanched spring shoots was proposed already in France in 1879 and Péron (1989) showed that blanched skirret petioles can be produced using the same techniques used for chicory and sea kale. Due to their lack of hardiness here, I have simply grown skirret in large pots that are moved into the cellar for the winter. It is then easy to either move the pot into a warmer room and force in the dark or just let the leaves grow out in the cellar in late winter.

Allium ursinum

FAMILY: Amaryllidaceae
ENGLISH: Ramsons, Wild Garlic, Stink Bombs
FRENCH: *Ail des Bois≈ Ail des Ours*
GERMAN: *Bärlauch*
ITALIAN: *Aglio Orsino*
RUSSIAN: *Medvezhiy Luk*

Ramsons will be familiar to many who live in Europe, as it is a common plant of damp humus-rich woodland occurring usually en masse where it grows. During the flowering period, you will smell it before you see it. The centre of ramsons-mania in Europe has been the small town of Eberbach, about 75km south of Frankfurt in Germany. In 2000, a month-long festival from mid-March to mid-April in honour of the *bärlauch* or, literally, bear onion (the *ursinum* epithet also pertains to bears) was arranged for the first time. During the festival, local restaurants serve a number of dishes using wild sourced local ramsons, you name it – sausages, wine, bread, ice cream – and you can purchase various products including this onion from butchers, bakers and greengrocers. Guided nature walks are also arranged to see and smell the wild plants. The festival has been an overwhelming success and people have come from all over the country for the experience. As a result, other ramsons festivals have also started up in other parts of Germany. A few plants have also found their way back into home gardens in Germany from this festival. This is all helped along by the recent popularity of garlic's health benefits and comparative medical trials that have shown that the bear onion is more effective than garlic in lowering blood pressure. People also believe that the origin of the German name is that bears would in the past come out of their lairs at about the same time that ramsons began to grow. They would then gorge themselves on the plant and this reputedly made them strong and healthy. It is said that 'Eating the plant gives you the strength of a bear!' The popular ramps festivals in North America are similar and this was possibly an inspiration. Ramps, *Allium tricoccum*, although similar in appearance, is not closely related in the large onion family.

Ramson leaves are broad (it is sometimes called the broad-leaf garlic) and it forms a dense carpet in the damp woods where it is found. Please make absolutely sure that the leaves smell of garlic, as there are a couple of poisonous look-alikes (lily of the valley, *Convallaria majalis* and autumn crocus, *Colchicum autumnale*). The wild distribution of ramsons is from the UK, southern and lowland Scandinavia, across Central Europe, and down into Italy. It reaches the Caucasus at the eastern extent of its range.

People have always planted useful wild plants in their gardens and it has become quite a popular garden plant over the last 10 years. However, some people regret having introduced it, as it can be a bit invasive if the conditions suit it. Nevertheless, this is obviously a potentially good one for the damper forest garden. I've also read of a dual culture of hops and ramsons where the latter forms a ground cover keeping deeper rooting weeds from establishing around the perennial hops.

76: A ramson wood is a fantastic site when the plants are in full bloom from March in the south to June in the north.

77: *Allium tricoccum* (ramps) is hugely popular as a wild harvested onion in North America and the subject of ramps festivals. Although superficially similar to ramsons, growing in similar habitats, it is only distantly related in the large *Allium* family. Unlike ramsons, ramps flowers after the leaves die down in mid-summer (Kew Gardens, London).

We have also seen increased commercial interest in ramsons over recent years. Here in Norway, the biggest dairy sells a ramsons cheese spread, one small company is selling a ramsons purée (used as pesto) and fresh leaves are also becoming available. A project has also been funded in Norway to investigate the genetic diversity of wild populations and to study how to cultivate the plant on a large scale. There is a worry that over-harvesting might become a problem (this is paralleled by the recent cultivation of *Allium tricoccum* in North America which is already suffering from overharvesting). Ramsons was last a valuable commodity during the Second World War, when it was collected from wild populations on a large scale throughout Europe.

For a pesto recipe, please see the description for *Allium victorialis* (Chapter 6), just use the leaves of ramsons instead. You can use the leaves in all sorts of dishes and salads. The flowers are also an attractive and tasty addition to a late spring salad (see photo 78). One of my favourite spring dishes is a simple nettle and ramsons quiche made with a mixed barley and rye wholegrain pastry. The immature green seed capsules can also be used as a kind of caper.

If you plan to grow ramsons in your garden, it is probably best to start with plants as it can take 4-5 years from seed to first harvest. There are many nurseries that now sell this plant, if one doesn't have access to a wild population or a friend growing them. Seed is also readily available, and this can be more cost-effective as many plants can then be produced. The seed should preferably be planted in the autumn and should

78 (above): Ramson leaves and flowers make a delicious salad.

79 (right): Edimental or weed? Allium ursinum *in flower in an emerging bed of cinnamon fern,* Osmunda cinnamomea *at the Brest Botanical Garden in France.*

then germinate the following spring (keep the seed trays outside as cold treatment helps germination along). It may however not germinate until the second spring, so don't give up. There is a Russian variety from the Caucasus called 'cheremsha medveshonok', but there's little information about how it differs. One subspecies is recognised, ssp. *ucrainicum*.

Armoracia rusticana

FAMILY: Brassicaceae
ENGLISH: Horseradish
FRENCH: *Cranson, Raifort*
GERMAN: *Meerrettich, Kren*
JAPANESE: *Seiyou Wasabi, Wasabi Daikon*
NORWEGIAN: *Pepperrot*

Horseradish is our best-known hardy perennial root vegetable. Nowadays I come across this plant more often in the wild than in gardens, although it's difficult to spot, as these plants don't often flower. I've found three locations where it grows within 1km of my house, along the seashore. Fittingly, the botanical name *Armoracia* actually means 'near the sea plant'. It's usually found on waste ground, places where people have dumped garden refuse in the past. Only a small piece of horseradish root can give a new plant. It has been cultivated both medicinally and for food for possibly 2,000 years and it probably originates in the wild from an area in southern Russia and western Asia. However, it is nowadays found escaped from gardens over much of the northern hemisphere.

There are at least two other species, *Armoracia sisymbrioides* (from Siberia) and *A. macrocarpa* (in Eastern Europe), which are used in the same way, although the

roots are smaller (e.g., *A. sisymbrioides* is mentioned on the Wild Edible Plants of Siberia website, http://sibrast.ru). A number of cultivars are available commercially, selected for disease resistance, yield and in the case of the variety 'Variegated', ornamental value. The latter can also be used for food and has the advantage of being less vigorous (horseradish has a bit of a reputation for moving around a bit too eagerly). Apart from the variegated form, cultivars are rarely available to the gardener, although the traditional variety 'Maliner Kren' (Bohemian horseradish) is available in the US.

'Maliner Kren' was one of the varieties cultivated in the St. Louis area in the US, an area settled by German immigrants and where some 60% of the world's horseradish root is produced. An International Horseradish Festival has been arranged nearby at Collinsville in Illinois since

80: Although there are a number of horseradish cultivars, only variegated horseradish is readily available. It is well worth growing for its edimental value.

81: Most of the work in preparing horseradish is in the digging. Once you have your roots, just peel and grind/grate them, adding pickling vinegar to control the strength (the quicker one adds the vinegar, the stronger the horseradish).

82: Collection of 27 horseradish clones at the Årslev Research Station in Denmark. The plants come from throughout Denmark and can be used to develop new resistant cultivars needed for organic commercial cultivation. There is more genetic variation than one would perhaps think from a vegetatively propagated plant.

83: Blanched horseradish can be produced by covering the plants in the spring to eliminate light. Notice the large difference the blanching pot has made on the growth.

84: Horseradish is also a beautiful edimental and the flowers and flower shoots are excellent raw.

1988. Commercially, it is normally cultivated as an annual, with root cuttings planted as early as possible in the spring and harvested in the autumn or following spring.

As a gardener, it's easy to produce enough roots for your own use from a plant or two in a sunny spot on the edge of the garden where its growth can be limited. In good soil, it can send out long shoots and invade new ground. I dig up roots in the autumn and store in sand or leaves in my cold cellar so that I have access to it even when the ground is frozen outside. I most often simply grind the root and add vinegar. A good alternative, particularly if you have your own apple trees is to mix the grated horseradish with steamed, mashed, preferably tart, apples. This is the Austrian sauce *apfelkren*. Another favourite is to mix in cooked ground beetroot for your very own bloody horseradish ... Finally, here in Norway, horseradish is often used in a sauce served with fish – either melt butter or mix sour cream (Norwegian *rømme*) with grated horseradish and a splash of lemon or lime.

Sushi restaurants have become very popular in recent years and wasabi paste is an essential accompaniment. In the West and in budget restaurants in Japan, *wasabi* paste is made from a blend of horseradish, mustard and food colouring. However, authentic *wasabi* is made from the Japanese horseradish (*Wasabia japonica*), one of the world's most difficult vegetables to cultivate, accounting for its high price. See more about *Wasabia japonica* in Chapter 4.

The leaves of ordinary horseradish can also be used. It has been recorded from the 19th century in Germany that the spring leaves mixed with other wild greens, to dilute the strong taste in salad, were good and the leaves could also be blanched in a similar way to that used for wild-type chicories as in *barbe-de-capucin*. I do this by putting aside a few roots when harvesting in the autumn and forcing them in a cool dark place during the late winter or placing a pot over the plants in situ. I also increasingly use the blanched and unblanched shoots in mixed cooked vegetable dishes. Later, the flower shoots and buds and flowers are excellent raw in salads.

Cirsium oleraceum

FAMILY: Asteraceae
ENGLISH: Cabbage Thistle
FRENCH: *Le Cirse Maraîcher*
GERMAN: *Kohl-Kratzdistel*
ITALIAN: *Cardo Giallastro*
RUSSIAN: *Bodjak Ogorodnyj,
    Bodjak Ovoščenoj*

I've had a patch of cabbage thistle in my garden for many years. The clump has only very slowly expanded, perhaps because I browse it too much in spring. It's not actually very thistle-like, completely lacking the spines that are characteristic of many of the species in the *Cirsium* genus. I'm reminded of a demonstration on a US foraging site of how to de-spine the aptly named *Cirsium horridulum*, the bull thistle! The first step was to invest in a full set of body armour with reinforced gloves ... Once the stems had been rid of their protective armament the writer assured us that the resultant vegetable was excellent fare, somewhat celery-like in taste. Maybe someone out there will set up a selection programme to breed the spines out of the bull thistle in the same way that the spines were removed from the wild cardoon in the development of today's cardoons and artichokes (see Chapter 2).

Cabbage thistle can reach 1.5m in ideal conditions and likes it relatively damp whether that is in open grassland or in light woodland, gradually spreading to a clump. Its native range is from Central Europe to southern Sweden, and south to northern Italy and eastwards to western Asia. It doesn't reach the far west of Europe apart from a few locations where it has naturalised.

I enjoy the young leaves and stems in various mixed spring vegetable dishes (see, for example, photo 404 on page 233 in Chapter 6). This plant was

85: Spring leaves of the cabbage thistle, Cirsium oleraceum.

86: The pale flower heads of cabbage thistle are attractive to bees.

87 (above): A vigorously growing cabbage thistle growing in ground enriched by compost in my friend Geir Flatabø's garden reaches 2m.

88 (right): Forced and blanched cabbage thistle shoots; unblanched leaves can be seen in the background.

undoubtedly collected from the wild as a spring vegetable throughout most of its range in the past, although those traditions seem to have all but disappeared. In Italy, its use has survived up to the present as one of many wild gathered ingredients in the traditional spring dish *pistic* (see Chapter 2; Dreon and Paoletti, 2009 show a picture of the plant). In a recent study from Poland, Lukzaj and Szymanski (2007) documented that it had formerly been used, but that it was considered to be a famine food. It was prepared in different ways: the leaves were scalded and fried with butter, flour or eggs; the leaves and roots were boiled with milk as a soup; and the plant was boiled in a mix of wild plants (so-called *warmuz*) and served with potatoes and butter. So, now you can start a new health trend: the famine food diet (sounds pretty healthy to me!). Otherwise there are old references to the plant having been formerly eaten in Russia. For example, Swedish botanist Carl von Linné wrote in 1760 that it was eaten by the Russians instead of cabbage, hence the English common name. There's also a report of it being cultivated in Japan (Mansfeld's World Database), but I haven't been able to find the source of this report.

Cabbage thistle can easily be propagated by division from spring to autumn and can also be started from seed that are probably best sown outside in the autumn or winter to stratify (cold treatment). It is available currently from a few nurseries in the UK and seed is also sometimes offered.

chapter 2

SOUTHERN EUROPE AND THE MEDITERRANEAN

There are long traditions of utilising perennial plants for food in the Mediterranean countries. The most well known temperate perennial vegetables, asparagus and artichoke, were both originally domesticated in this area, when their wild progenitors were moved into gardens for convenience. For both wild asparagus species and artichokes (*Cynara* spp., notably the fairly well known cardoon) have been collected from the wild since ancient times. This is a tradition that survives to the present day. It is a mystery to me, despite these two vegetables often being cited as the most delicious of all vegetables, that so few other perennials have reached the mainstream.

In 1995, a paper was published in the journal *Economic Botany*, 'Pistic, Traditional Food from western Friuli, N.E. Italy' by Maurizio Paoletti and co-authors. It documents, through interviews with elderly people living in the sub-alpine valley Val Colvera to the northeast of Venice, a traditional springtime vegetable dish called *pistic*. It had been found that as many as 56 different species were used, the greens being simply boiled quickly and then fried in butter with garlic. Only two of these species, *Rumex acetosa* (sorrel) and *Taraxacum officinale* (dandelion), are cultivated elsewhere commercially, albeit on a small scale. Over three quarters of the species documented in this paper are perennials. The authors actually suggest that some of this wide range of edible plants could be considered for the creation of new, local vegetables, to be grown on small scale farms in a sustainable way, so let's help make this happen.

Since Paoletti's paper, realisation that traditional knowledge was rapidly disappearing with the older generation and increased interest in 'the Mediterranean Diet' has led to an explosion of similar studies in several countries. In a review article, Rivera et al. (2006) find that as many as 2,300 species have been wild-foraged in the Mediterranean countries alone. Of these, some 1,000 species are only found in one area and only 30 are widespread across the region. Around two thirds of these are actually perennial plants, i.e. a total of some 1,500 species!

Apart from *pistic*, other remarkable spring multi-species dishes have been documented in recent years, mainly in the western Mediterranean countries (see table on page 59). Probably the best-known compilations of edible plants in the world are the online freely available Plants For A Future database (www.pfaf.org) and Stephen Facciola's (1998) *Cornucopia II*. However, both largely lack this new information, apart from *pistic* that is mentioned in Facciola's book. You won't therefore find some 30-40% of the wild gathered plants of the Mediterranean in these sources.

We can conveniently classify the Mediterranean perennial vegetables into two main groups.

The first group comprises plants collected as young asparagus-like shoots, including various widespread species of asparagus and its close relations, thorny evergreen climber *Smilax aspera* and *Tamus communis* (black bryony). Other much gathered shoot forming edibles in the western Mediterranean include *Bryonia dioica* (red bryony), *Humulus lupulus* (hops), *Ornithogalum pyrenaicum* (Bath asparagus; see Chapter 1), *Ruscus aculeatus* (butcher's broom), *Epilobium angustifolium* (rosebay willowherb) and *Clematis vitalba* (old man's beard). Note that *Bryonia*, *Tamus* and *Clematis* all contain toxic alkaloids that need to be neutralised before use. Despite this *Clematis vitalba* in particular is one of the most used wild edibles. Cooking or drying removes the toxins.

The second group is those plants where mainly the young leaves and stems are used.

89: *Anchusa azurea (large blue alkanet) is a perfect perennial edimental with superb azure-blue flowers in summer. Young leaves and flowering shoots of this species and others in the same family have been gathered from the wild in most Mediterranean countries. In Cyprus, for example, they were boiled alone, boiled with beans or fried. Like its annual cousin borage, Borago officinalis, the flowers are an attractive addition to salads or just freeze them in ice-cubes.*

Commonly used throughout the region are *Silene vulgaris* (bladder campion), *Cichorium* spp. (mainly *C. intybus*, wild chicory), *Nasturtium officinale* (watercress, see Chapter 1), *Malva sylvestris* (common mallow; Chapter 4), *Apium nodiflorum* (fool's watercress), *Scorzonera* spp., *Scolymus hispanicus* (Spanish salsify), *Reichardia* spp. (notably *R. picroides*, French Scorzonera), *Anchusa* spp. (alkanet), *Centaurea* spp. (knapweed), *Plantago* spp. (plantains), *Taraxacum officinale* and other dandelion species (Chapter 1), *Urospermum dalechampii/picroides* (goldenfleeces) and *Rumex acetosa* (common sorrel; Chapter 6), *R. scutatus* (buckler-leaved sorrel) and numerous other sorrel/dock species. Other species mainly used in the western Mediterranean include *Beta maritima* (sea beet, Chapter 1), *Chenopodium bonus-henricus* (Good King Henry), *Diplotaxis* spp. (wall rockets), *Hypochaeris* spp. (cat's ears), *Urtica dioica* (stinging nettle, Chapter 1) and *Ranunculus ficaria* (lesser celandine).

Several of these plants have secondary edible parts, such as the flower receptacles of the cardoons and roots of *Scorzonera*, *Scolymus* and *Reichardia*.

Table: Multi-species dishes of the Mediterranean

Dish	Area	Comments
Pistic, Frita, Lidum or *Litum*	Western Friuli, Italy	Up to 56 species, boiled and fried with garlic
Minestra delle 18 erbe selvatiche	Sardinia	A mixed vegetable dish with up to 18 species
Misticanza/Ervi maritate (married herbs)	Sicily/southern Italy	Often used to describe a mixed salad or other dishes with several wild species
Minestrella	Garfagnana, Tuscany, Italy	A vegetable soup with sometimes over 40 species, usually with yellow beans
Ensalada campanèla	Occitan, southeast France	More than 50 species salad
Salado campanello	Provence, France	Species rich Provençal salad
Ensalada del Campo/Ensalada de la huerta	Murcia, Spain	Multi-species salad
Boreklik/Kavurmalik	Bodrum, Turkey	Pies made with mixed wild greens, sold on markets
Suppa d'erbiglie	Corsica, France	Soup with a large number of wild and cultivated vegetables, served with rice or bread crumbs

Many of these wild gathered plants are sold on local markets in the springtime. I've seen bladder campion, nettle, hops, bulbs of tassel hyacinth (*Leopoldia comosa*) and annual corn poppy leaves (*Papaver rhoeas*) for sale in markets in Firenze and Venezia in early April.

For anyone interested in traditional wild gathered plants, I would thoroughly recommend a visit to the Orto Botanico (Giardino dei Semplici) in Firenze (Florence), Italy. I stumbled on this garden on a visit in early April 2007. Nestled between art galleries with hour-long queues to get in, I was the only visitor! And what a surprise to find a sign titled Edible Plants and announcing a collection of 150 wild edible plants of the Tuscany countryside, designed to help people identify and use this wild resource. Each plant was clearly labelled with botanical and Italian name as well as its use in the kitchen. A fascinating cultural-historic-gastronomic experience.

Across the Mediterranean, there are many ways used to serve these 'free' vegetables and I've summarised the main ones in the box overleaf:

90: Smilax aspera is a bushy climber, the young shoots and stems of which are commonly used like asparagus in the eastern Mediterranean countries. It can be worth trying in a forest garden at least as far north as the UK and Denmark.

91: Young spring shoots of rosebay willowherb, Epilobium angustifolium, are also widely used as an asparagus-like vegetable throughout its circumpolar range; chances are high that you will have this in your area. It can however be a very invasive species, so is probably best kept out of the garden. A variety with white flowers is nevertheless sometimes grown.

92: Clematis vitalba (old man's beard) is one of the most used wild edibles in Italy, harvested as the spring shoots emerge, despite the fact that it contains the toxic compound protoanemonin. However, this chemical is unstable and both drying and boiling detoxicates the plants.

> ### Some preparation methods used for Mediterranean wild perennials
>
> Boil, fry in olive oil/butter with garlic (and chilli), served over pasta
>
> Boiled and garnished with oil and lemon
>
> Boiled and fried in an omelette
>
> Vegetable soup, often with cultivated beans
>
> Raw or cooked in salad, dressed with oil, vinegar (and lemon)
>
> In local traditional pies
>
> Roast in the oven in oil with cheese and herbs
>
> Mix with onions raw and serve in folded unleavened bread
>
> In a *calzone*-type (folded) pizza
>
> Stuffing in *tortelli* or *gnocchi* (potato pasta)
>
> Cooked with onions and cracked (bulgur) wheat, eaten with yogurt

Many of the preparation methods are simple and quick. This is 'Fast Slowfood' and healthy with it! I often make a green vegetable pasta sauce following roughly the first method in the table above, although I omit the initial boiling, which was originally designed for strong-tasting and toxic-when-raw herbs. I fry the garlic and/or other Alliums with a couple of chillies, cumin/coriander (alternatively ground *Heracleum* seed, see Chapter 5) for a couple of minutes. Add some bay leaves, and then add the vegetables, a little salt and pepper, tomatoes in season (or dried), cooking for five more minutes or so. Plenty of green sauce is served over the pasta garnished with grated strong local cheese. Delicious, nutritious and this can take as little as 30 minutes from garden to table.

Traditionally, the season could be extended by preserving favourite spring wild harvested vegetables either by pickling in oil or vinegar or by sun/air-drying in the warm sunny weather that normally follows the main spring harvesting season.

93 (left): Scolymus hispanicus (Spanish salsify) and other species in the same family are popular wild edibles in the Mediterranean countries, worth trying in the warmer parts of northwest Europe and similar climates. Both the young leaves and roots taste good. It is also cultivated for the market on a small scale.

94 (above): Chondrilla juncea (skeletonweed) is a widespread wild gathered edible weed of the Mediterranean countries.

95-98: Other common wild edible genera which contain ornamental species: (clockwise from top left) Eryngium (campestre); Centaurea (aspera); Notobasis (syriaca) and Onopordon (acanthium).

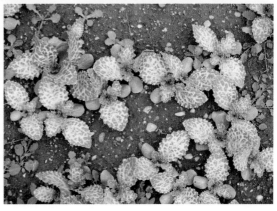

99: On a short visit to Firenze in early April, I stumbled on Orto Botanico, a small botanical garden that houses a collection of 150 wild edibles of the Tuscany countryside.

My selection for this chapter will include several of the 30 widespread species, some of which are also found in the wild in northern Europe, and will be biased towards those that are hardy enough to cultivate in my northern garden. There are more than enough exciting edibles to choose from; witness the species-rich dish which follows.

Inspired by the wild gathered plant traditions discussed above, I made a *calzone* (filled pizza) in June 2010 with 56 of the hardy species used in the Mediterranean area (see Appendix 2 on page 272 for all the plants used). This dish actually was five years in the making, as I first had to grow many of the plants! I used wholewheat spelt (it would have been even more authentic and traditional to use a sourdough variant). The filling was as in Sicilian *cudduruni*. The vegetables were first boiled and then fried in olive oil with chilli. The *calzones* were then assembled. The dough is rolled into 15cm rounds, brushing cold water around the edges, folding over and pressing the edges together to seal securely. Finally, slit the top with a knife and bake in a 220°C (430°F) oven for about 15-20 minutes. Easy and tasty once you have the ingredients (and you don't have to use 56).

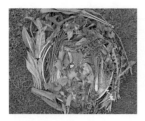   

100-103: Assembling the 56-species calzone.

Scorzonera hispanica

FAMILY: Asteraceae

ENGLISH: Scorzonera, Lettuce Salsify, Spanish Salsify, Black Oyster Plant

FRENCH: *Salsifis Noir, Scorsonère, Scorsonère d'Espagne*

GERMAN: *Schwarzwurzel, Winterspargel*

ITALIAN: *Scorzonera, Scorzonera di Spagna*

RUSSIAN: *Kozelets Ispanski*

SPANISH: *Escorzonera, Teta de Vaca*

....

Scorzonera (*Scorzonera hispanica*) is one of my top ten perennial vegetables. Most people think of it as a root vegetable, but it is much much more than that. Its biggest advantage is that it is one of the few vegetables that can be harvested fresh at any time of the year, an ever-ready permavegetable if you like. From late summer to spring, the long black cylindrical roots can be harvested. The young leaves, flower stems and buds can be used from spring to summer followed by the petals. In a cold climate where the soil freezes hard in winter, the roots can be lifted in autumn and stored in a cool place in slightly damp sand, leaf mould or similar. If too warm they will begin to sprout, but if they do you can just use the leaves or even deliberately force them.

The genus *Scorzonera* comprises some 160, mainly perennial plants, with close to 30 species in Europe, mostly in dry soils in the Mediterranean countries. Only one, dwarf Scorzonera (*Scorzonera humilis*), is a native of northern Europe. It is a rare plant in the UK. *Scorzonera hispanica* has a wild distribution ranging from Spain eastwards through Central Europe to the Caucasus and western Siberia. However, it has also frequently escaped from cultivation in other areas. The closely related genus *Tragopogon* is more familiar to northern Europeans, notably the wonderfully named biennial yellow-flowered Jack-go-to-bed-by-noon, *Tragopogon pratensis*.

104-106: Scorzonera hispanica, *useful throughout the season.*

107: Spring greens harvested early April in the author's garden. From top left clockwise: Allium senescens, salsify, sorrel, nettles, blanched horseradish, sweet cicely, ground elder, bistort and lesser celandine.

Salsify (*Tragopogon porrifolius*) is another Mediterranean species that has been domesticated as a minor biennial root vegetable, although new rapid growing varieties of Scorzonera seem nowadays to be preferred.

In the Mediterranean countries, various *Scorzonera* species have been wild-foraged for food from Spain in the west to the Middle East. In Spain, four species were recorded by Tardio et al. (2006), notably *S. laciniata* and *S. angustifolia*, but also, not surprisingly, *S. hispanica*. In the western Mediterranean, *Scorzonera* species are in fact among the 10 most common wild gathered vegetables. It is the tender young leaves, the sweet stems (my favourite part) and sometimes the unripe flower buds (the bottom part if used raw), which have traditionally been used rather than the roots. Use of roots seems to be rare apart from *S. hispanica* in Spain.

It seems that the greens are almost always eaten raw in salads. For example, in 1871, J.B. Gaut has *Scorzonera laciniata* and *Tragopogon pratensis* used together with a large number of other species in a Provençal country salad. Elsewhere, I've seen references to boiling the leaves, boiling the young shoots like asparagus and cooking the young flower buds in omelette.

Scorzonera hispanica seems not to have been domesticated before the 17th century when it became quite popular as a root crop, but perhaps at the back of people's minds was that the black root would somehow miraculously protect them from the Black Death. By about 1660 it was being cultivated in France and Italy. It had presumably reached northern Europe by the end of that century, as it was cultivated in England by 1683. It was mentioned in Norway's first gardening book, *Horticultura*, from 1694. Louis XIV of France was the best-known 'Scorzoneraphile' of the time. It never seems to have been more than a marginal crop in its homeland, Spain. Belgium is recognised as the largest producer of Scorzonera today, but it's also grown commercially in France, the Netherlands, Germany and Russia.

108 (top left): Scorzonera
laciniata *is the commonest wild
harvested Scorzonera species
in Spain, producing plentiful
succulent attractive looking
spring greens.*

109 (top right): I received
the plant on the right as
Tragopogon orientalis *but that
species is yellow flowered. It's
a large biennial which self-
sows and is closer to salsify,
T.* porrifolius, *but is a larger
plant than other name-variety
salsifies I've grown (notice the
lighter coloured flower at the
back which may be a hybrid).*

110 (above): Scorzonera
suberosa *ssp.* cariensis *is a
dwarf species sometimes grown
as an ornamental in the rock
garden.*

111 (right): Scorzonera purpurea
*is another attractive species for
the edimental garden.*

There are a number of varieties available commercially or from seed banks and seed savers organisations in Europe. Seed Savers Exchange in the US had, for example, seven varieties on offer in 2010. Selection has been made for uniformity of roots, earliness, length, colour, flavour and late flowering. However, only amateurs seem to have worked with selection for leaf production (read the interesting account on Dan Borman's work on what he calls 'Lettuce-Salsify' in Carol Deppe's book *Breeding Your Own Vegetable Varieties,* p.143). When growing Scorzonera for the roots, traditionally plants were harvested 2-3 years old. This is because it takes that long for the roots to get big enough, but quicker growing annual varieties have recently become available. After 2-3 years the older roots get a bit tough. Like Burdock (*Arctium* spp.) and Jerusalem artichoke (*Helianthus tuberosus*), the roots of Scorzonera contain the diabetic-friendly carbohydrate inulin. If your main emphasis is rather on the leaves,

112: A new wave of the young tasty leaves appear after cutting back Scorzonera (the picture was taken at the end of July in the UK).

113 & 114: My favourite vegetable from Scorzonera is the long flower shoots (left), crisp and surprisingly sweet, as are the flower shoots of another Aster family member, burdock (below) which just needs peeling to give you a fantastic vegetable that is hardly mentioned in literature. (See also artichoke flower stalks below.)

stems, buds and flowers, your plants can be left in the same spot for years. You can then harvest two or three times from the same plant each year, first the spring leaves, new growth subsequently appearing and you can later harvest the flower stems and buds. After flowering, the plant gets straggly and it's best to cut the plant back if you're a tidy gardener (I'm not). A bonus second crop of leaves then soon appears.

For root production, light, deep, sandy, stone-free soil is best to keep the roots from forking but for the leaves it is not important at all and I even have some plants on clay. They grow best in an open sunny location. Sow initially about 15cm apart, thinning to 30cm after a couple of years, harvesting the roots of the thinnings. The seed must be fresh as one-year-old seed of *Scorzonera* and *Tragopogon* species will generally not germinate. There are few pests or diseases affecting Scorzonera and it is therefore a trouble-free organic crop that is well adapted to drought conditions once established.

Cynara cardunculus var. *scolymus*

FAMILY: Asteraceae
ENGLISH: Artichoke, Globe Artichoke
GERMAN: *Artischocke*
ITALIAN: *Carciofo*
SPANISH: *Alcachofa, Alcaucil*

Cynara cardunculus var. *altilis*

ENGLISH: Cardoon, Artichoke Thistle
FRENCH: *Cardon, Artichaut à Cardes*
GERMAN: *Cardy*
ITALIAN: *Cardo Selvatico, Cardone*
SPANISH: *Cardo*

Years ago, I was attending a conference in San Francisco and had hired a car to explore the countryside around. I accidentally stumbled upon the self-proclaimed

'Artichoke Centre of the World', the town of Castroville in Monterey County. The surrounding area produces some 75% of the total US production. There's an annual artichoke festival there and also a giant artichoke sculpture. I remember popping into a small supermarket for something to eat and the counter was piled high with fresh artichoke pizza, my first and only time.

Alongside asparagus, the globe artichoke is the best-known temperate perennial vegetable. It is mostly cultivated commercially in areas with a Mediterranean climate, including Italy (the largest producer), Spain, France, Argentina, Chile, California and, increasingly, China. It has unfortunately limited winter hardiness which restricts where it can be grown as a perennial, although sheltering in some way from winter rain (cloches etc.) and/or mulching with leaves in autumn can be successful in northern gardens. In southern Norway, artichokes have been grown successfully in the past (for the King) and the roots were protected in winter by covering with a large slate to protect from precipitation. It's not impossible to grow artichokes successfully in even more severe climates. Here at 64.5°N, close to the Arctic Circle, I dig up the whole plant and overwinter in a large bucket in my root cellar which has a steady winter temperature of 2-5°C. A lot of effort, but well worth it to be able to harvest delicious home-grown sub-arctic artichokes, probably the tastiest on the planet!

Back to Castroville in California, where most of the production is perennial on a 5-10 year cycle, new plants being propagated vegetatively as offsets. However, there is an increasing trend to annual production. Plants are started from seed and they then occupy the land for a shorter period. This decreases maintenance costs and allows the farmers to use the land also for other crops in an area where the land is productive all year round. This has been made possible by increased uniformity of seed propagated plants in recent years. Annual production also allows artichokes

115: Sub-arctic green globe artichokes produced by overwintering the plants in a root cellar.

to be produced in areas where winter hardiness would be an issue. For example, artichokes were produced as annuals in the area around Stockholm in Sweden in the 18-19th century, starting the plants indoors with heat very early in the year.

It is nowadays considered that artichokes and cardoons are varieties or selections starting from the same wild species, *Cynara cardunculus*, the wild cardoon, which are large spiny plants with branched flowering stems. This species is found in the western Mediterranean countries as well as the Canary Islands and Madeira. Artichokes and cardoons can be crossed and in fact well-known plant breeder Alan Kapuler of Peace Seeds in Oregon has worked with trying to develop a hardier artichoke by crossing with cardoons that do tolerate somewhat lower temperatures.

In the recent studies of traditional wild gathered Mediterranean edibles discussed in the introduction to this chapter, the various *Cynara* species, including wild cardoon, figure strongly throughout the region. They have been widely collected from the wild for the table; most importantly the leaf stems are used. Flower stems and receptacles (the part of the artichoke most commonly eaten) are also used. It is collected during the damper cooler winter growth season and, at that time of year, the edible parts of the leaves are less bitter. Nevertheless, these wild gathered plants are first de-stringed (or peeled) to remove the longitudinal fibres on the outside of the ribbed petioles and are invariably either boiled and/or fried.

In the north of Europe, cardoons are grown in summer and leaves are then quite bitter, and it is therefore necessary to blanch them by wrapping the leaves in cardboard, newspaper or such-like for three weeks or more before harvest. Incidentally, artichokes are sometimes also grown for their edible leaf petioles and are then known as artichoke chard. As a by-product of my overwintering of artichokes in my cellar, I discovered that even in 3-5°C the leaves, cut down to ground level when moved to the cellar, would re-sprout from the root and grow away quite strongly (remember that artichokes are adapted to growing in the winter months in their home range, when temperatures are low). As it is completely dark in the cellar, I am able to harvest my own mid-winter blanched artichoke chard, a welcome treat for the time of year.

116: Cellar-blanched artichoke chards.

Other traditional wild gathered species in the same genus include *Cynara humilis* and *C. baetica* (southern Spain, Portugal and Morocco), *C. cornigera* and *C. sibthorpiana* (eastern Mediter-ranean islands and Greece) and *C. syriaca* (Turkey and the eastern Mediterranean). Some of these can also be found on local markets. Cardoon has unfortunately become a major weed elsewhere around the world, notably in some South American countries, southern Australia and also California. Therefore, you will find that Tim Low in his Australian book, *Bush Tucker*, advocates harvesting the cardoon thistle heads that abound around both Melbourne and Adelaide. Cardoons are also a foraging object in California, particularly for families of Mediterranean extraction.

The traditions of using wild cardoons in the local cuisine of the Mediterranean countries can be traced back to antiquity. However, neither modern day cardoon nor artichoke seems to have been domesticated in any big way by the time of the Romans. The best estimate seems to be that artichokes existed by the end of the first millennium, with the first definite sightings not before the early 15th century, whereas domestication of cardoon happened during the first half of the second millennium. From the wild cardoon gene pool, artichokes were selected for their large spineless flower heads, whereas cardoons were selected for spineless large leaf chards. This has resulted in cardoons being taller plants (up to 3m) with many small heads,

117: Cardoons at the market in Firenze, Italy in early April.

whereas artichokes are typically 1.5-2m with few larger heads. Cardoons were relatively well-known in the UK from the late middle ages to the 19th century, often mentioned in cookery books from that period. Interest returned in the 1970s with the boom in self-sufficient lifestyles, but they've never become mainstream vegetables.

Artichokes grown as perennials are started from offshoots or suckers in northern Europe in the spring and are planted usually about 1.5m apart, as these are large plants. If you start from seed you may not get what you expect, as there is often a lot of variation in seed propagated plants. Therefore, you may want to plant closer together to start with and then select the plants with the characteristic you're looking for. For example, I've had the odd inferior spiny plant from seed. A mulch of compost or manure each

118: Artichokes in early April interplanted with olive trees in the Tuscany countryside near Firenze; an inspiration for forest gardening in Mediterranean countries.

119: *Baby artichokes or* botoi *(the second pickings) on the Rialto market in Venice.*

120: Silybum marianum *is often planted as an attractive spring foliage plant, growing well in cool weather like most Mediterraneans.*

121: *Few realise that the young leaves of* Silybum marianum *are an excellent spring green and the young inflorescences are also used like baby artichokes, eaten whole.*

spring is worthwhile. Different authors suggest that artichokes should be re-propagated every 3-10 years. If your yield begins to decrease significantly, then you know what to do. Artichokes and cardoons are cultivated on a wide range of soils from sandy to clay. However, they don't like standing water and need to be in a fairly sunny location.

There are many varieties of artichoke, selected variously for spinelessness (e.g. 'Green Globe Improved'), hardiness (try 'Northern Star' in borderline areas), colour ('Violetto'; also attractive as an ornamental) and for annual production. There are also varieties developed for producing baby artichokes such as 'Purple de Jesi' and 'Purple Sicilian'. These are eaten whole either raw or steamed, as wild cardoon heads have been eaten for millennia in the Mediterranean region. The very closely related, but annual edimental *Silybum marianum*, the milk thistle, is also used in the same way. The young leaves are also a very good spring green, autumn sowed (used before the spines develop).

Although cardoons are usually grown as annuals, starting from seed as with annual artichokes some 8-10 weeks before you expect to be able to plant out, there's no reason why you couldn't grow them as perennials and harvest the leaf petioles when you wish. In fact, cardoons are often grown as ornamentals. Typically used at the back of a border, it's a fantastic foliage plant early in the year. Cardoon was actually awarded the UK Royal Horticultural Society's Award of Garden Merit in 1993 as an ornamental. Time perhaps for the RHS to introduce an edimental category I think. The cultivars 'Ivory Coast' and 'Gros Vert de Laon' are particularly fine foliage varieties.

A particularly interesting type of cardoon from Italy, which is more of a local cultivation technique, is the

122 (top left): Cardoon's silver grey-green foliage is at its most dramatic in the spring, here in mid-April in England.

123 (above): Cardoon is a tall plant, here towering to some 3m in a vegetable garden in Holland.

124 (left): The Scandinavian heirloom artichoke variety 'Herrgårds' growing in my friend Åke Truedsson's old garden in Malmø, Sweden.

125 (far left): The lavender stamens of various Cynara species have traditionally been used as vegetable rennet, for coagulating sheep and goat's milk.

so-called 'Gobbi' or 'Hunchback Cardoon' or 'Il Cardo Gobbo di Nizza Monferrato'. Nizza Monferrato is a municipality in the Piedmont region in northwest Italy. In this area, the cardoon stalks are bent towards the ground and covered with sandy soil that blanches them. The result is that the backs of the cardoons are strongly curved, apparently resembling the backs of the local gravediggers. It is now a Slow Food Presidium product. 'Gobbi' are often prepared simmered and dipped in *bagna cauda* sauce, which is a hot anchovy and garlic dip. This would certainly disguise any residual bitterness. Maybe this is the way to go if you find your cardoons too strong tasting (as many do).

Cynara cardunculus and its varieties have also been used in numerous other ways. Roots apparently have a good flavour and can be treated like parsnips or carrots and like many members of the *Asteraceae*, contain inulin, and are one of its medicinal sources. The inner part of the flower stem is also a delicacy (see the last section on Scorzonera) and has a sweet, nutty flavour. You can also grow your own vegetable rennet if you are interested in cheese making. The lavender stamens in the flower have traditionally been dried and used as the coagulant with sheep and goat's milk, both in France and Iberia. You can then finish off your meal with artichoke coagulated cheese and Cynar, the old Italian artichoke flavoured liqueur. Finally, you might even in the future be able to take the bus home fuelled by cardoon seed biofuel ... A useful plant indeed.

Myrrhis odorata

FAMILY: Apiaceae
ENGLISH: Sweet Cicely
FRENCH: *Cerfeuil Musqué*
GERMAN: *Süßdolde*
ITALIAN: *Mirride delle Alpi*
NORWEGIAN: *Spansk Kjørvel*
SPANISH: *Perifollo Oloroso*

When my kids were growing up, their favourite plant in the garden was without doubt sweet cicely. It was the immature seeds that attracted them as they have a very pleasant sweet aniseed taste, reminding most Scandinavians of a very popular old-fashioned sweet called King of Denmark. This seems to be universal. My friend Telsing in Canada told me that the green seeds are so tasty that her kids refer to them as candy. So much was the grazing pressure on my plants that it rarely self-sowed and it's only since the kids have left home that the invasive nature of this plant has become apparent. Here in Norway, it's on the national invasive species list that means it is an unwanted immigrant. Along with other invasive edibles such as Japanese knotweed, in my opinion this is a positive addition to our flora and sometime in the future when wild edibles are again an important food source, we will thank our ancestors for introducing these plants.

Sweet cicely hails from the South and Central European mountains and is found up to 2,000m. It was likely that the Romans spread it elsewhere in Europe including to the UK. Their ancestors have certainly until modern times continued to harvest this plant from the wild and it is noted by Rivera et al. (2006) as one of the 10 most important wild gathered perennials of the Mediterranean alpine zone. It was certainly cultivated in medieval herb gardens and the well-known English herbalist John Gerard was a fan, writing (in 1597), "The seedes eaten as a sallade whilest they are yet greene, with oile, vinegar, and pepper exceede all other sallads by many degree".

From introductions in gardens over the years, *Myrrhis odorata* has naturalised widely in Europe and also a few places in North America, although it is not so far considered a noxious species there. It is nowadays found mainly in colder areas of Eastern Europe, Scandinavia and northern Britain.

Given the right conditions, i.e. open to shady dampish locations, sweet cicely can grow to about 1.5m tall and it looks superficially like a large robust version of cow parsley (*Anthriscus sylvestris*). The leaves are large, triangular in shape with characteristic whitish flecks. The leaves and stems are usually softly hairy, but there is more variation in this species than is widely realised. My Danish friend Søren was surprised to learn that his hairless plant was unusual and he also told me of a red-stemmed plant that he had seen on an allotment. Hopefully, these forms will become available at some stage.

Sweet cicely is best propagated with fresh autumn seed sown outside, as old seed will probably not germinate. Otherwise, plants are readily available commercially or just beg a friend for a division, best taken from autumn to spring. You will probably find that one or just a few plants are sufficient. Plant it in a prominent place in your garden as it is an attractive plant and you will be snacking on it.

Back to its roots in Italy, *Mirride delle Alpi* is used today in a wide range of dishes as a flavouring for salads, soups, in omelettes, and even in a salt cod (*baccalà*) recipe (the Norwegian connection). The first flush of edible leaves appears very early in the spring (January in the south to April in more northern locations) and is unaffected by

126 (right): The spring leaves and stems of sweet cicely can be used in a wide range of dishes from salads to soups. Notice the characteristic white blotches on the leaves.

127 (far right): Blanched sweet cicely is very tasty raw in salads!

128 (below): The flowers and young green seeds of sweet cicely are excellent additions to summer salads or just as a garden snack.

129 (above): Sweet cicely and rhubarb are great companion plants in the garden and in the kitchen.

spring frosts. Later on you can harvest first leaves and later flower stems. The flower umbels are almost as tasty as the young green seeds (use, for example, in mixed salads). The seeds should be used while still young as they quickly become fibrous.

Experiment with it, it can be successfully combined with almost anything; I've even used it in curries (including in *raita*, Indian yogurt, the sweet taste combining nicely

with the other spices). As a sweetener, a bunch of sweet cicely sufficiently counteracts the sourness of rhubarb as in, for example, rhubarb crumble. There are otherwise numerous recipes to be found on the internet using this plant.

If you do forget to harvest the young seeds, collect them in the autumn and sow them densely in a large pot outside, bringing them into a warm room to germinate in the early spring. You will then have your very own sweet cicely sprouts.

Before we leave sweet cicely, let me give a quick plug for a group of seldom seen, mainly American perennial herbs also going under this name (or sometimes sweetroot), the genus *Osmorhiza*. These are smaller plants and have a slightly different sweet 'licquoricy' taste. To some people I've asked, they are even tastier. I've grown two species, *Osmorhiza longistylis* and *O. claytonii* (Longstyle and Clayton's sweetroot respectively). Why not seek them out?

130: Osmorhiza longistylis *is also commonly known as sweet cicely, a native of eastern North America. It is closely related to* Myrrhis odorata; *it can be used in a similar way and has excellent flavour, though it's not as productive as its namesake.*

Ranunculus ficaria

FAMILY: Ranunculaceae
ENGLISH: Lesser Celandine, Pilewort, Fig Buttercup
FRENCH: *Ficaire, Renoncule Ficaire*
GERMAN: *Scharbockskraut*
ITALIAN: *Ranuncolo Favagello*
NORWEGIAN: *Vårkål*
SWEDISH: *Svalört*
....

I steered clear of lesser celandine as an edible for many years due to the reputation of the genus *Ranunculus* for being poisonous to folk and livestock. It is often stated that all species of the genus are poisonous and Richard Mabey's *Food for Free* from 1972 repeats this. Neither does Mabey's *Flora Britannica* reveal any traditional use of this plant in the UK. I had always wondered how the plant had received its common Norwegian name *vårkål*, which literally means spring cabbage. No traditional uses of this plant seem to have survived here (Høeg, 1976). The German name *scharbockskraut* (scurvy herb) reflects its earlier use as a spring vegetable. Digging deeper, it turns out that the famous Swedish botanist Carl von Linné had referred to it being used in salads in the middle of the 18th century in Sweden. Hoffberg (1792) also refers to its use as a vegetable used in Sweden. More recently, its traditional use has been documented in several other European countries right up to modern times. Dreon and Paoletti (2009) record its use in six Italian studies both cooked and raw (including in *pistic* and *minestrella*) and Ertug (2004) notes it being wild collected in Turkey as a spring green; in Poland, Lukzaj and Szymanski (2007) say that it was used up until the late 20th century (young leaves boiled or raw, often simply with butter or lard or as a garnish with *barszcz*, beetroot soup).

What finally convinced me to try this herb was reading *Taste of the Wild Edible Plant Diary* published on the internet in April 2002 by Rosie Castle (who ran an interesting small nursery, Alternative Plants) and edible plant enthusiast, Ulrike Paradine. They wrote, 'Since February we have been enjoying the leaves and flowers of lesser celandine in salads. In fact it seems astonishing to us that the lesser celandine is not better known as a first-rate salad plant! The leaves are tender, with a mild, pleasant flavour and make all the difference to an otherwise boring supermarket lettuce – use them as a substitute if you want. They are rich in vitamin C and the choice of cultivated forms for leaf colour and flower is bewildering.' However, lesser celandine leaves do contain the toxin protoanemonin, which is commonly found in plants in the buttercup family. Although levels of this toxin are often quoted to be lower up to the time of flowering, I find no references to real measurements and therefore prefer to err on the safe side and therefore **only recommend their use early in spring before the flowers begin to appear and only boiled or dried, both of which destroys the toxins,** although I do regularly eat a few leaves in mixed salads!

131: Lesser celandine in full flower early in May in the author's garden. It was originally introduced in a damp spot under redcurrant bushes, but it has quickly colonised a neighbouring area planted up with ostrich fern, Matteuccia struthiopteris, and has actually outcompeted ground elder which once dominated here!

Ranunculus ficaria's wild range covers most of Europe from southern Scandinavia in the north, and south to the Mediterranean countries, including North Africa and East to West Asia. It has also been introduced to eastern North America and has been declared an unwanted noxious weed in Connecticut and Massachusetts as it is spreading rapidly there and in a number of other states. A number of subspecies are recognised, separated by whether bulbils occur in the leaf axils or not, whether the plants are straggling or upright, leaf size and shape and flower size. It thrives best on damp calcareous woodland soils, shaded banks of streams and more open moist disturbed sites.

In parts of Europe with mild, wet winters, the leaves appear after their summer rest in late autumn and the main harvesting period is from then until early spring. Here in Norway, the leaves normally don't appear until April and are available for 2-3 weeks before the flowers appear.

In my area, the form with bulbils is most common and if planted in the wrong place can be difficult to eradicate. Forms lacking the bulbils can also spread quickly by seed, so please only plant where it won't later become a nuisance. I inherited a garden with this species and removed it where I didn't want it by systematic digging over several years. It's impossible to find all the tiny tubers! I replanted it in a damp area of the garden under some berry bushes that already had a ground cover of ground elder. The celandine has well and truly defeated the ground elder and has invaded an area where I have planted ostrich fern (*Matteuccia struthiopteris*), but the two grow comfortably side-by-side.

132: Ranunculus ficaria's *small tubers supposedly resemble bunches of figs, giving the plant its scientific epithet* ficaria *(fig-like).*

I've also trialled the subspecies *chrysocephalus* from southeast Europe, a more robust plant that has been well-behaved here so far (it lacks bulbils). Perhaps this is a better bet if you are concerned with keeping control.

There are around 60 cultivars available from UK nurseries at present (RHS Plant Finder) and some collectors are known to grow over 100 varieties. Lesser celandine has been cultivated as an ornamental in Europe since the 16th century and it is claimed that in 1792 there were 800 varieties. It is most often grown for its attractive heart-shaped leaves that vary in colour from bronze to green and often have attractive silver or bronze mottled markings. The colour of the flowers also varies from the normal shiny yellow to cream and white and a number of double flowered varieties exist.

133: Ranunculus ficaria *'Brazen Hussy' is a popular bronze-leaved variant.*

Unfortunately, not all cultivars are as hardy as the species and I have lost several of those I've tried. You should also be careful when using the ornamental varieties for food, as we know little of their chemistry, but a few colourful leaves in a spring salad will not harm you.

I have personally so far used lesser celandine mostly in early spring mixed greens cooked dishes and mixed salads.

Finally, please do not confuse this species with greater celandine (*Chelidonium majus*), which is not related and is a poisonous yellow flowered plant in the poppy family, *Papaveraceae*.

Silene vulgaris (syn. *S. inflata*; *S. cucubalus*)

FAMILY: Caryophyllaceae
AMERICAN: Maidenstears
ENGLISH: Bladder Campion
FRENCH: *Silène Enflé*
GERMAN: *Taubenkropf-Leimkraut*
GREEK: *Stroufouthkia, Tsakridia, Strouthi*
ITALIAN: *Carletti, Strigoli, Silene Rigonfia, Bubbolini*
NORWEGIAN: *Engsmelle*
SPANISH: *Colleja, Colletas*

Bladder campion or *carletti* is one of the most commonly eaten wild perennial plants in the Mediterranean area, widespread across the region in meadows, along roadsides and on wasteland. It is otherwise found more or less everywhere in Europe where there is farmland, and is distributed far to the east into Siberia. It has also been introduced through agriculture to most other parts of the temperate world, including North and South America, Australia and New Zealand. However, common use as an edible seems to be almost restricted to the Mediterranean countries, although it is given a brief mention in *Food for Free* (Mabey, 1972). It is also known to have been used at least locally in the 19th century here in Norway.

Silene vulgaris reaches some 50-70cm with hairless grey-green leaves and stems with masses of white flowers with deeply cut petals and with the characteristic inflated sepal tubes.

In recent ethnobotanical literature, this plant is documented to be used traditionally

134 (left): **Silene vulgaris** *on a roadside verge in Norway.*

135 (above): **Silene vulgaris** *on sale on the Rialto market in Venice, Italy.*

in most if not all Mediterranean countries. It is used in a wide range of dishes, in fact most of those listed in the table on page 59; some examples are in *suppa d'erbiglie* (Corsica); *pistic* (Italy, along with two other family members *Silene dioica* and *S. latifolia*); *bqula* (Morocco; boiled, fried greens garnished with lemon and olives); *salado campanello* (Provence, France); *minestrella* soup (Garfagnana, Italy, also with *Silene alba*); in omelettes and scrambled egg (Spain, where it is one of the three most used wild edibles around Madrid); in *misticanza* salad (central Italy). In Cyprus, it is the most used wild gathered edible, added to small mixed vegetable pies together with boiled corn poppy (*Papaver rhoeas*), docks (*Rumex* spp.) and fennel (*Foeniculum vulgare*), and served with rice or couscous. Wild fennel (*F. vulgare* ssp. *piperitum*) is incidentally one of the most commonly wild-foraged plants in the Mediterranean region, literally from Spain to Palestine. For example, Della et al. (2006) recorded 10 different uses of the plant in the kitchen in Cyprus alone. This plant was so important to the Romans that it was cultivated in Britain and has since naturalised (Campbell and Hall, 2006) and is today widespread mainly in the south of the country (*F. vulgare* ssp. *vulgare*).

Seed of *Silene vulgaris* is currently sold as a vegetable by Italian seed merchants Franchi Sementi, under the common name sculpit (*Silene inflata*, which is a synonym). I've also seen it for sale on eBay as 'One of southern Italy's

Ingredients for **carletti risotto** *(left to right):* Allium babingtonii, Silene vulgaris *(carletti),* Levisticum *(lovage),* Allium x proliferum *(Egyptian onion),* Allium ampeloprasum *'Oerprei'* and Laurus nobilis *(bay leaves).*

Carletti Risotto

2 cups of cooked mixed whole grain rice and barley (mixed) (the rice and barley take the same time to cook, or just use barley, for the 'slowest' food outside of rice growing areas)

2 carrots

Carletti greens

Mixed perennial onions

Chilli (optional)

A few bay leaves

75g mature cheese

Small glass of apple juice or wine

Boil the carrots, adding the *carletti* for the last few minutes. Fry the onions with bay leaves in olive oil for a few minutes. Mix the cooked carrots and *carletti* greens with the onions and a little vegetable water and other mixed Mediterranean herbs of your choice. Then mix in the rice/barley mixture with the juice or wine, finally mixing in the cheese. Serve with garlic bread.

136 (above): Partly blanched carletti in my garden; good raw in mixed salads.

137 (above right): One of the commonest ways to serve wild greens in the Mediterranean countries is simply to fry the vegetables in olive oil with chilli, stir in eggs, salt and pepper and scramble. For a special occasion, decorate with flowers for a gourmet variant! Here I used Allium scorodoprasum, carletti and wild asparagus with dandelion, Chinese Allium humile and flowers of the North American spring beauty, Claytonia virginica.

138 (right): The pink-flowered form, Silene vulgaris 'Rosea', makes an attractive garden plant.

best kept secrets'. It is sometimes cultivated, also outside of its native range; for example, in California to supply Italian markets there.

In the perennial garden it is easily grown and reliably long-lived. It can be a bit invasive as it produces a lot of seed, just harvest the seedlings for food or remember to deadhead as soon as the flowers are over (the plant won't give up and will flower again so you will probably have to dead-head twice). *Silene vulgaris* is otherwise a variable species, so that a bit of selection work should pay off with more productive varieties for the home garden. It is best grown in a relatively sunny spot, but will tolerate some shade.

Humulus lupulus

FAMILY: Cannabaceae
CHINESE: *Pi Jiu Hua*
ENGLISH: Hop, Common Hop
FRENCH: *Houblo*
GERMAN: *Hopfen*
ITALIAN: *Luppolo Commune*
JAPANESE: *Hoppu, Seiyou Karahanasou*
NORWEGIAN: *Humle*
SPANISH: *Lúpulo, Espárragos de Zarza*

About 15 years ago, I was in Venice for a meeting in early April and was surprised to find bundles of hop shoots, *bruscandoli*, on the market there. I was later in Firenze and on a cycle trip into the countryside I quickly located wild hops growing along a riverbank. Hop shoots have no doubt been used in the western Mediterranean countries since ancient times, their use having been documented in remote communities and traditional dishes both in Italy, Spain and Morocco in recent years. It is, for example, used in the multi-species spring vegetable dish, *pistic*, in northern Italy and was traditionally most commonly cooked with egg as with other asparagus-like herbs.

Hops is a widely distributed plant in the northern hemisphere, and is found wild or escaped over most of Europe from the Mediterranean to northern Norway. Its range takes it east to western Siberia, and the distinctive var. *cordifolius* has an isolated distribution in Japan. Hops are also found as a wild plant and naturalised from cultivation over much of North America. It is originally a woodland climber and can reach six or even seven metres under optimal conditions in one season, dying back to ground level each autumn.

139: Hop shoots at the Rialto market in Venice, Italy in early April.

Further north in Europe, it is uncertain whether the use of hop as a vegetable pre-dates its cultivation for beer. Commercial cultivation started in the 16th century in Belgium. Herbalist John Gerard mentions the edibility of the shoots in his herbal of 1633 as follows, 'The buds or first sprouts which come forth in the spring are used to be eaten in salads'. Swedish botanist Linné notes in 1760 that the Dutch eat the shoots in particular. Hop shoots certainly later became popular amongst the migrant beer hop workers in Kent by the 19th century. When shoots were pruned out in the spring, the workers used the supple tops as food. The shoots are known to have been used in soup and served like asparagus with

140: Venice-inspired Pasta Nero de Sepia with hop-shoot green pasta sauce, parmesan cheese and pine nuts is a colourful combination; something for the death metal fan in your family, perhaps?

butter on toast (Davidson, 1999) and they were also sold on Covent Garden market in London. Roger Phillips (1983) includes an 18th century English recipe for Hop Top Soup. In recent years, hop shoots have also been spotted in supermarkets in the UK.

A renaissance in interest in hop shoots has been seen in the home of hop growing, western Flanders in Belgium. As so often, what was once peasant food is now served in local gourmet restaurants. It is sold for £65-85/kg ($110-135) as they are very labour intensive to produce and open field production only yields once a year. However, techniques have recently been developed giving two harvests a year in greenhouses. Unlike Italian *bruscandoli*, Belgian *jet de houblon* are blanched white by drawing earth over the roots and harvesting the shoots as they emerge.

Here in Norway, hops are a common site climbing up old farmhouse walls, a relic from earlier local hop production for beer making. However, there are no records of the shoots being used for food, apart from in a war-time book (Holmboe, 1941) that speaks warmly about them.

Native Americans mainly used hops medicinally, although there are some records of it being used as flavouring when baking bread and cooking potatoes (Moerman, 1998).

141: Golden hop vine is a perfect climbing edimental.

Anyone with land can easily grow their own gourmet hop shoots and later in the same season harvest hops for beer. Although seed is sometimes available, if you also want to harvest hops for beer, you will want one of the female cultivars. As far as I know, there are no cultivars developed for the shoots. It might be worth trying one of the more easily trained new dwarf varieties such as 'First Gold' ('Prima Donna') or 'Golden Tassels', although they still grow to about 2.5m. Hops are not that fussy about soil and tolerate both sunny conditions (up a house wall, for example), and deep shade. It could therefore be used as a climber in the forest garden.

The shoots grow quickly in warm spring weather; so don't turn your back as they quickly become too fibrous, although the tops are always good. You can also grow white (blanched) hop shoots by either earthing up or covering with a large pot. A second flush of shoots will emerge after the first are harvested and these can also be used letting a few shoots grow on. Golden hop shoots can also be produced using the golden hop vine *Humulus lupulus* 'Aureus', one of the finest climbing foliage edimentals.

Campanula trachelium

FAMILY: Campanulaceae
ENGLISH: Nettle-leaved Bellflower, Bats-in-the-Belfry
FRENCH: *Campanule Gantelée, Campanule à Feuilles d'Ortie*
GERMAN: *Nesselblättrige Glockenblume*
ITALIAN: *Campanula Selvatica*

In Chapter 6, I will discuss *Campanula latifolia*, the giant bellflower of northern Europe. *Campanula trachelium* (the nettle-leaved bellflower, no it doesn't sting like a nettle!) has a more southwesterly distribution than *C. latifolia* and replaces the latter species in the south of England, France, Italy, Spain and North Africa and eastwards into West Asia. It has also widely naturalised in northeast North America. It has similar ecological requirements to the giant bellflower, inhabiting open woodlands and hedgerows. It has a preference for alkaline soils and grows well on clay. It is also a large bellflower reaching over 1m when conditions are good. It is an excellent plant for the forest garden, also having edimental qualities like its giant namesake. It flowers from mid-to-late summer.

142: The nettle-leaved bellflower is a productive plant, growing quickly in early spring to over 1m.

It has been used traditionally in Italy in mixed species spring soups such as *minestrella* (see page 59) and is one of the ingredients in *pistic* (boiled and fried, see page 59). The young leaves and flowers can also be used in salads, having a mild slightly sweet taste.

Seeds and plants are readily available in Europe and North America. There are some particularly fine ornamental forms available in the trade which you might like to try, including a single-flowered white form (var. *alba*), a double white ('Alba Flore Pleno') and 'Bernice' (a deep purple-blue form).

Apium nodiflorum

FAMILY: Apiaceae
CYPRIOTE: *Arkoseleno*
ENGLISH: Fool's Watercress
FRENCH: *Ache Faux-Cresson*
GERMAN: *Knotenblütige Sellerie*
ITALIAN: *Sedano d'Acqua*
SPANISH: *Berra*

Strangely missed in the major databases and books on edible plants such as Plants For A Future and *Cornucopia II*, this perennial celery has traditionally been one of the most popular wild gathered edibles in the western Mediterranean countries from Spain to Cyprus. Otherwise, it is found in the wild in France and in the British Isles. Throughout this range, it cohabits with watercress (see Chapter 1) with which it is often confused (hence its common name). To me its taste is closest to carrot. It isn't particularly hardy and doesn't usually overwinter in my climate, although plants from the northern part of its range may fare better. I therefore started growing the plant in a large pot (without drainage holes to keep it damp) and overwinter it in a cold cellar where the temperature is normally 2-4°C in mid-winter. I discovered that it continued to grow slowly at this temperature and I could harvest fresh salad greens most of the winter.

In the Mediterranean, it is more often used in salads than many other wild edibles, but is also used in soups such as the Tuscan wild soup, *minestrella*. Nebel et al. (2006) recorded this species as the base of *Insalata di Spèlendra,* served with spring onion and oil and vinegar dressing. Like second-year garden celery (*Apium graveolens*), a bonus is that the seed is easy to collect and is good sprinkled on savoury dishes as flavouring.

143: Apium nodiflorum *posing in the snow in the author's garden; an excellent winter edible, growing well in quite low temperatures, but too low will kill it.*

It is important to be absolutely sure of your identification of this plant with a good flora if you are harvesting from the wild. There are poisonous look-alikes in similar habitats, such as lesser water parsnip (*Berula erecta*). Richard Mabey (1997) notes that he has found *Apium nodiflorum* seed in packets of commercial watercress on a couple of occasions, so you may already have eaten it. It is easy to propagate, the stems rooting easily in water or just start from seed. It is much easier to grow than watercress in my experience. This would make a good partner in the edible pond as ground/surface cover for cattails (*Typha* spp. see Chapter 5). I've seen it growing like this in Kew Gardens in London.

144: Apium nodiflorum *in flower in the author's garden; the seeds can be collected and used as flavouring and I decorate salads with the flowers.*

I have found it listed in one aquatics plant nursery in the UK. Seed are is difficult to come by.

Plantago coronopus

FAMILY: Plantaginaceae
ENGLISH: Buckshorn Plantain, Staghorn Plantain
GERMAN: *Krähenfuss-Wegerich*
ITALIAN: *Piantaggine Barbarella, Barba di Cappucino*
SPANISH: *Cuerno di Ciervo*

In one of my first Internet seed trade lists in 1998, I listed a large form of *Plantago coronopus* which I called giant. (I don't recall where the seed came from originally, probably an internet trader.) I had grown this species previously as an unusual edible, but the plants were tiny compared to this new monster. Unfortunately, the giant never produced seed. I only had one or two plants and it turns out that this species is what botanists call *gynodioecious*, meaning some plants in a population are bisexual, whilst others have female flowers only, so I guess I was unlucky. Although Larkcom (1989) does mention it, other comprehensive vegetable and culinary herb books from the 1990s do not. Nevertheless it has been cultivated in gardens for several centuries. Interestingly, I'd missed Hedrick's (1919) reference to it being cultivated in gardens in the late 17th century in England, the plants 'not differing except in size from the wild plant'. It was also grown in French gardens as a vegetable in the 19th century (Vilmorin-Andrieux, 1920).

Plantago coronopus is a common wild plant throughout most of the Mediterranean countries, as well as western France. Further north it is almost exclusively a coastal plant, as in the Low Countries, and southern Scandinavia. Even in southern Europe it is mostly found on sandy and saline lands near the sea. It has also been introduced both into the Americas, Australasia and South Africa. This is a potential cash crop halophyte (salt tolerant plant) (see the discussion in Chapter 6 on *Aster tripolium*).

145 (above left): 'Erba Stella' or 'Minutina' are giant selections of Plantago coronopus which have become available in vegetable seed catalogues in recent years. They are grown as cut and come again crops with three or four cuts possible in the summer. Here, a Minutina 'hedge' is used to separate the other vegetables (a perennial cultivar could be used effectively, rotating the other crops around from year to year).

146 (above right): The weird form Plantago major 'Rosularis' has been cultivated in gardens since at least 1629.

147 (left): Plantago maritima, the seaside plantain, is a common edible plant on beaches in northern Europe and North America; here on the beach below the author's house.

Buckshorn plantain shows a large genetic variability across its range and a number of botanical varieties are recognised. If you have grown one of the modern cultivars, you may be wondering why I have included this in a book on perennial vegetables, as 'Erba Stella' seems to be at best a biennial plant if you stop it from flowering. In the wild, populations can be annual, biennial or perennial. I suspect that there are forms that are perennial, as Joy Larkcom describes it as a 'pretty perennial' in *The Organic Salad Garden* (2003). In any case, in at least part of its range, the perennial buckshorn plantain is most common, so it should be possible to select for good perennial forms. Various authors suggest sowing the plant, either in spring or autumn, with between 13-25cm apart in rows and harvesting by cutting off the rosette three or four times during the season on a cut-and-come-again basis.

Whether from the wild or from the garden, buckshorn plantain is most commonly used in mixed salads, such as in the Italian *misticanza* or the French *mesclun*. It is often recommended to blanch it quickly in boiling water as the leaves can be a shade on the tough side, especially if harvested late. I don't find this necessary when using it in mixed salads. Numerous other perennial *Plantago* species are recorded as being used in traditional wild gathered dishes, the most common of which are *Plantago lagopus*, *P. lanceolata* and *P. major*, the latter two being widely distributed on disturbed lands worldwide and the chances are that you already have one or both growing in your garden. For salads, the youngest leaves are best; otherwise it is best to boil them first.

There are also numerous attractive garden cultivars of both species of these common weeds. *Plantago major* produces large numbers of seeds and these can be collected and used on bread (see page 252) and savoury dishes, useful for those needing to increase dietary fibre. Various other species of *Plantago*, including *P. psyllium* and *P. ovata* are cultivated for their seeds, used medicinally. The seeds can also be sprouted.

Further north in Europe, *Plantago maritima* is a very hardy and common seaside plant that has in the past been widely used over much of its range as a kind of spinach and was traditionally preserved in brine for winter use and for long journeys at sea. I'm sure this plant could be developed as a perennial vegetable for cold climates analogously to *P. coronopus*.

Rumex scutatus

FAMILY: Polygonaceae
ENGLISH: Buckler-leaved Sorrel, French Sorrel, Round-leafed Sorrel
FRENCH: *Oseille Ronde*
GERMAN: *Schild-Sauerampfer*
ITALIAN: *Romice Scudato, Acetosa Romana*
SPANISH: *Acedera Redonda, Acedera Romana*

Buckler-leaved sorrel is one of the ingredients of the Sardinian mixed wild vegetable dish, *minestra delle 18 erbe selvatiche,* where it is also used in a salad *turione crudo* (literally meaning raw spring shoots) together with *Crepis vesicaria* and French Scorzonera, *Reichardia picroides*. It is a hardy, low-growing, long-lived perennial hailing from the mountains of southern and central Europe as well as southwest Asia, east to the Caucasus.

It was formerly cultivated in Europe and sold on markets in the UK and France. However, it is nowadays a disappearing crop (Mansfeld's online database). Originally introduced to the UK in the 16th century, it is mentioned in *Gerard's Herball* from 1597. This sorrel is well-suited to home cultivation and leaves can be picked as needed through most of the summer and late into autumn too. I usually cut my plants back once in mid-summer to stop the plants seeding themselves as it can be a bit invasive. This initiates a second flush of leaves.

It is one of many *Rumex* species traditionally wild-collected for the kitchen in the Mediterranean countries and mainly in the west (Italy, Spain and France). Other commonly used species are *Rumex acetosa* (see Chapter 6),

148: Rumex scutatus.

149 & 150: Curled dock, Rumex crispus *and alpine dock,* Rumex alpinus*, are two of many docks/sorrels used in Mediterranean countries, but usually cooked.*

R. acetosella, R. crispus, R. alpinus, R. conglomeratus, R. induratus, R. obtusifolius, R. patientia and *R. pulcher.*

The leaves are much smaller than common sorrel (*Rumex acetosa*, Chapter 6), shield-shaped and similar to mountain sorrel, *Oxyria digyna* (Chapter 6). I've never seen higher yielding selections of this species offered, only the cultivar 'Silver Shield' with silvery leaves, sometimes grown as an edimental. The species is readily available as both seed and plants.

Diplotaxis tenuifolia

FAMILY: Brassicaceae
AUSTRALIAN: Lincoln Weed
ENGLISH: Perennial Wall-rocket, Sand Rocket
FRENCH: *Roquette à Feuilles Ténues*
GERMAN: *Schmalblättriger Doppelsame*
ITALIAN: *Ruchetta Selvatica, Rucoletta*
SPANISH: *Jaramago Silvestre*

Years ago, on a work visit to Venice, I remember enjoying *rucola* pizza. This was in the days before this vegetable went global. *Rucola* or rocket (*Eruca sativa*) is an annual plant in the cabbage family that was originally wild-foraged in Italy and other Mediterranean countries. In northern gardens, its biggest drawback is that it quickly bolts in the long days of summer with little yield. I had been aware that selections of long-day varieties had been made and, one year, I compared plants from different sources with the thought of perhaps selecting my own improved variety. The best variety I found in that original trial was called 'Long Standing', originating from Seed Savers Exchange in the US. However, I also received seed of 'Arugula Sylvett'. This one developed very differently and didn't bolt at all. It turned out to be *rucola*'s cousin, perennial *Diplotaxis tenuifolia*, also found common in the wild in Italy and collected and sold in small bunches on markets. According to Rivera et al. (2006), this is one of the characteristic wild edibles of the western Mediterranean region. I soon found that, although slower to first harvest than *rucola*, I could harvest the leaves for mixed salads all summer. The leaves are like concentrated *rucola*, certainly too pungent that you would want to make a pure *Diplotaxis* salad, but excellent diluted in mixed salads. Compared with *rucola* that provides usable leaves for a maximum of about two weeks here, *Diplotaxis* provided me with a nine month supply. Since then, my experience has been that it lives 2-3 years. It is also surprisingly hardy, surviving winter temperatures below -20°C. Nowadays, I sow *rucola* in very early spring for a quick crop of the long-standing variety, before *Diplotaxis* takes over for the rest of the season. It is unusual for a perennial to provide food for the whole summer (the mallows, profusion sorrel and *Reichardia* are exceptions). It can also be harvested in the wild over quite a long season, as it will germinate at any time that there is sufficient moisture, its long taproot allowing it to survive drought.

Perennial rocket is now cultivated for the market in greenhouses in Italy and presumably elsewhere. It is also found in supermarkets in northern Europe sold as *rucola*. It has also become commonly available in vegetable seed catalogues and improved varieties have also been developed, notably cultivars which grow more upright for ease of harvest (e.g. 'Napoli') but also for leaf shape and later flowering. A new variety qualifying as an edimental is 'Dragon's Tongue' with attractive purple veining on the leaves.

It is found in the wild over much of western Europe reaching into West Asia and has been introduced otherwise to North America and Australasia. It is a variable species with a wide range in leaf shapes, although typically with slender lobed leaves (the meaning of *tenuifolia*), although the variety *integrifolia* is lobe-less. The plant grows to 40-80cm and the aerial branches are densely covered in small leaves that can be used later in the summer.

In a taste trial organised by the RHS in the UK with a panel of leading chefs, vegetable gardeners and garden writers, *Diplotaxis* actually scored higher than *Eruca* for taste;

151: *Young leaves of* Diplotaxis tenuifolia.

152: *The yellow typical cruciferous flowers appear in late summer, are relatively large and are a tasty, attractive addition to mixed salads.*

see the panel's vivid description: 'Spectacularly peppery, slightly cabbagey, with a not-unpleasant bitterness, rounded out with acidity and sweetness' (McFadden, 2007).

It's best to start from seed and once established it should seed itself so that it will become a permanent feature. In some parts of the world it is a noxious unwanted plant (e.g. in Australia, where it is called Lincoln weed). It seems to be resistant to most of the pests of the cabbage tribe and can be planted in that spot in the garden with poor soil where little else will grow. It is also tolerant of dry conditions, having a long taproot and prefers an open sunny situation. It often grows out of walls in the wild, hence the common name wall rocket.

Although *D. tenuifolia* is the most commonly used *Diplotaxis* species harvested from the wild, there are a number of other annual and perennial species also used, including *D. muralis* (annual wall-rocket, which, despite its name, is often a short-lived perennial, with an almost identical range), *D. harra*, *D. erucoides*, *D. crassifolia* and *D. catholica*. In the Mediterranean, it is mostly used raw in salads, sometimes mixed with scrambled eggs and in mixed vegetable soups.

Cichorium intybus

FAMILY: Asteraceae
ENGLISH: Chicory, Succory
FRENCH: *Chicorée Sauvage*
GERMAN: *Cichorie*
ITALIAN: *Cicoria*
SPANISH: *Achicori*

Simple cooking is often the best as in *chorta tiganimena*, a dish from Calabria in Italy. Simply boil a mix of chicory leaves with other greens, drain and then fry in olive oil with garlic and chilli. Over the last 30 years or so, an amazing number of chicory and closely related endive (*Cichorium endivia*) cultivars have become available for growing. Facciola (1998) lists some 60 chicories, both heading, loose-leaf and raddichio (red-leaved) varieties, forms grown for their edible roots and also for chicons (the well-known compact spring shoots). Chicories tend to have hairy leaves and are derived from the perennial wild plant, whilst endives lack hairs and are annual or biennial. Phillips and Rix (1993) have a good overview with pictures, including blanching pots (similar to those used for rhubarb and sea kale).

Chicory is a common wild plant in most Mediterranean countries, in particular from Greece westwards, otherwise throughout Central Europe and the UK, becoming less common in Scotland, Norway and northern Sweden. It has been widely introduced in the Americas, South Africa and Australasia. It is often found in northern Europe growing on dry, disturbed soils, notably roadsides, with a preference for calcareous soils.

Until the development of the *Witloof* forcing varieties in Belgium in the mid-19th century, cultivated chicory was probably close to the wild perennial form. The first mention of cultivated chicory (from Germany) seems to have been in the early 17th

153 (left): There are a myriad of forms of chicories derived from the wild species Cichorium intybus; from left to right: 'Red Rib' or 'Italian Dandelion' and 'Galatina' (Catalogna loose-leaf types) and 'Lusia' (a heading type).

154 (below left): Edible rooted chicory.

155 (below right): Witloof type grown for the winter-forced chicons.

century, although it is known to have been used wild-harvested back to ancient times.

Not surprisingly, the chicories, also including annual *Cichorium pumilum* and the perennial spiny chicory, *C. spinosum*, are very frequently reported as being collected from the wild for food in the Mediterranean countries. They are often used in soups (e.g. in the Italian *minestrella*) and in boiled and/or fried mixtures, for example, mixed *liakra* (a wild green mix) and boiled and fried with broad beans (Pieroni et al., 2002). It is also commonly eaten raw and in salads, for example accompanying onions, olives and bread and as a salad with yoghurt (in Palestine).

From Crete, perennial *Cichorium spinosum* (*stamnagathi*) was traditionally gathered from the wild, but is nowadays so popular and in demand from the best gourmet restaurants that it is also cultivated. In Greece, wild greens are known as *horta*. Again the commonest recipe is simple. Boil for five minutes, just covering with water, drain and coat with a dressing made of the cooking water mixed into olive oil in the proportion 2:1, adding a little lemon juice and serve warm. The cooking water was also traditionally saved and taken as a healthy drink. This is another traditional fast but slow food taking all of 10 minutes from garden to table.

In North America, chicory has naturalised in a big way, a common wild plant in most states. Already in 1962, Euell Gibbons in *Stalking the Wild Asparagus* dedicated a chapter to this plant and informs the reader that it is best to cut the spring shoots

156: Wild perennial chicory is a prime edimental and is nowadays often sold by nurseries as an ornamental for late summer flowers at the back of the border. The flowers also liven up salads.

below ground level as the best bit is the blanched part which can be used in salads, whereas the stronger tasting aerial parts should be cooked.

The lovely blue flowers are also a colourful addition to late summer salads, livening up the vegetable garden at that time. Wild chicory is nowadays readily available from nurseries and in seed catalogues and is advocated as a great ornamental perennial for the back of a border where it will year after year provide colour in late summer. There are also ornamental cultivars available including the white and pinkish-flowered variants 'Alba' and 'Rosea'. Thompson and Morgan are also currently offering seed of a form 'Electric Blue'. Most vegetable varieties today are biennials.

If you manage to overwinter them then blanching in the spring with a large pot for a milder salad leaf is worth trying.

Both Ken Fern (1997) and Eric Toensmeier (2007) mention the lack of hardiness of some cultivars and the wish for better perennial varieties bred as vegetables (mild-leaved, productive etc.). Fern mentions that the variety 'Grumolo Verde' and 'Rossi di Verona' are hardy with him and Toensmeier notes 'Cerolio', 'Dentarella', 'Italian Dandelion', 'Grumolo', 'Italo Rossico', 'Red Rib', 'Puntarella', 'Rossa di Treviso', 'Rossa di Verona' and 'Spadona' as perennials in his climate. However, both 'Red Rib' and 'Italian Dandelion' bolt in the first year here and are not winter hardy. This would certainly be a worthwhile breeding project for the adventurous amateur looking to make his name!

Allium triquetrum

FAMILY: Amaryllidaceae
ENGLISH: Three-cornered Leek, Three Corner Garlic
FRENCH: *Ail à Tige Triquètre*
GERMAN: *Dreikantiger Lauch*
ITALIAN: *Aglio Selvatico, Porro Selvatico, Aglio Triquetro*
SPANISH: *Lagrimas de la Virgen*

The next two plants, *Allium triquetrum* and *Chenopodium bonus-henricus* introduce the wild-gathered plant traditions of Albania, as they are traditionally the two most commonly wild-foraged edibles there (Hadjichambis et al, 2008). Three-cornered leek has traditionally been gathered from the wild in its home range throughout the western Mediterranean. It has a mild garlic flavour and the flowers also make a pleasant and attractive addition to spring salads.

I remember years ago being struck by the mass flowering of this species along roadsides in New Zealand. It is, however, a native of the western Mediterranean (including North Africa), but has been introduced as an ornamental around the world, escaping in a big way both in the UK, West Coast US and in Australasia. It is not that hardy and is therefore found in milder temperate climates, but can be overwintered in colder climates by using a leaf mulch or similar. Three-cornered leek has its name because the flower stems are triangular in cross-section. It is one of the earliest Alliums to come into flower.

This is a species to consider for the forest garden, growing well in shady conditions (it is, however, sometimes mistaken for the white flowered form of bluebell, *Hyacinthoides non-scriptus*, so please make sure it has that characteristic onion odour before eating). It also grows well in more open sites. *Allium triquetrum* is available from several nurseries in the UK as bulbs or plants. I've never heard of any cultivars.

There are in total at least 11 Mediterranean Alliums being collected for food; two of those that have proved worthy edimentals in my garden are *Allium moly* and *Allium nigrum*.

Chenopodium bonus-henricus

FAMILY: Chenopodiaceae
ENGLISH: Good King Henry,
   Lincolnshire Asparagus,
   Lincolnshire Spinach
FRENCH: *Chénopode Bon-Henri*
GERMAN: *Guter Heinrich*
ITALIAN: *Farinello Buon-Enrico*
SPANISH: *Espárrago de los*
   Pobres

Carol Deppe (2000) writes, 'I've read a number of descriptions of and accounts relating to Good King Henry, and no one mentions that it tastes horrible. Is all Good King Henry as unappetising as my line?' I will, Good King Henry tastes absolutely disgusting! I struggle to think of another plant of the thousands I've

157: **Allium triquetrum** *is collected from the wild in its native Italy, here in full flower in the first week in April in Orto Botanico in Padua, Italy. Three-cornered leek is not hardy in my garden, but I have managed to overwinter it by covering it with a winter mulch.*

158 & 159: Two other wild-gathered edimental onions: **Allium moly** *(top) is a common easy perennial garden onion used in Spain; the flowers are tasty and attractive additions to salads. Black garlic,* **Allium nigrum,** *(bottom), used in southern Italy, is also nowadays readily available as bulbs.*

sampled that comes near to this in the inedible league. If I eat a couple of leaves raw, a strong unpleasant bitter taste quickly ensues and doesn't leave me again for at least 15 minutes. I therefore call it Bad King Henry or *Chenopodium malus-henricus*. Why include it here then? Well, its taste is really bad only in the raw state, cooking making it much more appealing, and it is also probably the best perennial grain crop for cool climates. Nevertheless, there are authors who actually recommend it as a salad plant. Either there are varieties that lack the bitterness of Carol Deppe's and my plants, or the authors in question haven't eaten it! Fern (1997) and Toensmeier (2007) both of which came out after Deppe's original book in 1993 also note that the raw leaves are bitter. Blanching in spring by covering your plants or earthing them up (Vilmorin-Andrieux, 1920) will decrease the bitterness.

160: Good King Henry is a compact and quite attractive plant; the young leaves are best harvested until the young flower spikes appear, but beware of eating them raw, they don't taste good!

161 (below): Good King Henry produces masses of saponin-rich seed which can be cooked and used like the seed of its better known annual sister, Quinoa, Chenopodium quinoa.

162 (bottom): Spring blanched shoots of Good King Henry have a milder taste.

163: Ingredients for a spring Chinese-style soup with: Allium nutans, *blanched* Crambe cordifolia *and* Chenopodium bonus-henricus, *Golden Needles (*Hemerocallis, *see Chapter 5), Mibuna and Mustard Greens 'Ruby Streak'.*

Its original wild range is probably mountainous areas of the Mediterranean and the Caucasus. It has otherwise naturalised, mainly near to human settlements, over much of Central Europe, the UK and southern Scandinavia, as well as northeast North America. It has no doubt been gathered from the wild for millennia over its wild range. In a recent study in a remote mountain village in Albania, Good King Henry was the most frequently wild-gathered edible (Hadjichambis et al., 2008). It figures in traditional dishes also on the other side of the Adriatic in Italian *garfagnana* (Pieroni, 1999), boiled or *frittata* (a kind of omelette); in *pistic* (northeast Italy, see page 59, Paoletti, 1995) and in the Alps (Pieroni and Giusti, 2009) where it is boiled in soups and in omelettes. Clifford Wright (2001) includes a recipe for *omelette bon-Henri*, from the Languedoc in southern France, in his excellent *Mediterranean Vegetables* (2001). François Couplan (1983) also notes a green *gnocchi* made with Good King Henry from Haut-pays Niçois, a mountain area north of Nice in France (see the nettle *gnocchi* recipe on page 33 and just replace the nettles with Good King Henry).

This plant is probably also the best perennial grain crop for cool climates producing masses of seed that can be cooked just like homegrown quinoa (*Chenopodium quinoa*). First rinse the seed well, and then boil a couple of times, discarding the soapy water each time. Aim for about 15 minutes total cooking time. It really is tasty and attractive. I just mix it with fried garlic and chilli with a little salt. The seed has also been used in the past, ground into flour.

Good King Henry would certainly have been familiar to the Romans and it is not inconceivable that they took seed with them as they moved north. It seems that it was quite commonly grown in gardens in England in the 17th century. It became less popular in the 18th century, although it was still grown locally. In Lincolnshire, people continued to prefer it to spinach (known as Lincolnshire asparagus). It was described as an English vegetable by Vilmorin-Andrieux (1920).

There are a few records of it being sold on local markets in the 20th century outside of the Mediterranean area; e.g. Luczaj and Szymanski, 2007, record it being sold on a market in Poland in 1953, the leaves being eaten alone or with potatoes or with *kasza* (cracked cereals).

Both seeds and plants are easy to source and plants can also be propagated vegetatively by division. Seeds are best sown in autumn as they benefit from cold stratification. Plants readily self-seed and you may want to cut off the flowering stalks, as they can be a bit invasive in a garden setting. Once established, your Good King Henry could well outlive you, just keep the plants nourished with an occasional mulch of compost and they will be happy. It tolerates growing in fairly shady spots too. This is a very hardy plant and can probably survive down to about -30°C without snow cover. Aim for about 20-30cm between plants as individual plants form a mound of about 30cm diameter after a few years.

Asparagus officinalis

FAMILY: Asparagaceae
ENGLISH: Asparagus
FRENCH: *Asperge*
GREEK: *Sparaggi*
ITALIAN: *Asparago*
SPANISH: *Espárrago*

Asparagus acutifolius

FAMILY: Asparagaceae
ENGLISH: Lesser Asparagus, Wild Asparagus
FRENCH: *Asperge à Feuilles Aigües*
GREEK: *Agrio Sparaggi*
ITALIAN: *Asparago Selvatico*
SPANISH: *Espárrago Triguero, Esparraguera
Silvestre*

On a visit to Athens I was invited to an ex-colleague's home for dinner. He knew of my interest in edible plants and took me for a walk on the hills above the city. He wanted to show me a local wild delicacy that grew there. It turned out to be *Asparagus acutifolius*. Nowadays, the spring shoots of this species are actually preferred to cultivated asparagus by local gourmet restaurants in Athens. It has also long been one of the most commonly used wild-foraged species in the Mediterranean, used from Turkey to Spain.

The genus *Asparagus* has around 300 species in Europe, Asia and Africa. Several of them have been used locally for food, including *Asparagus laricinus* (South Africa; van Dyk and Gericke, 2000) and *A. filicinus* and *A. racemosus* (Nepal; Manandhar, 2002). Several other species are also used in the Mediterranean countries, including

164: Asparagus filicinus *is a fern-like woodland species found in Nepal, and elsewhere in the Himalayas and southeast Asia, where the young shoots are collected for food in the springtime.*

165: *These berries were collected for seed to establish a wild asparagus bed in my garden.*

166: *If you are lucky enough to have easy access to seaweed, this is a fantastic free perennial resource to which salt-tolerant plants such as asparagus respond well to as a fertiliser.*

167 (above): Asparagus tenuifolius.

168 (right): The climbing West Asian species, Asparagus verticillatus.

Asparagus albus, *A. aphyllus*, *A. stipularis* and the common asparagus, *A. officinalis*. The latter has a wide geographical range from West and Central Europe, locally in the Mediterranean countries and eastwards to the Caucasus and western Siberia. However, there is often a mix of wild plants and plants naturalised from cultivation. For example, in the UK, the prostrate subspecies *Asparagus officinalis* ssp. *prostratus* is rare, only found in a few coastal locations, whereas the naturalised plant is much more common. Asparagus was first moved into gardens a long time ago. For example, Cato the Elder (234-149 BC) described asparagus cultivation. The word asparagus can be traced back to the Persian word *asparag* that simply means a shoot or sprout.

In other parts of the world, *Asparagus officinalis* has also naturalised as the red berries are sought after and spread by a number of bird species (such as pigeons). In eastern North America, this non-native species has spread to such an extent that North America's best-known foraging book is called *Stalking the Wild Asparagus* (Gibbons, 1962).

Most vegetable gardening books cover asparagus cultivation, so I won't repeat this here, however I'd encourage you to seek out the wild species mentioned, for your own gourmet asparagus experience. Being smaller plants, they can be planted closer together. Asparagus has other qualities too. It is an impressive plant that can be grown at the back of your mixed edimental perennial border. Its feathery foliage can

169 (above): Summer asparagus plumes.

170 (above right): British asparagus on sale at Cambridge Market.

171 (right): Assembling asparagus sushi.

be used in flower arranging, and it also bears attractive red berries in autumn if you have male and female plants. Here in Norway, we've found asparagus in many old gardens and often owners aren't aware of its identity, believing it to be a poisonous ornamental (due to the red berries).

There are three main types of commercial *Asparagus officinalis* available today. Green and white asparagus dominate the market, the main difference between the two determined by the cultivation method, the white being blanched to remove light. Italian violet asparagus is becoming increasingly popular. Facciola (1998) lists over 25 cultivars. Some varieties are used for white asparagus production only, others for both, there are early varieties, high yielding types, those for extended harvest, others selected for taste and/or sweetness and there are also low fibre varieties.

In Italy, so-called sprue asparagus has long been popular. Sprue has pencil thin shoots, similar to the shoots on wild plants, and is the first pickings of young commercially grown plants. They have also started appearing in supermarkets in northern Europe. The easiest way to use your asparagus or other asparagus-like plants is the commonest Mediterranean preparation method, *asparagus frittata* (or omelette).

chapter 3

THE CAUCASUS TO THE HIMALAYAS AND SIBERIA

This chapter covers a vast area of Asia from the Caucasus in the west to the mountains of Central Asia, the Himalayas and Siberia. This region contains three so-called biodiversity hotspots, areas with a significant percentage of endemic (found nowhere else) plant species. The Caucasus with its 1,600 endemics is one, and so too are the mountains of Central Asia (Tien Shan and Pamir) with 1,500 and the Himalayas with over 3,000. There are certainly thousands of species that have been used for food in this region. Rivera (2006) notes, for example, 565 species of gathered plants and fungi in the Caucasus region from an old and hardly complete 1952 overview by Grossheim (in Russian).

In the Himalayas, Manandhar's *Plants and People of Nepal* (2002) really stands out with a comprehensive and fascinating catalogue of how more than 1,500 species are used by the Nepalese. People don't often have large areas to grow vegetables and therefore wild foraging is still important. Vegetables are preserved either by simple drying or by making *gundruk*, fermented leafy vegetables. Unlike, for example, *kimchi* in Korea (Chapter 4), *gundruk* is dried after the fermentation. Some commonly wild-gathered green vegetables (not featured in the following) include:

- *Diplazium esculentum* (*pani nyuro*, a fern, unlikely to be very hardy, as it is found at lower elevations).
- *Fagopyrum acutatum*, syn. *F. dibotrys/cymosum* (perennial buckwheat; this is available in the UK and is definitely worth trying as the taste is excellent; it hasn't proven hardy here, but I've seen it in botanical gardens in London and Paris and I can overwinter root cuttings inside).
- *Girardinia diversifolia* (Himalayan nettle; a giant herb reaching 3m high, used in the same way as common stinging nettle, *Urtica dioica*, which is also commonly used).
- *Megacarpaea polyandra* (*rubi ko sag*; this giant plant in the cabbage family is so popular in the Himalayas that it has been overharvested in some areas, it should survive down to -20°C, but it is reputedly very slow growing).
- *Ranunculus diffusus* (*mardi jahr*, commonly used despite being poisonous raw; it must be cooked).

- *Rumex nepalensis* (Nepalese dock or Halhale).

Another Himalayan study is Sundriyal et al. (2004) from Sikkim (India). They found that the following species were commonly collected, but only at higher elevations: *Diplazium esculentum*, naturalised watercress and stinging nettle (both Chapter 1), another nettle, *Girardinia palmata*, as well as the onions *Allium caesium* and *A. wallichii* (this chapter). Other familiar plants include *Polygonum viviparum* (alpine bistort) and *Rheum nobile* (both Chapter 6).

The best resource to Siberian edibles I've found is the Edible Wild Plants of Siberia website, in Russian (see http://sibrast.ru). Of the 193 non-woody edibles described, 73% are perennials. The most interesting leafy green species are listed below, several of which are described elsewhere in the book:

- *Adenophora liliifolia* (and other *Adenophora* species closely related to the bellflowers, *Campanula*, the sweet rhizomes are also used).
- *Aegopodium podograria* (ground elder, common forest species of western Siberia, Chapter 6).
- *Armoracia sisymbrioides* (horseradish wild relative, Chapter 1).
- *Cacalia hastata* (Chapter 4).
- *Chamaenerion* (*Epilobium*) *angustifolium* (rosebay willowherb, Chapter 2).
- *Cichorium intybus* (chicory, Chapter 2).
- *Crambe tatarica* (this chapter).
- *Equisetum arvense* (field horsetail).
- *Humulus lupulus* (hop, Chapter 2).
- *Hypochaeris maculata* (spotted hawkweed, a dandelion relative found in the wild from western Europe to western Siberia, wild-foraged in Sweden and one of the ingredients of *pistic* in Italy).
- *Lamium album* (white dead-nettle).
- *Matteuccia struthiopteris* (ostrich fern, Chapter 5).

*172: **Rumex nepalensis** is one of my Himalayan vegetables, here in early May in the garden. It doesn't look at all 'low altitude sick' does it?*

173 & 174: Perennial buckwheat, Fagopyrum dibotrys, in Paris Botanical Gardens (top), and Megacarpaea polyandra in Gothenburg Botanical Gardens (bottom) – two of the most frequently wild-gathered perennials in the Himalayas.

175: **Adenophora liliifolia** *is one of the wild-foraged plants of Siberia, an attractive edimental, although it and other species of the genus can be invasive, spreading vegetatively.*

176 & 177: **Polygonum alpinum** *flowers (above) and spring shoot (right), wild-foraged from Siberia to Alaska.*

- *Plantago major* (greater plantain, Chapter 2).
- *Polygonum alpinum* (also used by native tribes in Alaska where it is known as Alaskan wild rhubarb).
- *Polygonum viviparum* (alpine bistort, Chapter 6) and *Persicaria bistorta* (bistort, Chapter 6).
- *Primula elatior* ssp. *pallasii* (Russian form of oxlip).
- *Taraxacum* spp. (dandelions, Chapter 1).
- *Rheum* spp. (rhubarb, Chapter 1).
- *Rumex crispus*, *confertus*, *acetosa* and *thyrsifolius* (docks and sorrels, Chapters 2 and 6).
- *Silene nutans* ssp. *dubia* (subspecies of the Nottingham catchfly).
- *Typha* spp. (Chapter 6).

Bunias orientalis

FAMILY: Brassicaceae
ENGLISH: Turkish Rocket, Warty Cabbage, Hill Mustard
FRENCH: *Bunias de l'Orient*
GERMAN: *Orientalische Zackenschote*
ITALIAN: *Cascellore Orientale*
NORWEGIAN: *Russekål*
RUSSIAN: *Sverbiga Vostochnaya*

I've grown a single clump of Turkish rocket in my garden for many years, an easily grown and well-behaved acquaintance, the clump slowly increasing in size from year to year. It was therefore a surprise when I learnt that this species had been placed on the Norwegian blacklist as an invasive species. In the south of the country, *Russekål* (literally Russian cabbage) has spread dramatically with seed and also with pieces of root moved by construction machinery. Although this naturalised species is mainly found in grassy fields, roadside verges and wasteland, it has occasionally also invaded species-rich dry calcareous habitats. The threat to local biodiversity has led to its unwanted status.

It is not widespread in Turkey and is restricted to the far east of that country bordering the Caucasus region. Its native range includes the Caucasus, western Russia east to the Urals and northern Kazakhstan. It is believed that *Bunias orientalis* spread to Europe in a big way in horse forage that followed the Russian army that was victorious over Napoleon in 1814, reaching France. However, this species was being grown in the Chelsea Physic Garden in London as early as the 1730s. It is now naturalised in most European countries and is currently spreading and being monitored in the US (Wisconsin). In its natural range, Turkish rocket is said to be

found in open woodlands, forest edges and riverbanks and is therefore a good plant for the sunny border of the forest garden. It grows well on both sandy and clay soils. It is a long-lived hardy perennial and a member of the cabbage family. It reaches about 1m in mid-summer when it is conspicuous with its typical yellow cruciferous flowers.

In its home range, *sverbiga* as it is known in Russia, was traditionally harvested as a wild vegetable. Retzius (1806) reports that the Russians eat the young stems with kale. More recently, the fresh leaves are boiled

*178: **Bunias orientalis** is a black-listed invasive species in some countries such as Norway, here seen in full flower in Oslo.*

179 (left): Spring basal leaves of Turkish rocket in the author's garden ready to harvest early in May.

180 (above left) : Blanching the emerging foliage gives a milder product.

181 (above right): Turkish rocket broccolis are milder than the spring leaves and very tasty.

and eaten in Armenia. In Chechnya/Ingushetia the roots and peeled stems are eaten (the latter were apparently formerly loved by children) and the roots are grated and pickled like horseradish. On Russian back to nature websites these traditions are clearly being kept alive and numerous recipes can be found, e.g. puréed stems, sometimes with sorrel (*Rumex acetosa*), seasoned with salt and pepper; and dried leaves are used as a flavouring in winter soups and other dishes.

Cultivation of this plant as a vegetable began at some stage in the 1800s as Vilmorin-Andrieux (1920) reports: 'the young and tender leaves and shoots are eaten either boiled or as salad. This plant has been highly spoken of as a kitchen-garden plant. It commences to grow very early in spring, when other fresh green vegetables are scarce, resisting both cold weather and drought well.' The reader is also informed

182 (above): Mid-summer flowers can be used in salads; if the plant is cut back to prevent flowering a second flush of leaves will soon appear.

183 (top right): Turkish rocket roots are a good size and can be used like horseradish.

184 (right): These Turkish rocket roots I used here were a bit too old and fibrous, but the taste was very good and similar to horseradish.

that '...the seed is sown in drills in autumn or spring, and the plants will continue vigorous and productive for several years.' I can add that it is also easy to propagate by taking root cuttings or just dividing the plant, preferably from autumn to early spring. Plants can be purchased at a few nurseries in Europe and seed is also sometimes offered.

Probably due to Vilmorin-Andrieux's recommendation, this plant continues to be included as a minor vegetable in popular books on kitchen gardening (for example, Phillips and Rix, 1993). Some people may find Turkish rocket to be too strong tasting eaten raw. Blanching in the spring by covering with a large bucket or boiling for 10 minutes reduces the strength. The taste is then similar to oriental mustard greens. I usually use this plant mixed with other spring vegetables (it is one of the perennial vegetables shown in the photo on page 233, Chapter 6). Some selection work would be worthwhile also with this species as it is reported that strength varies a lot between plants. Another positive feature is that I have never seen it attacked by typical brassica pests!

I've mentioned the invasive nature of this species around Oslo. This is something that the local Thai community has quietly taken advantage of. I was told that large quantities of Turkish rocket are picked in the early summer before it flowers, taking the top 10-15cm of the shoots, best when the plants are 20-30cm high. New shoots then emerge and they harvest one more time. It's used particularly in connection with big celebrations. They blanch the vegetable (i.e. it's thrown briefly in boiling water) and use it as a side dish, dipped in chilli and fish sauces. It is described as tasting like broccoli.

Family member *Bunias erucago* (corn rocket) is a smaller annual or biennial species that is commonly gathered from the wild in southern Europe. It is, for example, one of the ingredients in the Tuscan dish, *minestrella* (Chapter 2).

Hablitzia tamnoides

FAMILY: Chenopodiaceae
DANISH: *Spinatranke*
ENGLISH: Hablitzia, Caucasian Spinach
FINNISH: *Köynnöspinaatit*
GERMAN: *Kaukasische Spinat*
NORWEGIAN: *Stjernemelde*
RUSSIAN: *Gablitsiia Tamusobidnaia*
SWEDISH: *Rankspenat*

I first heard about Hablitzia in 1999 when someone in Norway offered me it as part of a trade. At that time I couldn't have known of its edibility. Nevertheless, I requested seed, but it didn't germinate. A couple of years later I received an email from a Swedish author, Lena Israelsson. She told me that she had written several books on vegetables and herbs and that she was very interested in trying out new species, in particular various perennial onions (Allium) that would be hardy in the Stockholm area where she lived. I sent her selected Allium seed that had grown well for me and to my great surprise she sent me two of her books in return as a thank you. One of those books, *Köksträdgården: Det Gröna Arvet (The Kitchen Garden: Our Green Heritage)*, written in 1996, was one of the most interesting books I had read on vegetables. Unfortunately, it has never been translated into English. Among the more unusual vegetables, there was one that was completely unknown to me apart from those seed that I'd tried, *Hablitzia tamnoides*. I searched for this species in the most important reference works on edible plants (e.g. Ken Fern's Plants For A Future database and Stephen Facciola's *Cornucopia II*), but drew a complete blank. Neither was it possible to source this plant in any of the UK nurseries covered by the comprehensive RHS Plant Finder, although it had been offered by one nursery in 1999. *The European Garden Flora* (with 17,000 taxa) surprisingly didn't mention this plant either. The same year I obtained some seed through trading with another Swede and one plant resulted.

185: Hablitzia tamnoides *climbs to 2-3m or more early in the summer. Its botanical epithet,* tamnoides, *reflects its similarity to* Tamus communis, *an important but mildly toxic wild edible of the Mediterranean countries.*

Hablitzia tamnoides (incidentally spelled *thamnoides* by Israelsson) is a perennial herbaceous climber from the Caucasus both in the south and north. It is found particularly in spruce and beech woods, among rocks and in ravines and along rivers. Gabrielian and Fragman in *Flowers of the Transcaucasus* (2008) give its habitat as 'forests, rocky places, shady places and roadsides' between 900 and 2,100m and state that it is common throughout the Caucasus and northeast Turkey. Hablitzia is named in honour of Carl Ludwig Hablizl, an 18th century naturalist who was also vice-governor in the Crimea. The epithet *tamnoides* refers to the resemblance of the leaves to another climber, black bryony (*Tamus communis*), a native found in southern England and further south in Europe. In antiquity, the young shoots of *Tamus* were apparently preferred to asparagus and they are still used today in various spring dishes throughout the Mediterranean area. They must, however, be cooked as it is mildly toxic raw.

Botanically, Hablitzia belongs to the goosefoot family (*Chenopodiaceae*) and is the only species in its genus (monotypic). It is therefore related to other well-known vegetables such as beetroot, Swiss chard, spinach and garden orach (*Atriplex hortensis*). It is also a cousin of the South American grain crop, quinoa (*Chenopodium quinoa*), the herb epazote or wormseed (*Chenopodium ambrosioides*) used in Mexican cuisine and also Good King Henry (*Chenopodium bonus-henricus;* Chapter 2).

Unusual for the goosefoot family, Hablitzia climbs to 2-3m in the course of a very short period during spring/early summer. The lowest leaves are heart-shaped with a long stalk and have sensitive leaf stalks that make them well adapted to climbing into trees. The flowers are small and green, held on long racemes emerging from the leaf axils. The seeds are small (about 1.5mm), shiny and black.

Lena Israelsson describes the history of Hablitzia in Sweden in her book. The plant was originally introduced to gardens as an attractive climber around 1870. It took only a few years, however, for people to discover that the leaves were also edible. The plant never became very popular, but was grown in some of the biggest manor house gardens.

In the UK, Hablitzia was being grown by both Kew Gardens and the Cambridge Botanical Gardens by 1828 only a decade after it was first described. In 1840 it was noted that it was killed (by frost?) but quickly recovered. In 1879, the magazine *The Garden* had an article 'The Common Hop as a Climber'. Apart from hop, other equally good hardy climbers are noted: edible North American *Apios tuberosa* (ground nut), *Tamus communis* and 'Tamus-like *Hablitzia tamnoides*'. Hablitzia is described as 'a plant of rapid growth, and one that is covered for some weeks in summer with a profusion of small blossoms produced in dense racemes.' In 1881, the *Journal of Horticulture and Practical Gardening* describes it as 'a fine pillar plant of Hoplike appearance' and *The Gardeners' Chronicle* mentions 'a fine specimen at Kew'. RHS magazine *The Garden* in 1888 has a positive profile of Hablitzia, probably inspired by 'the thriving specimen of this Caucasian Hablitzia near the alpine house at Kew', and continues that it '...is graceful, and we may say beautiful ... dense in growth, exceedingly free,

186: *Hablitzia is well adapted to climbing up into trees in its native habitat in the Caucasus (photo: Sergey Banketov).*

and surmounted throughout the summer with a great mass of greenish flowers, that individually are quite inconspicuous, but collectively give the plant a graceful, informal aspect…' In 1891, *The Garden* again refers to its graceful profusion and notes that the Kew specimen '…never till this year has attracted so much attention, as it has never attained such a large size, a circumstance owing to its having been planted two years ago in a deep bed of loam and manure'. *The Gardeners' Chronicle* again mentions Hablitzia in 1893 and suggests, 'a mass of it tumbling over the rougher parts of the rockery or rootery is very pleasing'. It is also included in *A Practical Guide to Garden Plants*, by John Weathers in 1901 and Samuel Arnott's *The Book of Climbing Plants and Wall Shrubs* from 1903. It was still being grown at Kew in 1902. It had also found its way to the Chateau de Crest near Geneva in Switzerland in 1896.

Hablitzia also found its way across the Atlantic and was in the living collections at the New York Botanical Garden in 1898 and was being trialled in Ottawa, Canada in 1908. Despite all the glowing reports it probably never became popular and it seems not to have survived the First World War in gardens. I had a giggle at the only report of it in England between the wars which says simply: "We will not worry about weeds". None of these references, apart from in Scandinavia, mentions its use in the kitchen.

I have also been unable to find any reference to the use of Hablitzia as a wild edible in its home territory in the Caucasus. In the *Flora of the USSR* (1968), the economic importance of this species is stated only as an ornamental garden plant used for pergolas, porches etc. It turns out that Hablitzia was also grown, or at least trialled successfully, in Norway in the late 19th century. It was even cultivated in the very far north of the country in Finnmark, vouching for its complete hardiness. The plant is also mentioned in various Scandinavian gardening books from the early 1900s.

187-189: Hablitzia can be propagated either by seed (left), by autumn division, by shoot cuttings with a sliver of root crown taken in late spring (centre), and even young plants can be multiplied by cutting vertically through the root with a sharp knife leaving at least one bud on each division (right).

191: Hablitzia shoots appear in the late autumn and grow slowly in mild periods in winter. Over 250 shoots can arise from one plant.

192: A small mid-winter treat of Hablitzia with spring leaves of Allium paradoxum.

There is also one reference from the late 19th century suggesting that Hablitzia spreads like a weed. It is also known that relic populations or individual plants have survived to the present day in several places in Sweden, Finland and one location in Norway to the 1970s, probably vouching for the longevity of individual plants.

Propagation is easiest from seed. Hablitzia emerges very early in the spring and seed germinates at very low temperatures, just above freezing. This is an adaptation to its woodland habitat where it is important to put on as much growth as possible before the leaves appear on the trees. Sowing in high temperatures in spring isn't successful. One can sow the seed and put outside for the winter, and it will then germinate in very early spring. Alternatively sow, water and put the pot in the fridge in a plastic bag. The seed will then start germinating after 1-2 weeks. You can then take it out and germination can continue in a cool room. Make sure you only just cover the seed (1-2mm). The resultant plants grow slowly during the first year but growth accelerates and full height can be reached in the second year. Plants can also be propagated by division in autumn; I have also successfully propagated young shoots with a little sliver of root crown (hops can also be propagated in this way) and have even successfully divided one year roots into three or four separate plants using a sharp knife.

190: My oldest Hablitzia grows quickly up the south side of the house in early summer; even at this stage the top part of the shoots can be eaten.

My original plant grows up a south-facing wall of my house, although it only gets sun in the afternoon. I also now have plants thriving equally well in completely shady conditions growing up into an old birch tree. In order that the first harvest is as early as possible, it's preferable to plant in a relatively sunny position. A baking hot spot isn't advisable, as it may get too dry in summer. Some 19th century advice suggests a well-drained good, rich, loamy soil, bearing in mind that there should be sufficient moisture in summer, but not waterlogged in winter. Once established, the plants don't seem to need much feeding. The most noticeable feature of this plant is its incredible growth rate early in the year. It seems also to be perfectly hardy and should tolerate late frosts, but even if shoots are killed, new shoots should quickly appear from the root. Examination of the root crown will reveal hundreds of reserve shoots waiting to take over. Short Hablitzia shoots actually appear already in late autumn and grow on slowly in mild periods during winter, allowing for a very early treat one year when the air temperature was below -15°C. In my garden, only Alliums can be harvested at that time of year. These winter shoots seem hardly affected by air temperatures down to at least -24°C.

From my oldest over 10-year-old plant, there are now some 250 shoots in spring and the root crown is now an elevated mound. Two years ago there was a mild April here. I was able to harvest the young shoots three times in the course of the month (cut-and-come-again) before allowing the plant to grow on. I have grown thousands of edibles and I know no other plant that is anywhere near as productive so early in the season. That alone is reason enough to grow it!

When I only grew one plant, it rarely produced seed and I believe it is self-incompatible. Now having several plants a lot of seed is produced each year and they do self-seed quite prolifically. Seedlings have appeared even at quite some distance from the mother plants and I think this is due to the shiny low-friction seed whizzing across the ice, blown by the wind in winter.

One can use the young shoots in all kinds of dishes for which one would have used spinach or asparagus – in soups, salads, pies, pizza, Indian and oriental dishes etc.

In November 2012, somebody asked me if the roots were edible. I'd seen that the roots were a good size as I'd tried once to propagate from them, but I'd never tried to eat them. I therefore carefully excavated around the roots and cut off a few of the very long roots. I prepared them by just scrubbing them. Raw they had quite a pleasant slightly sweet texture. I steamed them, but cooked they weren't so sweet or tasty. Served with the garlic/chilli/Cuban oregano (*Plectranthus amboinicus*) butter that I'd made, they tasted great.

The Hablitzia Revival

Thanks to Lena Israelsson's book, there was a bit of a renaissance in the use of Hablitzia as an edible in Scandinavia. A small group of enthusiasts had been keeping this old and unique Nordic tradition alive. Lena told me that she had originally obtained seed through the Swedish seed exchange run by Sällskapet Trädgårdsamatörerna (STA, literally Swedish Amateur Gardening Society) around 1995.

Recognising the potential for this shade tolerant plant for the Forest Garden and Permaculture planting schemes, I decided it was time to spread the word about

193-196: Hablitzia is a versatile vegetable and can be used in all dishes you would use spinach. Top left: With Hosta ready for a Hosta-Hablitzia spinach pie (see also Hostakopita, *Chapter 4). Top right: the purple coloured spring shoots adding a splash of colour to a January salad. Below left: Ingredients for traditional Norwegian/ Portuguese* bacalao/bacalhau *with a Hablitzia twist: spring onion, Hablitzia, potatoes and rehydrated dried and salted cod. Below right: With biennial garlic mustard,* Alliaria petiolata, *which is also available very early in the year.*

the Caucasian spinach and an article resulted in *Permaculture* magazine in 2007. Independently, Jonathan Bates in the US, friend of author Eric Toensmeier, had picked up *Food Plants of the World* by South African Ben-Erik Van Wyk (2005). On page 25 a picture captioned 'Climbing Spinach (*Hablitzia tamnoides*) from the Caucasus' leaped out of the page at him, as it was a plant he wasn't familiar with. Van Wyk's book includes one page profiles of 354 plants, but Hablitzia is only included in the one picture and in a list of some 120 common leaf, stem and flower vegetables. It is unknown where Van Wyk had heard about this plant.

Jon Bates set out to try to source seed and this took him to the Danish Seed Savers whom I'd recently sent seed to and we were in touch. Jon was also intrigued by the Hablitzia story and this resulted in an article in *Permaculture Activist* in 2008 in which he tells his story and includes three recipes, two of which are adapted spinach recipes from Georgia (*ispanakhi pkhali*), a spinach salad, and Finland (*pinaattiohukaiset*),

197 & 198: Owner of Draglands Nursery, Kjell Dragland (left), showing his **Hablitzia** **tamnoides** *used for propagating the plants sold in the nursery (right).*

spinach pancakes. In summer 2007, Justin West and Li An Phoa of Schumacher College in Totnes, Devon visited me. They were so inspired by the Hablitzia story that they mounted a private expedition to the Caucasus in search of the elusive Caucasian spinach. They did find the Hablitzia grail, gathered seed and they are still the only souls known to have foraged and cooked wild Hablitzia leaves in the wild.

I also managed to source wild seed of Hablitzia from a botanist, Sergey Banketov, who collected seed for me from a mountain overlooking Pyatigorsk in the North Caucasian Federal District. He hadn't, however, heard of this plant being used for food in his area. The resulting wild sourced plants look quite different to the old Scandinavian material. They have reddish stems (only red at the base on the Scandinavian types), the flowers are smaller and it also flowers earlier. I lost one plant in a cold winter that may suggest that this wild accession is less hardy and therefore perhaps more suited for milder climates. It is suggested that the Scandinavian type may have adapted to its environment over the 140 years that it has been cultivated here.

The Nordic Genetic Resource Centre (Nordgen) funded a small project in 2009 to collect old material from the Nordic countries. This resulted in a total of eight accessions, four from Finland, one from Norway, one from Estonia, and the others of unknown origin. In Norway, Hablitzia has been adopted as a national heritage plant (Plantearven). The PLANTEARVEN® logo is used when marketing such plants and one nursery, Draglands, sells plants under this scheme, rescued from the only known relic Norwegian plant, found in the local Hadsel vicarage garden.

You can share your experiences of this plant on the 'Friends of *Hablitzia tamnoides*' Facebook group that I started in 2010. It is usually possible to source seed and plants through the group on both sides of the Atlantic.

Crambe cordifolia

FAMILY: Brassicaceae
ENGLISH: Greater Sea Kale, Colewort, Ornamental Sea Kale, Heartleaf Crambe
FRENCH: *Chou Nuage Blanc*
GERMAN: *Herzblättriger Meerkohl*
RUSSIAN: *Katran Serdtselistny*

Growers of giant vegetables would do well to grow the greater sea kale for it is naturally a true giant and will have visitors to your perennial veggie garden gasping (well, Stephen Lacey in his book *Scent in Your Garden* claims this is the effect this plant has...). It has been given the Royal Horticultural Society's AGM (Award for Garden Merit), a giant edimental, cultivated in Europe from about 1820. It is an impressive and much planted herbaceous perennial.

In the same area where *Hablitzia tamnoides* is unknown as an edible, Pyatigorsk in the northern Caucasus, *Crambe cordifolia* has been declared endangered because of indiscriminate harvesting from the wild.

In the wild, *Crambe cordifolia* ranges from the Caucasus in the west (ssp. *cordifolia*), eastwards through Kazakhstan, Iran, Afghanistan, western Pakistan, Tibet and northwestern China. In the east, *Crambe cordifolia* ssp. *kotschyana* (sometimes known as just *Crambe kotschyana*) is found, differing only in small details such as leaf shape and hairiness. They are treated together here as both have been used in similar ways. It is described as being found on mountain slopes, rocky hillsides and

199 & 200: Crambe cordifolia is a popular ornamental, but under-appreciated as a productive edible.

201: Blanched Crambe cordifolia has that distinctive sea kale taste and has a pleasant mild taste when cooked.

grassy foothills in the east (China) from 700-4,000m, and on steppes, rocky slopes in woods and among bushes in the foothills of the Caucasus up to 700m.

There's only limited information on the extent to which this plant has been wild-gathered for food across its range. This might be due to the lack of ethnobotanical studies. I haven't found any evidence either of it having been domesticated for food. I mentioned above that it had been almost harvested out of existence in the Caucasus, but here it was the roots that were collected and sold on markets, used like horseradish. Harvesting the leaves is a kinder form of foraging, as it doesn't kill the plant. In the few available references there is scant information about how this plant was used. Von Mueller (1891) says simply, 'the root and foliage of this kale afford an esculent.' Similarly in the online Flora of China it has 'the leaves and roots used as a vegetable'. In *Global Research On Underutilized Crops* (2002) by Williams and Haq, a priority list is given for underutilised vegetable and pulse crops and *Crambe cordifolia* is on this list.

This is an easy plant to grow (RHS Skill Level: Beginner); plants are readily available in Europe and North America as are seeds. The seed can be sown in both autumn and spring outside in a cold frame or similar. Established plants can be divided in early spring. I started my plant from a root cutting in autumn. It is a pretty hardy plant and can probably take winter temperatures down to -30°C. As long as it isn't too damp, it isn't too fussy on soil conditions, but will grow bigger with deeper, fertile soil. My plant is growing on shallow soil, no more than 15cm on the edge of my garden over rock, somewhere I wouldn't dream of growing traditional annual crops. The yield is astonishing for such a place! It is also tolerant of light shade. Despite having a windy garden I haven't had to stake my plant. Pests of brassicas such as slugs, caterpillars and flea beetles can attack it, but my plant has proven pretty resilient. It is noted as 'seeding itself to excess' in one book I read and has naturalised in a few places in the UK. However, my single plant doesn't seem to produce fertile seed.

In Phillips and Rix's *Vegetables* (1993) it is suggested, 'the giant inflorescences would make a fine perennial vegetable if blanched and tender and would be suitable for cold continental climates.' The broccolis or unopened flower clusters are indeed excellent and much milder than the spring leaves, not needing to be blanched. I have been blanching my greater sea kale by putting a large bucket over the plant in spring. After a few weeks, masses of stalks can be harvested. I have used it successfully in various stir-fry and other oriental and spiced dishes.

Crambe cordifolia has also been cultivated as a fodder crop and you'll really need to know that camels love it.

There are various other perennial species in the same genus worth checking out if you can find them, e.g. *Crambe tatarica*, *C. orientalis* and *C. koktebelica*.

Levisticum officinale

FAMILY: Apiaceae
ENGLISH: Lovage, Spring Celery
FRENCH: *Ache des Montagnes, Lévistique Officinale*
GERMAN: *Liebstöckel*
NORWEGIAN: *Løpstikke, Kjærlighetsurt*
RUSSIAN: *Ljubistok*
SPANISH: *Apio de Montaña, Levístico*

202: Lovage in mid-summer. Most of the summer you will be able to find a few young shoots if you search around at the base of the plant; these are milder than the older leaves and stems.

Lifting the forcing pot off the erect virginal lovage shoots at the end of April always uplifts the spirits. Now it is really spring and it is easy to understand why this great perennial vegetable is known as the 'love herb' in several languages. Indeed I've read that if you wear a sachet of lovage and orris root (*Iris germanica florentina*), it won't fail to make you attractive to your secret love. I call it spring celery when blanched like this, for it doesn't look nor taste that unlike celery. Until I learnt this trick, I didn't use this plant much as the unblanched shoots have such a strong taste. Otherwise, there really is no comparison between this perfect unspoiled vegetable and my conventional celery bed in autumn with stems gnawed by slugs.

Although some authors state that lovage hails from the eastern Mediterranean, it seems nowadays to be accepted that its wild range is West Asia, in particular in the mountains of Iran and Afghanistan. I certainly haven't found any references to it being foraged from the wild in the Mediterranean area at least not in modern times. Since at least the time of the Romans, it has been used as a flavouring in food and they probably spread it across their empire. It later became a common plant in medieval monastery gardens. It has subsequently spread from or appears as a relic of these original plantings. In my garden, it has certainly popped up here and there from seed. Until relatively recently it hadn't been used in the kitchen here in Norway. It was traditionally planted in gardens, but rather due to the belief that its strong taste would keep snakes away. Farm animals would also have lovage added to their feed for the same reason. It is found as a relic right to the very far north of Norway and also in the mountains, vouching for its hardiness. It is also found introduced and spread across North America.

The commonest way to use lovage has been as a flavouring in soups or like a vegetable stock cube. In fact, in several countries the plant has the popular name

203 (above left): Cover your lovage bed with a large bucket or a rhubarb/sea kale forcing pot and you can have spring celery, it's as easy as that. Compare the yield with traditional celery and you can see that perennials can produce more food than annuals – these plants are about 20 years old and have never had any fertiliser. Celery, on the other hand, is a hungry crop. Notice also the lower unblanched lovage at the front right – covering also gives an earlier crop, as it's warmer under the pot.

204 (above right): Unblanched spring lovage shoots can also be used, but use sparingly, the taste being described as strong yeasty celery, a good description I think.

205 & 206: Diced blanched lovage leaf stalks make a tasty vegetable curry.

'Maggi Herb' as it tastes a bit like the commercially popular Maggi vegetable stock cubes. Both the flowers (fresh) and seeds (dried and ground) are also used as a flavouring in sauces and soups, often with fish like mackerel. Try also the ground seed as a savoury topping on bread. The seed is also apparently sometimes used instead of celery in commercial celery salt. It's certainly worthwhile getting into the habit of harvesting the seed before it falls to the ground in any case. If you're a real fan of lovage, you can also cut down the whole plant in mid-summer and new shoots will soon be available for harvesting. However, it's a strong good-looking foliage plant, so I normally let it go and use the flowers and seeds instead.

Levisticum officinale is easy to propagate from seed as long as the seed is sown fresh in the autumn and given the cold treatment or you can take offshoots from an established plant with a bud and piece of root. It is readily available in the herb section of many garden centres in Europe and seed is also available, also in North America. There is one cultivar 'Magnus' which has been offered in Europe in recent years, described as 'an extremely uniform selection' and I have two Russian cultivated varieties, 'Odyssey' and 'Udalets', which I hope to compare in a few years. I've also heard that a variegated form exists, but haven't located it yet. Perhaps someone would like to try selecting for a milder or even a self-blanching form?

Lovage can grow well both in open and somewhat shady locations, needing dampish conditions when it is putting on most growth in spring to mid-summer. It is a tall herb reaching well over 2m in my garden. It's sometimes suggested that you should replant your lovage every few years, but given fertile land this probably isn't necessary. My plant is still vigorous after 20 years and it has never received fertiliser of any form apart from that which nature provides.

207: Namesake Scots lovage (Ligusticum scoticum) *is a close relation, also strong tasting but with a good mild flavour after blanching.*

Allium sativum **var.** *ophioscorodon*

FAMILY: Amaryllidaceae
ENGLISH: Serpent Garlic, Hardneck Garlic, Pskem River Garlic
FRENCH: *Ail Rocambole*
GERMAN: *Großer Schlangenknoblauch*

In 2000, American food historian William Woys Weaver published a great little (red) book *100 Vegetables and Where They Came From*. One of his 100 vegetables was Pskem River Garlic (*Allium longicuspis*). The Pskem River is in a remote area of Uzbekistan and the garlic was collected by an expedition to the area in 1989. In 2003, Will Weaver offered this garlic through Seed Savers Exchange in the US and he kindly sent me a few cloves. It didn't unfortunately grow too well in my cool climate (not many garlic varieties do). It survived the winter but it gave a rather poor yield. I therefore planted it in one of my perennial beds.

Garlic (*Allium sativum*) is actually a perennial; it's just that we normally cultivate garlic as an annual or biennial, replanting vegetatively by cloves each year. The Pskem River Garlic multiplies so quickly that within one year, there were almost 100 bulbs from the eight cloves I originally planted. Spring garlic shoots are excellent fare with a nice garlicky taste. From then on, my Pskem River Garlic was grown for its spring shoots which can be cut a couple of times (cut-and-come-again, like most Alliums).

Pskem River is classified as a hardneck or serpent garlic. In the simplest classification of garlic we have hardnecks and softnecks, the difference being whether they bolt or not, although climate does play a certain role in whether flowering is initiated. Normally, bolting is a negative trait amongst vegetables, but garlic is an exception I think and I will explain why below. Hardneck garlic sends up long flower stems, except that flowers and seeds are normally replaced by small bulbils. The flower stems or scapes can be rather spectacular as described by the following authors: 'the scapes twist and bend' (Small, 1997); 'the stems lose their sense of direction when forming

208 & 209: Allium longicuspis, *Pskem River Garlic, growing as a perennial in the author's garden as it would in the wild.*

the flower stem ... perform acrobatics and loop the loop' (Fern, 1997); 'the beak shaped flower heads writhe upward in elaborate curves and coils imitating a flamingo at its toilet and sometimes tying themselves in knots' (Davies, 1992). Get the idea?

It was long thought that *Allium longicuspis*, which was first described in 1875, was a distinct ancestral species from which all garlic originated. However, it now seems (from genetic techniques) that it is not distinguishable from modern day garlic *Allium sativum*. It is therefore more likely to be a primitive strain of garlic which naturalised in the past as did the wild clifftop cabbages (Chapter 1). Nevertheless, the *longicuspis* group of *Allium sativum* does exhibit a relatively high diversity of forms and some even sometimes produce real seed in the wild.

There is currently a lot of interest amongst amateur growers trying to develop new garlic varieties suited to local conditions through true seed. In 2012, Seed Savers Exchange published a fascinating article by Ted Jordan Meredith and Avram Drucker about their successful attempts to produce true seed by removing the bulbils (see http://garlicseed.blogspot.no/p/growing-garlic-from-true-seed.html for details).

The garlic cultivars sold commercially in supermarkets are non-bolting, softneck forms which have been selected to be easy to grow and harvest (flower scapes of hardneck forms would just be a nuisance when harvesting mechanically) and not for flavour and other characteristics. Having tested many types of garlic over the years in my borderline climate – Seed Savers Exchange in the US listed over 350 varieties in their 2011 yearbook – I have ended up with a couple of varieties which give the best yield in my climate; both are hardneck varieties and one is a Scandinavian heirloom called 'Aleksandra' which can be traced back over 100 years.

In 2002 a Finnish woman, Jenni Leväsvirta, offered me this variety. She told me its story: 'It comes from St. Petersburg in Russia and was brought to Pertunmaa, Finland, by a lady whose name was Aleksandra in the first decade of the 1900s. When she died, this garlic grew wild in her former summer cottage kitchen garden, where the neighbour found it years later among the weeds and took some to her own garden. She propagated it and gave it to members of the Finnish Useful Plants Society.' The lady turns out to be a well-known Finnish pomologist, Aleksandra Smirnoff, who had a Russian father and Finnish mother. She sent many plants between the two countries including this garlic.

That 'Aleksandra' should grow so well in my climate is not surprising as Finland has a similar climate and this variety has no doubt been selected for this characteristic. It is incidentally always the first garlic to appear in the spring. It is planted in autumn, as it needs a cold winter period to give optimal yield and is very hardy.

The scapes or flower stalks can grow as high as a person. This bolting characteristic of the hardneck garlics actually provides us with two gourmet foods in addition to the garlic bulbs. First, the immature scapes can be harvested and used in a wide range of dishes from salads to stir-fry dishes. They have a delicate pleasant garlic taste, but make sure you harvest them young, as they get tough as they mature. Removing the scapes is in any case often recommended as the plant then puts all its energy into producing bulbs, although my trials with and without scape removal

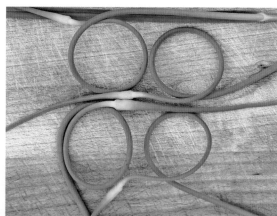

210-212: Scapes of the Finnish garlic heirloom 'Aleksandra' in my garden are as tall as I am!

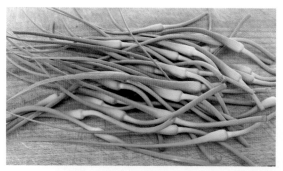

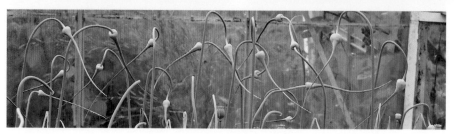

haven't shown more than a relatively minor difference. Therefore, I usually remove about half of the scapes and leave the others to produce the third edible product that is provided by the bulbils that form instead of flowers.

The colour, size and form of the bulbils in different garlic varieties are distinguishing features and bulbil diversity really is quite large. They can be planted in the autumn in pots which are kept cold until say January and then they may be brought into a cool room in the house where they will quickly sprout and one can then harvest fresh delicious garlic sprouts in mid-winter when there is little else fresh available. They can be continuously cut, soon re-sprouting each time, for a couple of months. I also sow them in the autumn in my cold greenhouse for a second harvest in the very early spring. The variety 'Aleksandra' is ideal for this purpose as the individual bulbils are relatively large but small enough that there are still a lot of bulbils on each head. Being genetically identical to the parent plant if left to grow and progressively given more space, they will after about 2-3 years provide full size garlic bulbs.

Another characteristic of homegrown garlic which varies enormously and is extremely important if you want to be self-sufficient is how well different varieties store. Luckily, 'Aleksandra' also passes this test and bulbs can be stored for about six months. The message here is that the variety that grows best in my conditions is unlikely to be the best one for you. Seek out local heirlooms to your area and trial

213-214: Different hardneck garlics have very distinct bulbils in different colours, sizes and shapes. 'Aleksandra' has relatively large purplish-red bulbils (left) and can be forced indoors in winter to provide tasty winter garlic shoots (right).

different ones before deciding which varieties to concentrate on. There are now a number of specialist garlic growers offering different varieties. The largest diversity can, however, be tapped into through various seed saver organisations in North America and some European countries.

I have now also planted 'Aleksandra' as a perennial in different parts of my garden. This variety is particularly worthwhile growing for the very early young shoots and the scapes are also a nice edimental feature for a perennial bed that visitors always comment on. It will probably be necessary to thin out every few years so that they don't get too crowded.

Allium obliquum

FAMILY: Amaryllidaceae
CHINESE: *Gao Ting Jiu*
ENGLISH: Twisted-leaf Garlic, Oblique Onion
FRENCH: *Ail à Feuilles Obliques*
GERMAN: *Schieferlauch, Scharfer Gelblauch*
MONGOLIAN: *Sarmisan Songino*
RUSSIAN: *Luk Kosoy, Dikii Chesnok*

Eric Block (2009) tells us that the chemistry of *Allium obliquum* is similar to that of common garlic, *Allium sativum*. It is then not surprising to learn that it was traditionally wild-foraged in western Siberia as a garlic substitute and was so popular that it was also cultivated for its bulbs in home gardens in this region. It was preserved by lactofermentation (as is *Allium victorialis*, Chapter 6).

Like real garlic, twisted-leaf garlic is a harbinger of spring, starting into growth as soon as there is a little warmth in the air. In the wild, this species ranges from an isolated population in Romania in Eastern Europe where it is a rare plant of gorges, through the southern part of European Russia to Kazakhstan, western Mongolia and northwest China. It grows in both open and shady habitats in meadows, on mountain slopes and along mountain streams.

Twisted-leaf garlic arrived in England in the middle of the 18th century and has since then been grown on a small scale as an ornamental. Some gardening authors at

215-217: Allium obliquum, the twisted-leaf garlic, tastes similar to garlic and is cultivated in home gardens in western Siberia.

the time loved it; others thought it was a waste of time. Personally, I think it's an attractive plant from the time the shoots appear to the end of flowering. The greeny-yellow flowers are unusual, the scapes rising under good conditions to over 1m above the curiously twisted leaves, which gives it its English name. It is very hardy and doesn't object to heavy soil. I have mine in full sun, but judging from its native habitat it should also be able to tolerate some shade.

Both seed and plants are currently readily available. Seed should be given cold treatment in order to germinate. Plants can be divided and/or thinned in the autumn. No cultivars are currently available. Selection of better forms would certainly be worthwhile and work on the domestication of this plant has been recommended in Russia.

Allium wallichii (syn. A. wallichianum, A. bulleyanum)

FAMILY: Amaryllidaceae
ENGLISH: Himalayan Onion
GERMAN: *Himalayazwiebel*
NEPALESE: *Jimbu Jhar, Ban Lasun*
RUSSIAN: *Luk Valliha*
SIKKIM: *Dung-Dunge*
TIBETAN: *Yang*

You will of course be familiar with the seminal study 'The High Altitude Ethnobotany of the Rolwaling Sherpas' (Sacherer, J., 1979)? No, perhaps not! We don't hear much about the way of life of the Sherpas when they're not climbing Everest. However, wild-gathered food has always been an important component of the diet for these isolated mountain people. The aforementioned paper reviews this and one of the more important plants that was wild-foraged in this area is a tall onion, *Allium wallichii*, which purportedly also offers alleviation for altitude sickness! I first saw this handsome onion in the Tibetan Garden at the Hillier Arboretum in Hampshire, England. Soon after I obtained seed and although it takes a few years to establish, this has become one of my favourite edimentals and probably the most unusual Allium I've grown. It is certainly hardly ever grown as a vegetable in the developed world, which is a shame I think.

Allium wallichii (named after the Danish botanist Nathaniel Wallich) is a widespread species found at high elevations in the Himalayas including India, Nepal, Tibet, Bhutan, Sikkim and China. It grows in scrubby,

218: *Spring shoots of* **Allium wallichii**. *It grows quickly to full height that can exceed 1m in good conditions.*

219-220: Harvested spring shoots of Himalayan onion (top) and the flower buds above the triangular scape (bottom).

rocky areas in clearings, liking damp summers (as it is adapted to monsoon conditions). There are two named varieties, var. *wallichii* and the Chinese var. *platyphyllum*, the main difference being whether the leaf has a petiole (leaf stalk) or not.

So, what is unusual about this onion? First, every year I think it has died on me as it is extremely late in appearing in the spring, usually at the end of May. I suspect that this is because it is adapted to the monsoon weather conditions in the Himalayas, as the onset of the rains is usually after mid-summer. However, it grows away quickly and the peculiar scape (flower stalk) with triangular cross-section appears. The irregular star-like flower umbels, which appear in late summer, come in a range of colours from pink to almost black, the latter being much sought after by plant collectors. Finally, the seed capsules on some varieties are an attractive black colour. One other peculiarity I've noticed that I haven't seen referenced anywhere is that these plants develop very long rhizomes and new shoots can emerge 30cm or more away from the parent plant. I've seen descriptions in ornamental gardening books saying that it's not an outstanding plant. I disagree.

Throughout its range, *Allium wallichii* is one of the most sought after wild-foraged edibles due to its pleasant tasting garlicky leaves. Not surprisingly, it is also cultivated in home gardens, although I have been unable to find information on cultural practices or varieties. In both northern India and Nepal, the young spring leaves are most sought after and are dried for later use. Harvest is in mid-summer before the monsoon rains start as it is ideal solar drying weather.

In India, these dried leaves are used to flavour *dhals* whilst in Nepal they are used in curry and pickles. Our Sherpa friends mix this onion with chilli and salt to spice up potatoes. In addition,

fresh green shoots are also used in season. Later in the summer the young inflorescences, flowers and seed pods are also used in succession. Paul Barney (Edulis Nursery) tells me that the long rhizomes are also dug and eaten. The Sherpas have a strong attachment to this plant and decorate their high altitude huts with the attractive flowers in late summer. The flowers are also a perfect addition to late summer salads, tasty too. Other species are also used in a similar way, including endemic (to Nepal) *Allium hypsistum*. *Allium hookeri* (hooker's onion) is another large promising onion which I'm currently trialling. It is from Tibet and northwest China and is also cultivated in mountainous areas.

Cultivation is easy where it feels at home, which is probably most of northwest Europe and cooler parts of North America where regular cool wet spells occur in summer. It likes full sun, but it can tolerate some light shade. It seems to be hardier than some authors suggest. Plants For A Future say it isn't hardy in colder areas of Britain with a minimum of -5 to

221-223: The inflorescences are very attractive and brighten up the autumn garden; the size, number and colour of the star-like flower umbels varies a lot; the seed pods are also an attractive black colour.

-10°C, yet my plants have successfully negotiated -24°C with little insulating snow cover. However, I have also lost plants from other seed sources, so my form is perhaps a particularly hardy one? Plants and seed, including a dark-flowered form, are available from some nurseries in Europe, with at least 12 currently in the UK. Seed should be stratified (cold treatment) and plants can be divided in spring.

224: Hooker's onion, Allium hookeri, *is another interesting species which is cultivated in home gardens in the eastern Himalayas; the plant on the left was found on a market in Mizoram, Eastern India by Paul Barney of Edulis Nursery in the UK.*

Allium nutans

FAMILY: Amaryllidaceae
CHINESE: *Chi Si Shan Jiu*
ENGLISH: Siberian Garlic Chives, Steppe Onion, Blue Chives
RUSSIAN: *Luk Ponikaiushchii, Luk Slizun*

Allium senescens

FAMILY: Amaryllidaceae
ENGLISH: Broad-Leaved Chives
JAPANESE: *Miyama Rakkyou*
RUSSIAN: *Luk Stareiushchii*

This is a group of Alliums which to the non-botanist is a confusing group and more often than not what you buy or see in botanical gardens is wrongly labelled. Several species including *Allium nutans, senescens* and *angulosum* (mouse garlic) also readily hybridise in gardens so that the horticultural trade ends up offering a hotchpotch that confuses even more. Further, I'm told by US based Allium guru Mark McDonough that these species will even hybridise with unrelated North American *Allium cernuum* (see Chapter 6) and *A. stellatum*. So, please be aware of this and go for vegetatively propagated plants wherever possible. Although this isn't a guarantee, it decreases the chances of you getting a mediocre hybrid, although hybrids can have superior qualities (due to hybrid vigour) as we will see in the discussion of Norrland onion below. Mark has utilised this to his advantage and has selected numerous excellent hybrid forms that have more or less randomly turned up in his mass Allium plantings in his garden in Massachusetts.

Again I have to thank Swedish author Lena Israelsson for introducing me to *Allium nutans*. In her 2002 book, she describes special varieties associated with kitchen gardens in different parts of the world. Under Russia, she includes what she calls Siberian onion (or 'Slizun') – *Allium nutans*. This is another plant that has been largely missed from compilations of edible plants such as Facciola (1998) and Hedrick (1919).

225: Allium nutans *from Seed Savers Exchange with typical nodding flower stalk with winged edges.*

226 & 227: Broad leaved Allium nutans *'Lena' (left) which I've renamed after Lena Israelsson and* Allium senescens *(right) with narrower twisting leaves.*

Allium nutans has its wild range in the south of western Siberia from the western flanks of the Altai Mountains (within China, Mongolia, Kazakhstan and Russia) roughly west to the major Yenisei River, growing in meadows and damp places. The Chinese name *shan Jiu* simply means mountain onion. This makes it one of the hardiest vegetables, but it is quite happy with milder areas such as the UK. It has been wild-gathered for food across its range presumably for a very long time. However, it has also been moved into gardens and is cultivated as a vegetable, prized for its young mild tasting leaves as they can be harvested as soon as the snows melt, at a time of year when little else is available. This and the other Alliums mentioned above usually begin to send up shoots in the autumn and the green shoots are extremely hardy and stand through the winter. In my climate, with variable snow cover, I am able to harvest these green shoots at any time they are accessible during the winter. It is said that one can cut the plants (down to ground level) up to four or five times in a season as long as they are well nourished; they just keep on coming. In recent years its popularity has spread outside of its home range to other parts of Russia, the Ukraine and Belarus. Cultivated forms are also said to be found. The only information I have found on this is from a member of Seed Savers Exchange in Belarus who sent me seed of a variety called *Belaruski Botanichny*. He told me, 'There was a special expedition of Belarussian botanists to the Russian Altai mountains in the 1990s where they found local wild *Allium nutans*. They took some seeds and then selected for several years in Belarus, calling the final variety *Belaruski Botanichny*.' Sadly that seed never germinated. However, ornamental cultivated forms of *Allium nutans* held in private collections (e.g. Mark McDonough) vary considerably, so selection of some good vegetable forms shouldn't be difficult.

I've also obtained another form of *Allium nutans* through Seed Savers Exchange in the US. This plant has been offered since 1989 and is described as a 'striking edible ornamental, tastier than *A. tuberosum* (garlic chives)'.

In my cold climate, there is a hungry gap after stored bulb onions are finished in late winter until the first shallots are ready in mid-summer, a gap readily filled by perennials and these along with *Allium cernuum* (Chapter 5) are used most frequently as they are all productive.

Lena kindly sent me seed of her 'Slizun' that she had obtained in Russia (she mentions in the book that commercial seed is also available there). Experts I have shown pictures of this to agree that it definitely has a lot of *nutans* 'blood' but it might also be a hybrid with *senescens*. *Allium senescens* differs from *nutans* in generally having narrower

228 (right): The Russian vegetable form of Allium nutans *'Slizun' is now renamed 'Lena'.*

229 & 230 (below): Allium senescens *ssp.* montanum *(now A.* lusitanicum*) (left) and* Allium angulosum *(right).*

leaves and hemispherical rather than spherical inflorescences. *Nutans* flower stems nod strongly, *senescens* only weakly, quickly straightening on flowering and the flower stems are strongly winged or keeled on *nutans*.

Previously, *Allium senescens* was used to describe one species of similar appearance found in two distinct areas: an eastern area (ssp. *senescens*), hardly overlapping with *nutans* and further to the east including Trans-Baikal, Manchuria and Korea; a western area over much of Europe (ssp. *montanum*). Modern genetic analysis has shown that the western and eastern populations are actually only distantly related in the Allium world, despite outward appearances. The European *senescens* is now correctly referred to as *Allium lusitanicum*.

The eastern *Allium senescens* has been an important wild-foraged food plant, for example, it was a favourite pot herb of Chinese cattle herders in northern China (Hu, S-Y., 2005). The online Edible Wild Plants of Siberia (Anon, 2011) says, 'The bulbs and young leaves are eaten fresh and are harvested for winter by drying and fermentation.'

All the species mentioned here are available as plants from UK nurseries at present (with a proviso of them being correctly identified). I will try to make some good forms of *Allium nutans* available (Facebook group Edimentals). Plants can otherwise be divided at any time and all can be seed propagated (sow seed in winter, keep cool and they should germinate in spring). All prefer sunny spots, but all tolerate some shade.

Before we leave this group of Alliums, I have to tell you the story of one more onion, quite possibly the most exciting new onion to appear for many years, tasty, productive and beautiful, and this means returning to Scandinavia again, where its secret has been kept since its discovery in the 1970s. I can now reveal all, it is...

Norrland Onion

In 2004, I visited plant collector Magnar Aspaker at his home in Harstad in northern Norway. One of the plants I came away with was a large unidentified onion which he called simply *Allium Ex-Råneå* as it came from a garden in the village Råneå in Luleå municipality in the far north of Sweden. The plant grew vigorously in my garden into a fine clump of a tall *Allium senescens*-like plant. A couple of years later I heard from Swedish Allium guru Åke Truedsson in Malmö about an unidentified perennial onion that had been found in Sweden. He thought that it could be a form of *Allium nutans*. In 2008, I visited Åke and the nearby Botanical Gardens in Lund where Åke told me I might find the plant. I didn't have much time and didn't find it, but when I went into the cafe in the garden, I found a little booklet produced by the garden, *Lökar på bordet* (onions on the table). To my surprise, this onion and its story is described on page 16 under the title 'Norrlandslök (Allium senescens?)'.

It turned out that it was the garden's director Marie Widén who had discovered this special onion in the north of the country in the 1970s. The description in *Lökar på bordet* fitted very well with my onion. In addition, it was apparently sterile, as mine also seemed to be. I therefore contacted Lund and sent some photos of my *Ex-Råneå* onion. She agreed it was the same.

Lund had never managed to positively identify which species their Norrlandslök belonged to despite much searching in the literature. In spring 2009, I therefore sent a sample of our onion to Allium expert Dr. Reinhard Fritsch at Gatersleben in Germany who had agreed to grow it out and try to identify its parentage. His analysis suggests strongly that Norrland onion is a hybrid between *Allium senescens* and *A. nutans*, and possibly a third so far unknown species is involved. He also concludes that 'your plants represent a good selection for domestic use – vivid growth and vegetative multiplication, without becoming weed-like by masses of seedlings, are very positive characters for a garden plant'.

In 2011, I received an onion of the Lund plant from Marie Widén and grew it out and so far it looks identical to the plant

231: Norrland onion in the author's garden.

I obtained from northern Norway. This plant has been made available through the Norwegian Seed Savers over the last couple of years and there are now several people that grow it here, but there are not any nurseries that offer it at present. I will try to make it available.

chapter 4

THE FAR EAST
AND AUSTRALASIA

When Joy Larkcom's *Oriental Vegetables* was first published in the early 1990s, a new world opened up to the adventurous vegetable gardener. Alongside the amazing diversity of oriental brassicas, incidentally mostly progeny of wild species from Europe and West Asia, we could read for the first time in English about a number of cultivated and wild-foraged perennial vegetables. I remember reading her section on wild plants and, in particular, the first plant, *Aralia cordata*, stuck in my memory. She writes, 'When I first saw the 2ft long white stalks of this plant in a wholesale vegetable market in Tokyo I was completely mystified...' I had also recently got hold of a copy of *Sturtevant's Edible Plants of the World*. This book enhanced my interest in this mysterious vegetable further when I read, 'The young shoots of this species provide an excellent culinary vegetable ... this plant is universally cultivated in Japan...' Unlike those oriental brassicas, *udo* (its Japanese name) has remained practically unknown in the West, although other *Aralias* are used as ornamentals. I managed eventually to get hold of some seed in the late 90s. *Udo* turned out to be a giant of a herbaceous plant, annually producing a dozen or more of Larkcom's 2ft long stalks from the one plant, and is today my most productive vegetable.

At the time of Larkcom's book, Chinese cuisine was already widespread in the West and many of us had eaten the most well-known oriental perennial vegetable, bamboo shoots, strangely not mentioned by Larkcom. Over the last 20 years, Japanese sushi restaurants have opened in the West in a big way and another oriental perennial vegetable is an essential ingredient with authentic sushi, *Wasabia japonica* or *wasabi*. Unfortunately, it is a very difficult plant to grow at home successfully, although this does help maintain *wasabi*'s exclusivity. I was very happy to produce 1oz of the stuff at the peak of my home production.

Other well-known East Asian perennial vegetables are the Welsh onion (*Allium fistulosum*, see Chapter 6) and garlic chives (*Allium tuberosum*, this chapter). Common for all perennial vegetables is that they have at some stage been domesticated and selected from wild plants. In the case of the latter onions, selection has been carried out over such a long time that the vegetable is distinct from the wild ancestors, *Allium altaicum* and *Allium ramosum* respectively. Others such as the Korean aster,

Aster scaber, has only been domesticated in the last few years in response to demand from health conscious city dwellers looking back to their countryside foraging roots. The six indigenous Korean plants with most acreage in 1992 were *Platycodon grandiflorus* and *Codonopsis lanceolata* (for the roots), *Aster scaber*, *Aralia elata*, *Allium grayi* and *Youngia sonchifolia*, all but the last one being perennials. I will also mention (see also Chapter 6) the revival in interest and recent cultivation of *Allium victorialis* (gyoja-ninniku), one of the most important wild sourced food plants of the long-repressed Ainu people in northern Japan.

It is within these ancient foraging traditions that we can look for novel perennial vegetables. East Asia is particularly rich in such traditions, with a particularly species-rich natural flora. Japan is one of the so-called biodiversity hotspots of the temperate world with nearly 2,000 endemics (i.e. plants found only in Japan). The wide range of climates from the subtropics to temperate, largely mountainous and ranging from sea level to the 3,776m of Mount Fuji contributes to this. These wild-foraged vegetables are known as *sansai* in Japan and *sannamul* or *chwinamul* in Korea, both meaning literally 'mountain vegetables'.

Some of the species listed in the following have already been introduced to the West, but as garden ornamentals, and one, alfalfa (*Medicago sativa*) is a major agricultural forage plant. Japanese knotweed even became a major invasive species and is now well-established in western Europe and North America, but few are yet aware of the food and health value.

> ## *Sigumchi Namul*
> ## Korean Style Wild Vegetables
>
> This is a simple delicious way used to prepare wild perennial vegetables in Korea:
>
>   Oil
>   Sesame seeds
>   Vegetables
>   Garlic (a few cloves, minced)
>   Salt
>   Pepper
>   Soy sauce
>
> Stir-fry the sesame seeds and garlic in oil; add the greens and stir-fry until wilted; remove and mix with soy sauce, salt and pepper.

The main selections presented in this chapter are perennials that I've personally succeeded with in my relatively cold climate in Norway. Others which I've either been unable to source seed for or am still trialling are listed below.

Japanese *Sansai*

- *Adenophora triphylla* (tsurocaneninjin) related to the bellflowers (*Campanula* spp.).

- *Allium ledebourianum* (asatsuki/giant Siberian chives) and *Allium macrostemon* (nobiru).

- *Anemone flaccida* (nirinsou) must be cooked or dried to detoxify like other plants in the buttercup family.

- *Angelica keiskei* (ashitaba).

232-238: Selected Japanese and Korean perennial 'mountain vegetables' not discussed in detail in this chapter, clockwise from top left: Allium ledebourianum, Adenophora triphylla var. japonica, Angelica keiskei, Petasites spp., Cacalia nikomontana, Cacalia delphiniifolia, Codonopsis spp.

- *Cacalia delphiniifolia*, *C. hastata* ssp. *orientalis* (*inudouna*/Indian plantain). *C. hastata* is also used in Manchuria.

- *Elatostema umbellatum*, a nettle relation.

- *Oenanthe javanica* (water dropwort) also used in Korea (*minari*) and Manchuria.

- *Petasites japonicus* (*fukinoto*/Japanese butterbur) (unopened buds). One of the commonest wild foods in Japan and also cultivated, although long-term use may be unsafe due to the presence of pyrrolizidine alkaloids. It is also an invasive plant, spreading vegetatively (also very commonly used in Korea, known as *mowi*).

- *Synurus pungens* (*oyamabokuchi*).

Korean *Sannamul*

- *Adenophora divaricata* (*nolbunjandae*). *A. verticillata* is used in Manchuria.

- *Adenophora triphylla* var. *japonica* (*t'oljandae*).

- *Aster tataricus* and *A. yomena* (*kaemich'wi* and *ssukpujaengi*).

- *Codonopsis lanceolata* (*todok*) roots and spring shoots, also cultivated, related to the bellflowers (*Campanula* spp.).

- *Ixeris japonica* and *Ixeris dentata* (*bodunssumbaguwi* and *ssumbagwi*) roots and greens, also cultivated.

- *Pimpinella brachycarpa* (*ch'mnamul*).

- *Smilacina japonica* (*p'ulsomdae*).

- *Smilax nipponica* (*sunmilnamul*).

Allium tuberosum

FAMILY: Amaryllidaceae
CHINESE: *Jiu*
English: Chinese Chives, Garlic Chives, Chinese Leek
JAPANESE: *Nira*
Korean: *Bu Pu*

Allium ramosum (syn. *Allium odorum*)

FAMILY: Amaryllidaceae
CHINESE: *Ye Jiu*
ENGLISH: Fragrant Onion, Fragrant-flower Garlic
RUSSIAN: *Luk Vetvistyi*

Chinese chives (*Allium tuberosum*) are considered by botanists as a purely cultivated species derived from its nearest wild relative, fragrant onion (*Allium ramosum*), a very hardy species found in northern China, Mongolia, Kazakhstan and Russia. Fragrant onion flowers early, in late spring to early summer, and the flowers are bell-shaped when open and last a long time before developing seed capsules. On the other hand,

239 & 240: A comparison of the flat star-like flowers of Allium tuberosum *in early September (left) with the campanulate flowers of* Allium ramosum *(right), in bloom in early June.*

241: Chinese chives can be planted as a perennial edimental, here used as an attractive edging to the herb/vegetable garden at RHS Rosemoor in England.

Chinese chives flower in late summer and they open right up, are flat and star-like and quickly form seed capsules. You can also see from the two pictures that the inner three petals (tepals) are significantly narrower on *Allium ramosum*. There are several other differences too including the fact that only *A. ramosum* has multiple growth points from each bulb.

In East Asia there are many varieties of Chinese chives, with two main groups, those used for leaf production and those cultivated for the tender flowering stems. I would recommend Larkcom (1991, 2007) for detailed cultivation instructions for the different forms that are still unfortunately rarely available in the West. In the perennial vegetable garden, *Allium tuberosum*, once established, can be used as a multi-purpose plant, using both the leaves and flower stems as needed and enjoying it as an ornamental.

In the Far East, blanched Chinese chives are very popular with a milder aromatic flavour. Blanching is easily achieved at home. If you have several plants, you can successively blanch the new emerging shoots on individual plants using either a special clay blanching pot similar to but slimmer than those used traditionally in the West for blanching sea kale and rhubarb, or just use a large plastic bucket or pot with light excluded from any drainage holes, alternatively earth up or use a deep straw mulch. After cutting the plants back to ground level (not necessary if you are starting in the spring), it will take a few weeks for the plants to grow ready for harvest. This process shouldn't be repeated with the same plant in the same year so as not to weaken it. Why not experiment with blanching other perennial onions?

If you prefer a more formal edible garden, you can simply harvest the young leaves from your plants in the spring before leaving the plants to flower in late summer. The relatively large white star-like flowers make Chinese chives an attractive late-summer edimental. The flowers also make an attractive addition to late-summer salads.

Allium tuberosum can be rather slow to establish from seed but will gradually divide into a clump that will live for many years. New plants can be started or it can be revitalised if the plant is getting less vigorous, by simply digging up and dividing the clump and replanting with compost added. Plants (and seed) of both *Allium tuberosum* and *ramosum* are readily available in Europe and North America, but be aware that these two species are often mixed up in the trade, in private gardens and even botanical gardens.

Hardiness varies widely between the different cultivars of *Allium tuberosum*. Most of the named Japanese cultivars I've tried have not proven very hardy (as I've similarly found with *Allium fistulosum* cultivars from Japan, Chapter 6).

Over its natural range, wild *Allium ramosum* has been traditionally foraged for food (e.g. in Manchuria, see Baranov, 1966) and there is a tradition of using the inflorescences in a traditional Mongolian cold vegetable dish, *soris* (Khasbagan et al, 2000).

Aralia elata

FAMILY: Araliaceae
ENGLISH: Oni's Walking Stick, Japanese Aralia,
  Japanese Angelica Tree
FRENCH: *L'Angélique du Japon, Aralie Japonaise*
GERMAN: *Die Japanische Aralie, Japanischer
  Angelikabaum*
JAPANESE: *Taranoki*
KOREAN: *Dureup, Turup*
SPANISH: *Arbol de Angelica*

To the uninitiated, the Japanese angelica tree (*Aralia elata*) would at first glance be an unlikely candidate for an edible plant. Anyway, who would want to eat a plant probably made by the devil? For this plant is very closely related to the North American *Aralia spinosa* (devil's walking stick) due to its straight very thorny stem as a young tree. Angelica tree is far too nice a name! Angels and devils don't really belong together. I've therefore given *Aralia elata* a new name, Oni's walking stick – Onis are Japanese devil-like demons with long nails, wild hair, a fierce look and two horns on their forehead. The use of the name angelica derives from the similarity of the leaves to wild Japanese plants in the genus *Angelica*.

Aralia elata has been introduced to North America as an ornamental and has spread widely particularly in the north where *A. spinosa* doesn't grow naturally. Under ideal conditions it can spread vegetatively by rhizomes and can quickly cover quite large areas. Note that it is considered an invasive species that shouldn't be planted in some states. The two species are often confused, as there are only relatively minor differences in the inflorescence and size of the fruit and/or seed, not that it really matters as they are equivalent foodwise. If you are in North America and want to grow this, it would

242-244: As a young tree, Aralia elata *(left) grows with a long single thorn-covered stem. The young shoots (centre) are harvested before the leaves have fully unfurled (right).*

be best to plant the native *spinosa*, although it is probably not as hardy as *elata*.

In the Far East, *Aralia elata* is found in China, Japan, Korea and far eastern Russia and throughout much of its range it is recognised as one of the best food plants. It is also a curious ornamental in a garden, but will not be anything near as productive as its cousin, *udo* (*Aralia cordata*) that we will soon get acquainted with, so grow that one by choice. In the wild, Oni's walking stick grows best on the edges of woodland, along riverbanks and roads, and so doesn't mind an open location in a garden, but as with *udo*, it prefers moist soil in spring. An excellent tree for the forest garden.

As food, *Aralia elata* is particularly popular in Korea, where it is also cultivated on a small scale to help meet demand. The shoots are picked from the end of the branches at the stage when the leaves are unfurling and **before any thorns have hardened**. (Thornless forms are also available in Japan.) They do, by the way, regrow after picking.

Preparing *Aralia elata*

In Korea, it is called *dureup* or *turup* and it is prepared in the following ways:

- Scald the shoots, dip in cold water (to preserve the colour), serve with a simple dressing of soy sauce, vinegar and sesame oil (optional red pepper, chilli, garlic and/or ginger root).

- Parboil and season with Korean chilli pepper paste (*gochujang*), a traditional home fermented paste made with dried chilli powder, rice powder (alternatively barley flour) with fermented soya beans and salt.

- Deep fry in a glutinous rice paste (*dureup bugak*).

In Japan, the shoots are known as *taranome* (the plant is *taranoki*) and it is prepared as follows:

- Dipped in batter and fried as *tempura*, see below (probably the easiest and best way to enjoy this plant; you can call it devil's *tempura* to 'impress' your friends...).

- Boiled with leaves from *Zanthoxylum piperitum* (Japanese pepper tree, *kinome* or *sanshō*), the seed pods from which are the main source of Sichuan pepper, a spice widely used in the Far East, a small easily grown attractive thorny shrub which should be grown more often.

- Raw after dipping in *miso* (preferably the thornless form; Brussell, 2004).

Devil's *Tempura*

1 egg

1 cup iced water

1 cup white flour

Beat the egg and add the ice water in a bowl. Add the sifted flour and mix lightly. Dip the *Aralia* shoots in the batter so that they are lightly covered and fry in oil at 170-180°C until lightly browned.

Dip in *tempura* dipping sauce (three parts *dashi*, one part *mirin*, and one part soya sauce) or just soya sauce or salt. Serve over rice.

There are other members of the Ginseng family (*Araliaceae*) that are also used in the Far East. During a seven year stay in Japan, David Brussell (2004) tried several others, none of which I have personal experience with yet. Brussell's favourite of all was *Chengiopanax* (syn. *Acanthopanax*) *sciadophylloides* (*koshiabura*), a forest tree, currently available from one nursery in the UK. Young shoots were served as *tempura*. Others noted were *Eleutherococcus* (syn. *Acanthopanax*) *spinosus* (*yamukogi*); *Evodiopanax innovans* (*takanotsume*) and *Kalopanax pictus* or *K. septemlobus* (*Harigiri*); the latter at least is available in the UK, but there is some concern of it becoming invasive in the US. Brussell also notes that he didn't find that *Oplopanax japonicus* was used for food, although its brother, devil's club, *Oplopanax horridus*, from Alaska has been used in a similar way there.

As it can take some years to establish it is wise to start with a plant. *Aralia elata* is readily available from nurseries and there are also a number of attractive and less vigorous cultivars with variegated and coloured leaves available. Currently, the RHS Plant Finder lists the following five cultivars available from UK nurseries: 'Aureomarginata', 'Aureovariegata', 'Golden Umbrella', 'Silver Umbrella' and 'Variegata'. The 'Variegata' cultivar has been awarded the RHS Award of Garden Merit, a good one for the edimental garden.

Aralia cordata

FAMILY: Araliaceae
CHINESE: *Shi Yong Tu Dang Gui*
ENGLISH: Japanese Asparagus, Udo
FRENCH: *Aralie à Feuilles Cordées*
GERMAN: *Japanische Bergangelika*
JAPANESE: *Udo*

Aralia cordata (*udo*) deserves to be much more popular in the West. For what is basically a wild plant, it is remarkably productive, and the highest yielding vegetable that I have grown. It is a herbaceous perennial reaching 3m tall in the course of the summer months. *Udo* is wild-foraged in Japan, Korea and China. It is a close relative of ginseng (*Panax ginseng*) and is in fact sometimes used as a substitute for the latter. There are about eight herbaceous *Aralia* species restricted to North America and Asia.

Udo is so popular that it is nowadays also cultivated in Japan. As I mention in the introduction to this chapter, Joy Larkcom had stumbled over cultivated plants in a market in Tokyo, describing them as 60cm long with white stalks when researching her book. Behind Larkcom's blanched *udo* stalks lies a very unusual production method. So-called *nanpaku-udo* or simply *Tokyo-udo* is cultivated mainly *under* western Tokyo (Tachikawa and Kokubunji City). The roots are forced during the winter months in naturally warm subterranean caverns excavated in the special Kanto loam, of volcanic origin, which can be excavated without danger of collapse. These caverns were originally used to store vegetables, but have been used for forcing *udo* off-season since about 1927. A pit is first dug 3-4m deep and then several horizontal tunnels are excavated from the bottom of the pit. *Udo* roots are planted in these tunnels and the resultant white stalks are sold locally on markets. A number of novelty food items are also available locally. I simply put one of those large black buckets used by builders (about 45cm deep) over the roots before the shoots appear in the spring. The temperature is also raised by the bucket giving an earlier harvest. The bucket is eventually lifted by the plant, a sign that it's time to harvest. Otherwise, you can cultivate *udo* as you would asparagus with perhaps 1.5m between plants in a row. In spring you can also earth up the plants as the shoots grow to blanch them.

245: *The first young leafy shoots are preferred by some people and are known as* Meudo. *They resemble* Aralia elata *shoots and can be deep fried in* tempura *in the same way at this stage.*

Nevertheless, many people in Japan prefer the stronger 'better flavoured' green *udo*, often foraged in the wild. There are at least three types recognised; *yamaudo* (or mountain *udo*), *miyamaudo* (high-mountain *udo*, actually a different species, *Aralia glabra*) and *meudo* (the young leafy shoots, similar to *Aralia elata* shoots).

The first time I tried *udo*, I followed a recommendation in the short entry in the *Oxford Companion to Food* (Davidson, 1999). Here it states that *udo* is 'usually simply peeled and steeped in cold water and then eaten almost raw'. Some people find the raw shoots slightly unpleasant and soaking disguises this as does using a dressing. I prepared a Japanese style *aemono* dressing for the sliced *udo* stem, made from 3 tablespoons of water, 2 tablespoons vinegar, 2 tablespoons soy sauce and sesame seeds (best roasted and crushed in a mortar). I have since found that *udo* salad dressings vary widely in Japan and may also contain mustard, garlic, sake, chilli and sugar. *Udo* salad has a crispy texture and it was delicious. The flavour of *udo* is mild and is variously said to be lemon-fennel like or asparagus-like. In Japan, stem slices are also commonly added to soups a minute or so before serving (*miso-shiru* is a popular soup in Japan in which it is often used). *Udo* stalks

246: *Udo stems, blanched under a large builder's bucket, are at harvest about half a metre high and 3-4cm in diameter. A mature plant can easily produce over 20 stems.*

are ready to harvest at about the same time (mid to late May) as Hosta shoots and could therefore be used as a starter to accompany a Hosta meal (later this chapter).

I've also used *udo* in western-style dishes. For example, the mix of international permaveggies in the photo overleaf were used in a simple green pasta sauce (see recipe on page 60).

Preparation of green *udo* usually involves boiling for a few minutes to reduce the stronger flavour, although different people will tend to like different strengths. It is often served deep-fried in *tempura* batter, in particular the leafy tops (like *Aralia elata*). The flower bud umbels are also a delicious vegetable available in mid-summer, also used in *tempura*. The roots are also reported to be used, but I think you would only want to try this if you had too many plants.

247: Udo salad is easy to prepare: just peel, slice and add the dressing!

It is often recommended to soak the *udo* in a water/vinegar mix if you won't be preparing food for a while, both to maintain the colour and keep it from becoming bitter.

The closely related *Aralia continentalis* (syn. *Aralia cordata* ssp. *continentalis*) can be used in a similar way. In Baranov (1967) this species is reported to be used occasionally by the Chinese in Manchuria and it is also used in Korea.

Udo is also cultivated in North America to a limited extent for oriental markets and UK company NamaYasai, specialising in Japanese vegetables, is growing *udo*. It doesn't travel well and this is therefore a natural slow food that needs to be grown locally!

Udo grows away quite quickly starting from seed, taking perhaps 3-4 years to the first harvest. It is basically a shade-loving plant, so it is ideal for a forest garden, but doesn't mind open sunny conditions provided that the soil doesn't dry out. It is also, luckily for me, considerably hardier than the UK hardiness zone 8 given in the Plants For A Future database (it has been reported to survive Finnish winters below -30°C).

Aralia cordata and *A. continentalis* are available from a handful of UK and US based nurseries at present and seed is also sometimes available in Europe. Paul Barney of Edulis in the UK exhibited *udo* at the Chelsea Flower Show in May 2012. A recent ornamental introduction from Japan is the cultivar 'Sun King', with bright gold leaves and, I quote '...is truly one of the most amazing new perennial introductions in the last decade'. It is available from 22 nurseries in the UK at the time of writing.

248: *Left to right: Japanese* Aralia cordata, *North American* Allium validum *(Chapter 5), Caucasian* Hablitzia tamnoides *(Chapter 3) and Afghan* Crambe cordifolia *(Chapter 3) can all be harvested at the same time and form the basis of a truly international round the world perennial dish.*

If you are starting from seed as I did originally, it is probably best to give them the cold treatment. Plants can also be propagated easily by dividing the roots.

Aster scaber (syn. *Doellingeria scabra*)

FAMILY: Asteraceae
ENGLISH: Korean Aster
JAPANESE: *Shirayama-Gik*
KOREAN: *Chamch'Wi*
....

Korean aster is hard to beat as an edimental, producing masses of white flowers in late summer and autumn until the first frosts. That this should be one of my favourite vegetables comes as a big surprise to people visiting my garden in the autumn.

This is a very popular wild-foraged species (Pemberton and Lee, 1996) and, in recent years, a cultivated vegetable in Korea. In fact, it is *the* leafy indigenous vegetable with highest cultivated acreage in Korea. It is grown in greenhouses and exported to the Korean markets in the US, both dried and frozen. It is also reportedly now cultivated on a small scale in Japan. However, unless you're a Plants For a Future trainspotter like me, you're unlikely to have heard of it before. The plants produce a good quantity of mild-tasting leaves in spring and after removing all the leaves, it will still rebound to flower later in the summer.

In Korea, wild vegetables or *chwinamul* are used in a dish called *bibimbap*. The vegetables are stir-fried in sesame oil with various seasonings such as salt, vinegar and *gochujang* (red pepper paste) and are served over rice. Fried egg is also often added. The dried leaves are often just soaked in water and seasoned with soy sauce and sesame oil (there's even a YouTube video explaining how to prepare the dried imported product in the US). People generally believe that these wild vegetables are very healthy and I'm sure they're right!

Aster scaber is available currently from three nurseries in the UK – don't all rush at once though. Seed is, unfortunately, more difficult to come by.

249: **Aster scaber** *is a fantastic combined edible and ornamental (edimental), producing masses of typical white aster flowers in late summer.*

250 & 251 (left): Korean aster at the harvesting stage in spring; mid-May in Norway.

252 (below): Aster ageratoides in Kew Gardens is another species wild-collected locally as a vegetable in spring in China.

My oldest plant came from the excellent wild seed list of the Russian Far East of botanist Dr. Alexandra Berkutenko, sadly no longer produced.

In February 2012, I received a completely unexpected telephone call from Misoni Sandvik in Oslo. She was a refugee from Korea when she was young and remembered foraging with her grandmother near Seoul. One plant she remembered fondly was *Aster scaber*. She had recently bought a cottage with a plot of land where she wanted to grow some of the plants she remembered from Korea. She had searched unsuccessfully for some time for seed of this Aster until one day she discovered that this guy in Norway had it on his internet seed trade list! She told me that the leaves were picked in spring and her grandmother had two ways of preparing it. First, the leaves were quickly blanched in boiling water and served with a dressing of soya sauce, crushed garlic, a little sugar, a little sesame oil and sesame seeds with a few spring onions. In the second variant, the same ingredients were used but the leaves were raw and they were 'crushed' together. She also remembered the fantastic taste of the leaves that they also nibbled on as they foraged.

This plant isn't mentioned by Larkcom and, in my opinion, given too low a rating in the Plants For A Future database.

Other closely related species, *Aster glehnii* and *A. tataricus*, are also eaten in Korea and are also sold dried. The latter is available in the UK. *Aster yomena* (syn. *Kalimeris yomena*) is also used in Japan (Pemberton and Lee, 1996), a cultivar of which 'Shogun' is quite a popular ornamental in the UK. *Aster ageratoides* is another that is used locally in China (Hu, S-Y, 2005), and is also available in the UK. I have not tried any of these so far. See also *Aster tripolium* (Chapter 6).

Hosta sieboldiana

FAMILY: Agavaceae / Hostaceae
ENGLISH: Plantain Lily
JAPANESE: *To Giboshi*

Hosta montana

ENGLISH: Large-leaf Hosta, Tall-Cluster Plantain Lily
JAPANESE: *Oba Giboshi*
Korean: *Keun-Bi-Bi-Chu*

Hosta sieboldii

ENGLISH: Small-leaved Hosta
JAPANESE: *Koba Giboshi*

Hosta longipes

ENGLISH: Rock Hosta
JAPANESE: *Iwa Giboshi*

That Hosta should prove to be such a good spinach plant came as quite a surprise, as Ken Fern in the book *Plants For A Future* wrote simply that he had only tried two species and that they are 'somewhat fibrous but have a sweet flavour'. The genus Hosta as a whole is given the lowest usefulness rating on the online Plants For A Future database: www.pfaf.org. Other references I had read indicated that the leaves were either sour or bitter. That the species I have so far tried didn't have a hint of bitterness and weren't at all fibrous was therefore unexpected.

I must admit I like to surprise visitors to my garden. As we pass my largest group of mature Hosta plants, I don't say anything and usually someone will pipe up, 'Surely you don't eat those'. Hosta is a common ornamental throughout Norway and it has never occurred to folk that they could be eaten. So, when I tell them that Hosta is one of my absolute favourite edible plants, they leave convinced that I AM crazy...

The genus Hosta consists of some 45 species of clump-forming perennials from Japan, Korea, China and east Russia, previously classified in the Lily family (known as Plantain Lilies). Their natural habitat is along rocky streams, in woodland and also in more open habitats such as alpine meadows. They are very hardy and can be grown throughout northwest Europe. As the natural habitat indicates, Hostas are shade-tolerant and as we will see perfect for the edible forest garden herb layer.

They were introduced to Europe as ornamentals in the 18th century and are today one of the most popular garden plants. They are also one of the best-known families used in the woodland garden, in particular the larger species, which act effectively to suppress weeds. They are mainly grown as foliage plants, with a large range in leaf size, shape, colour (from green to yellow to grey blue) and many different variegated forms are also available. With an estimated 5,000 or more cultivars, there are an enormous number of varieties to choose from. The latest UK based RHS Plant Finder lists over 1,800 varieties of Hosta available currently in British nurseries!

Hostas are propagated easily by division in late summer and spring, and they can also be raised by seed, although cultivars will not necessarily come true. However, it will take several years from seed before plants are ready for harvest. The main problem with their cultivation is that slugs are also partial to a Hosta salad, although in my climate this is only a problem in late summer when the plants are on the wane. However, the problem can also become a solution, see box to the right.

Over the years, I had planted various Hostas in my edible garden, both cultivars and a growing number of species Hosta, the latter mostly seed propagated. As mentioned earlier, Plants For a Future didn't rate Hosta

Hosta-Leaf Slug Trap

Try breaking off a few leaves of the largest Hosta species and place them around your Hostas and other susceptible plants and regularly collect the slugs that will congregate underneath – this is more effective than beer! Another great Japanese vegetable, biennial burdock (*Arctium lappa*) is also useful in the same way, and as the leaves are available much earlier than Hosta are better if you have them.

Burdock leaves can, like Hosta, be used as a slug trap for exposed young plants, here guarding a young courgette.

very highly and *Cornucopia II*, a comprehensive sourcebook of edible plants, only has one entry, for the species *Hosta longipes*, stating, '...the sourish leaves are cooked and eaten. In Korea they are used for *namul*, a side dish commonly seasoned with soy sauce and toasted sesame oil'. I looked in various other reference books and I remember that I didn't find much that really inspired me to try Hosta.

Later, searching the internet, I did find some interesting articles. I learnt that *Hosta sieboldiana* was cultivated in mountain villages in Japan and was sold as a cash crop vegetable in the cities. Another website in particular attracted my attention; an amusing article by a guy called Ernie Flippo from the US Hosta Society called 'Hosta Cookery'. He had prepared a couple of Hosta dishes for meetings of the New England Hosta Society, including cream of Hosta soup and *hostakopita*, the latter inspired by the Greek *spanakopita* (spinach pie), using Hosta leaves rather than spinach. He ends his article with, 'Now for lunch ... there's nothing like a nice plate of free-range, Hosta-fed slugs sautéed in garlic butter...' This I had to try – no, not the slugs, the *hostakopita*.

Hostas are ready to harvest here in late spring around the middle of May, and I finally got round to experimenting with them at the end of May in 2006. I thought that I

253 & 254: Hosta shoots in my garden in mid-May (top) and newly harvested shoots or Hostons, known as Urui *in Japan (bottom).*

had probably left it a bit late and had expected that the leaves would be fibrous and bitter. However, I tasted the raw leaves and they were neither.

You can take all the shoots from a plant and it will quickly shoot again and still manage to flower later in the season. In fact some Hosta gardeners will deliberately mow their Hostas as it is the young leaves that are the ornamental attraction. I used three of my larger plants for this experiment, *Hosta sieboldiana* 'Elegans', the yellow-variegated *Hosta montana aureomarginata* and *Hosta fortunei*. The *hostakopita* pie was a great success despite being served to a group of sceptical family members and guests, an excellent spinach green with a good taste.

Since then, I have unearthed a lot more information on the internet about the culinary use of the genus Hosta, particularly from the increasing number of Japanese sites in English. One can also find a lot of information in the book *The Genus Hosta* by W.G. Schmid, which was published in 1991 (new edition in 2009). It includes an Appendix on the use of Hosta in the kitchen and other uses.

Not being skilled in the intricacies of filo pastry making used in Greek spinach pie, I bought some in a Turkish supermarket. Having bypassed the difficult part of

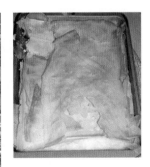

255-257: The beautiful blue green foliage of Hosta sieboldiana *'Elegans' (left),* Hosta montana aureomarginata *(centre), both used in the Greek Hosta pie,* hostakopita *(right).*

258: Homegrown blanched Hosta montana *(snow urui) is easy to produce using an upended bucket.*

259: Hosta montana *lightly cooked with soy sauce is the easiest way to enjoy this excellent vegetable.*

hostakopita construction, the rest was pretty straightforward. Wash, chop finely and drain about 1kg of Hosta shoots. Sauté a few spring perennial onions in olive oil (I used a bunch of shoots from one of my best perennial onions, *Allium obliquum*, twistedleaf garlic, see Chapter 3). Mix four eggs with 1lb. of crumbled feta cheese and melted butter, adding the onions, Hosta leaves and salt and pepper. Line a large greased pan with half the filo sheets (about 10), brushing with melted butter between each sheet. Place the filling on the pastry and finally cover with the remaining filo sheets, again with melted butter. Bake at about 350ºF (180ºC) for about 45 minutes.

In Japan, it is mainly the young leaf stems (petioles) that are harvested and these are sold in Japan in vegetable shops as *urui*. The commonest species are *Hosta montana* (*oba giboshi*) and *H. sieboldii* (*koba giboshi*) and both are found throughout Japan. *H. sieboldiana* (*to giboshi*) is also common. *To* and *oba giboshi* are the largest species and naturally therefore also the ones most used for food. The latter is commonest and is so common in some areas that it has become a weed in rice fields. Farmers exploit this by harvesting and selling the weed as a by-crop in spring. Due to its commonness, the plant itself has also become known as *urui*. The green-leaved wild collected *oba giboshi* is also often preferred to the grey-green leaves of *to giboshi*. In the wild *montana* is mostly found on the east, Pacific side of Japan whilst *sieboldiana* is found in the west, and both are utilised by local populations.

I call them hostons due to their resemblance to chicory shoots or chicons. In recent years, *urui* has become more popular and to meet the demand they are now cultivated in greenhouses. This has lead to the production of novelty blanched Hosta shoots, known as '*yuki urui*', or literally snow *urui*, and this is reckoned to be gourmet food. The white petioles are tender and are often used raw in salads, but are also used in a whole range of other dishes. The simplest way that *urui* is enjoyed is to boil it and add soy sauce, or, as with most vegetables, use as *tempura*.

260-262: *Assembling* nori-maki-sushi *filled with marinated* urui.

Hosta has also been used in sushi and there are several recipes. In spring 2007, with a little help from my friends, I tried one of these recipes. The dried hostons are first boiled and then marinated in soy sauce, salt and (optionally) sugar and are used as the centre filling for *nori-maki-sushi* (this is the familiar sushi wrapped in *nori*, the seaweed related to Welsh laver). In another recipe, the Hosta leaves are used instead of nori as the outer casing for rice prepared with purple *perilla* (*shiso*) leaves (called *shiso-giboshi-sushi*).

Hostas have also been considered to be the best wild vegetables for pickling and they have also been preserved by drying. The flower stalks have a good crisp texture and flavour and finally, Hosta flower buds are also sometimes used in *tempura*.

One of the most popular ornamental Hostas today is the cultivar 'Sagae'. This is a large-leaved variegated form of the species *Hosta fluctuans*. It was apparently found amongst cultivated Hostas being grown for food in the garden of a resident of Sagae City, located inland on the main island in Japan, Honshu. The gardener potted it up as he liked it and grew it in his front garden until a passing nurseryman noticed it. *Hosta* 'Sagae' now has pride of place at the entrance to my garden.

Urui is often collected from the wild in Japan. There are, however, occasional cases of mistaken identity leading to poisoning as Hosta leaves can be mistaken for the leaves of false hellebore (*Veratrum* spp.), although it is not difficult to tell the difference.

263: *Purple shiso (Perilla frutescens) is an easily grown annual, used with shiso-giboshi-sushi.*

264: *The young purple shoots of* Hosta montana *cultivars are especially attractive in a woodland garden.*

This could also be a problem in a garden setting, so please be absolutely sure that you have Hosta in front of you. Note that all the leaf veins of *Veratrum* go from base to the tip of the leaf, not so with Hosta.

If you want to try Hosta for food and don't already have a plant, I would suggest that you try one of the large-leaved *Hosta montana* or *H. sieboldiana* cultivars, such as 'Elegans', 'Big Daddy' and 'Blue Umbrella'. You can check the species of many cultivars on the MyHosta database.*

265: **Hosta montana** *is a vegetable in spring, foliage plant in summer and ornamental flower in autumn – a perfect edimental. Both the flower buds, stalks and the flowers themselves are edible too and can be added to salads.*

Cryptotaenia japonica

FAMILY: Apiaceae
CHINESE: *San Ye Quin*
ENGLISH: Mitsuba, Japanese Wild Parsley, Japanese Honewort, Trefoil
JAPANESE: *Mitsuba*

Cryptotaenia is a genus consisting of two species in the carrot family. The Japanese *mitsuba, Cryptotaenia japonica,* is the most important edible species as this widespread woodlander, found in Korea, Japan, China and Taiwan, has been domesticated in a big way in the Far East. It reaches about 30cm tall and my experience with the purple-leaved cultivar *Atropurpurea* is that it can stand winter temperatures down to a least -15°C and self-seeds. The very closely related honewort, *Cryptotaenia canadensis,* is found throughout eastern North America also in moist, shady places. This is a somewhat hardier plant in my experience. They are very difficult to tell apart, the main difference being in the number of flowers in the umbels. There are more in *japonica*. Different botanical forms of *japonica* are recognised over its range, with variations in leaf and umbel form.

Mitsuba is nowadays commonly available in herb and vegetable seed catalogues in the West and it is relatively easy to start from seed as long as the seed is fresh. Once it is established as a perennial it will readily seed itself and may behave in an invasive way if allowed to escape into woodland. So, keep your eyes on it. However, I've not found it to be a problem, I just eat the seedlings that come up in unwanted spots. The plant that seeded itself miraculously right next to a purple leaved form of *Plantago major*, greater plantain, in the middle of my species-rich lawn was allowed to stay.

In Japan, *mitsuba* has been cultivated for a little over 100 years, originally being one of the *sansai* or mountain vegetables. It is still wild-collected locally. Nowadays,

* http://myhostas.net

266 & 267 (above): I have been most successful with this purple form of Cryptotaenia japonica (above left). As with ground elder (Chapter 6), the shinier leaves are best and even the emerging flower heads are good. Its seedlings (above right) seem to vary in colour to some extent, so it's best to select for the darker colours to maintain the variety. The colourful leaves add a splash of colour to spring salads along with red-leaved dandelions (see Chapter 1).

268: Purple mitsuba sowed itself in the middle of my species-rich lawn one year, right next to a purple-leaved cultivar of greater plantain, Plantago major 'Atropurpurea'; presumably, the seeds had hitched a ride on the sole of my boots!

it is produced year-round in greenhouses. It is both cultivated as a perennial (on a 5-6 year rotation, Larkcom, 1991), harvested for leaves and stems at about two months from seed (kiri-mitsuba) and in the first spring with the roots attached (ne-mitsuba); the latter two types are also blanched by earthing up, and are grown in full sun for stems and leaves (ito-mitsuba).

Growing mitsuba as a perennial you'll be able to try all these variations yourself, as it will seed itself. If you harvest the supple top growth throughout the summer, it will continue to send up new shoots. In this way, you can have fresh mitsuba from spring to autumn. My plant of the purple-leaved cultivar 'Atropurpurea' is over 10 years old and is still producing, although it probably won't be the original plant as it self-sows each year. Although purple mitsuba is mostly grown as an ornamental, it is perfectly edible and it gives a nice splash of colour to salads from very early spring to autumn.

269 (left): Purple mitsuba *on sale as an ornamental at the National Trust's Knightshayes Court Garden Centre in Devon, England.*

270 (above): Honewort, Cryptotaenia canadensis, *is a good replacement if* mitsuba *doesn't make it through the winter. It is often mistaken in its early stages for ground elder (Chapter 6) as both have leaves divided into three leaflets.*

Use it also as a garnish as you would parsley, or add to various cooked dishes, including soups, at the last moment. I've not had so much success with standard green *mitsuba* as it doesn't seem as hardy. However, the North American honewort grows well, so I use that instead, although it does taste milder than purple *mitsuba*.

The Japanese use this plant in a whole range of dishes from soups to salads to tempura to sushi and in some dishes it is considered to be absolutely essential, no replacement being possible. The flavour is difficult to describe, milder than, say, coriander leaf, it's simply *mitsuba* tasting...

You can also experiment with the seeds as a seasoning on or in bread, home-made cheeses, goodies etc.

Strangely, there don't seem to be records of Native Americans using honewort. Steve Brill (1994) in New York describes it and says that this is one of his favourite plants to dry for using later in bean soups as it's easy to pick in quantity, growing abundantly in the wild.

Wasabia japonica (syn. *Eutrema wasabi*)

FAMILY: Brassicaceae
CHINESE: *Shan Yu Cai, Shan Kui*
ENGLISH: Japanese Horseradish, Wasabi
JAPANESE: *Wasabi*
KOREAN: *Wasabi*

Wasabi is probably the most well-known indigenous Japanese perennial root vegetable. Even though you may be familiar with wasabi as the green 'explosive' paste served at sushi restaurants, it is by no means certain that you have eaten genuine *Wasabia japonica* root, as wasabi paste is usually a mix of horseradish, mustard and food colouring, outside of gourmet restaurants. This is due to the fact

271 (above): Wasabi in my garden in Norway survives from year-to-year, but roots remain small. The spring leaves and flowers can be used however. The plant flowers very early and this picture is taken in the first week of May.

272 & 273 (right): The yield was nothing to write home about, but to have a micro-taste of home-produced wasabi was a treat.

that it is difficult to produce, supply falling well below demand, with subsequent prices being sometimes 100 times that of horseradish. The highest quality wasabi is grown in specially constructed beds with constantly flowing cold mountain water (at about 11-14°C), reminiscent of watercress beds in the UK (see Chapter 1), but in more shady conditions. This requirement means that there are limited areas where wasabi can be grown successfully, mainly in Japan, but also in China, Korea and in British Columbia and North Carolina in North America. Hydroponic production in greenhouses has, however, been mastered in recent years, particularly in New Zealand.

If you just happen to have a stream, it might be worth having a go. Plants are available in Europe and North America, but be prepared that it can take several years before the roots reach a usable size. I've grown wasabi in various parts of my garden over the last few years. They are hardy, grow very slowly but the roots remain very small. Nevertheless, you can use the tasty spring leaves, stalks and flowers in salads, sauces etc. A popular pickle called *wasabi-zuke* is made in Japan from a mix of all parts of the plant and the flowers are also used in *tempura*. In my garden the plant dies right back in the autumn, but starts into growth again in the very early spring and flowers early.

Fallopia japonica
(syn. *Reynoutria japonica* / *Polygonum cuspidatum*)

FAMILY: Polygonaceae
CHINESE: *Hu Zhang*
ENGLISH: Japanese Knotweed, Flowering Bamboo
FRENCH: *La Renouée du Japon, Renouée à Feuilles Pointues*
GERMAN: *Japanische Staudenknöterich, Zugespitzter Knöterich*
JAPANESE: *Itadori*
KOREAN: *Hojanggeun*

Fallopia sachalinensis
(syn. *Reynoutria sachalinensis* / *Polygonum sachalinense*)

FAMILY: Polygonaceae
ENGLISH: Giant Knotweed, Sakhalin Knotweed
JAPANESE: *Ooitadori*
KOREAN: *Wanghojang*

These two giant herbaceous plants from the Far East have in the past been widely introduced in the northern hemisphere as ornamentals. They have proven to be invasive both in Europe and North America and are difficult to eradicate. Forgetting for a minute the possible impact on native vegetation, this has been one of the best introductions for the wild (and garden) forager. Think also about a future scenario where wild foraging once again becomes vital. What plants would you introduce given our present access to more or less any plant worldwide? It is, however, illegal in the UK to introduce these species into the wild (even accidentally from garden waste), although there is no restriction on you growing it in your garden. Interestingly, the Botanical Society of the British Isles (BSBI) states the following on its website:

> 'DEFRA (Department for Environment, Food and Rural Affairs) … claims that Japanese knotweed harms the native flora. This seems questionable, and no references ever seem to be attached to such statements. Ford (2004) eradicated a stand of F. japonica but found that bluebells had been thriving under it in Cornwall.'

Despite this, an insect has been foolishly released to control this unwanted plant.

Japanese knotweed is found in about 2,500 x 10km square survey areas in the UK according to the BSBI. Giant knotweed, on the other hand, is less widespread, mainly concentrated in southeast England. This means that most people in the UK will have access to wild plants in their local area, so apart from easier access, there probably isn't much reason for planting this in your garden.

So, this is very much a plant of the 'if you can't beat it, eat it' brigade, for I've discovered, along with many other foragers in North America, Europe and the Far East that this is an excellent perennial edible. A gourmet nuisance plant as someone once described it. Shouldn't a perennial vegetable that just keeps on coming despite repeated harvest be very attractive? In fact, such is the enthusiasm for this plant as an edible in the US that a Knotweed Festival has even been arranged in Pittsburgh.

274: Knotweed stalks are persistent through the winter. Here is a typical spreading colony which has escaped from the old Hadsel Vicarage garden in northern Norway. In the foreground can be seen two other good perennial vegetables, giant bellflower, Campanula latifolia *(Chapter 6) and rosebay willowherb,* Epilobium angustifolium.

These giant knotweeds are related in the knotweed family to many other cultivated and wild sourced edibles such as annual buckwheat (*Fagopyrum esculentum*) and perennial buckwheat (*Fagopyrum dibotrys*, Chapter 3), as well as rhubarb, bistort, alpine bistort and sorrel (Chapter 6). They do contain some oxalic acid, so it's advisable not to overdo your attempts to graze this to death.

Fallopia japonica can reach 3m, whereas *F. sachalinensis* is the real giant reaching 4m in one season under ideal conditions. They both have large, hollow, jointed stems giving them their alternative name of flowering bamboos to which they are unrelated. The stems are persistent through the winter and that will help you localise colonies in your area. In Japan, it is called *itadori*, literally the strong one.

You don't really need to tell these two species apart as they are used in the same way but for the curious, *F. sachalinensis* has a leaf which is heart-shaped at the base and has hairs underneath. The leaf base of *F. japonica* is straight and lacks hairs. However, a hybrid between the two species is also quite common confusing identification.

In the wild *F. japonica* is widespread in China including Taiwan, Japan and Korea, whereas *F. sachalinensis* is found in Japan and eastern Russia, notably in Sakhalin and the Kuril Islands. This is a popular *sansai* vegetable, particularly in Japan. I have seen recipes where the peeled shoots (harvested young at about 30-40cm) are (a) eaten raw with salt; (b) lactofermented as *kimchi*, (c) used as *tempura* and

275 & 276: These shoots were about 40cm and were perfect for eating.

(d) used in *nimono* (a special Japanese stew). The very young or supple top part of the shoot is also served as *tempura* with the leaves intact (without peeling). It is easiest to peel the shoots from the root upwards.

In the West, knotweed is mostly cooked as a sweet dish as we would use rhubarb, which it both resembles in appearance and taste when cooked, although the taste is distinct. The shoots shown harvested in the picture cooked down perfectly and weren't at all fibrous even though I didn't peel the shoots. I also used the leaves, although some prefer not to use them, due to possibly higher levels of oxalic acid. Well-known American forager Euell Gibbons pioneered its use in the West already in the early 1960s with a whole chapter devoted to 'Japanese Knotweed: A Combination Fruit-Vegetable' (Gibbons, 1961). He includes various recipes for using it as a kind of spinach, as a soup (sweet and savoury), as salad, and as a dessert and jam. A North American way of preparing knotweed is with maple syrup. The Cherokees had also incidentally already started to use this foreign species as a vegetable (Moerman, 1998).

It is also interesting that knotweed contains a powerful antioxidant, resveratrol, and it is today the main source of this as a nutritional supplement (resveratrol is otherwise found in red grape skins/red wine). Some beekeepers have also actually planted knotweed as it's one of the few nectar producing plants in the autumn. Not really such an evil plant after all, is it?

277-279: Different stages in the preparation of knotweed crumble.

Hemerocallis citrina

FAMILY: Hemerocallidaceae
CHINESE: *Huang Hua*
ENGLISH: Citron or Long Yellow Daylily

Hemerocallis altissima

ENGLISH: Tall Daylily

Hemerocallis fulva

CHINESE: *Xuan Cao*
ENGLISH: Orange Daylily
KOREAN: *Wonchurri*

Hemerocallis lilioasphodelus

CHINESE: *Bei Huang Hua*
ENGLISH: Yellow Daylily

Hemerocallis or daylilies have become possibly the most popular ornamentals in the temperate world thanks to their showiness and their adaptability to a wide range of climates. From a range of some 20 recognised species, there are today over 40,000 garden cultivars. However, they have been cultivated for food and medicine in China for several thousand years. The most important part used is the dried flowers or flower buds, so-called golden needles or *jin-zhen*. About 10 years ago, I contacted Hemerocallis expert Dr. Juerg Plodeck in Switzerland as I understood he was married to a Chinese lady and might know more about which species were cultivated. He was a great help and told me that he had been told on a visit to Beijing Botanical Garden that it is the citron daylily or *H. citrina* which is used in cooking. However, from looking at the golden needles sold in shops in China, he had concluded that it could also either be the yellow daylily, *H. lilioasphodelus* or the tall daylily, *H. altissima*. He was also kind enough to send me offsets of both *H. citrina* and *H. altissima*. Plodeck's website[*] is an excellent resource on species Hemerocallis. There does not, however, seem to be any evidence for the various double flowered cultivars of *H. fulva*, favoured by Ken Fern in his taste trials (Fern, 1997), such as 'Kwanso' (or *chang ban xuan cao*), having been cultivated for food in China.

Searching Chinese websites with Google Translate today certainly confirms that the citron daylily is widely cultivated, typically on open rolling farmland in upland areas such as in the Qinling Mountains, the home of the Qinling panda. We can find packets of golden needles with a picture of a panda in oriental suppliers in the West. However, *H. lilioasphodelus* is apparently also used and long-flowered cultivars have been selected for this purpose according to Hu (2005). Whatever the species, a daylily farm must be a sight to behold during the harvesting period and I wish I could share with you some of the pictures I've found browsing Chinese websites. In Taiwan, there is one area that has become a tourist attraction due to the daylily farms!

The flowers and buds of *H. citrina* are particularly long. Golden needles from this species are known as *Huang hua cai*, or simply 'yellow flower vegetable'. It is also one of the

[*] www.hemerocallis-species.com

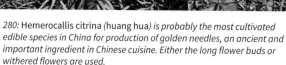

280: **Hemerocallis citrina** (huang hua) *is probably the most cultivated edible species in China for production of golden needles, an ancient and important ingredient in Chinese cuisine. Either the long flower buds or withered flowers are used.*

281: **Hemerocallis citrina** *in my garden with withered flowers ready to pick.*

most striking of the species and a worthy addition to the edimental garden. It's rather strange that this species isn't more often used in gardens. A bonus is that you can still enjoy the flowers, particularly if you harvest the flowers after they have wilted!

Some claim that species like *H. citrina* are night-flowering, the flowers emerging in the evening and wilting by morning, but that's a fallacy. In reality, it seems that yellow flowered species tend to start coming into flower in early afternoon so that they are in full flower at night, but they may remain in bloom for up to three days. *H. citrina* is also a fragrant species, which will enhance the taste, another reason for trying to get this one. Hu (2005) relates that the flower buds are best harvested early in the morning before they would have opened in the afternoon. They are quickly scalded to kill the cells before they are dried to give the best product. These techniques were originally developed by Taoist and Buddhist monks for use in their vegetarian dishes, but the market has spread in modern times to cities in China and to Chinese markets internationally.

Now, a warning about eating daylilies, because they can make you ill! The person who originally suggested that I contacted Juerg Plodeck for information wrote to me saying, 'Only the other week I ate a lot of them raw and it had a devastating effect on my digestive system an hour later'. I have seen numerous similar reports of people contracting gastrointestinal symptoms of poisoning, particularly when eating large amounts of fresh daylilies (e.g. Peter Gail reports various episodes in the US in his booklet, *The Delightful Delicious Daylily*). The cause seems to be that daylilies contain an alkaloid. Some people, myself included, do get an almost immediate burning sensation in the throat after eating raw daylilies and in my experience this isn't species dependent as suggested by Fern (1997) who says that, 'The species

282: **Hemerocallis citrina** *and* **H. altissima** *withered flowers picked for drying (note that the best product is obtained by drying the flower buds).*

H. lilioasphodelus is especially to blame. The flowers of the other species are free of this aftertaste'. Eating a few petals in a salad should however be perfectly safe, but just have a taste the first time! Dried and cooked daylilies are safe to eat and they are usually cooked well in China. I have also found a number of public warnings on the web in China from experts against eating fresh daylilies.

Therefore, I would advise that you should use daylilies as the Chinese have for millennia as follows:

- Use either well cooked or pre-dried.
- Use species rather than modern cultivars (we can't possibly know the chemical composition of all the 40,000 cultivars out there).
- Use preferably the better tasting yellow flowered species.
- Don't use a lot of the spring leaves or raw tubers (both are sometimes used in China and elsewhere).
- Try only a few the first time.

I hope that the above doesn't completely scare you off! Remember that the Chinese have been using them for a very long time and in a diverse permagarden they will never be a significant part of your diet. Personally, it's the daylily flower buds that I find most useful. There are many alternative perennial leaf edibles available at the same time as daylilies, whereas the flower buds are available at a time when there isn't much else available in the perennial garden. With a mix of species, they can also be available all summer (and winter if you have enough to dry). The following table gives a rough guide as to when the main species of interest are in flower:

Flowering times for species *Hemerocallis*

H. dumortieri	spring
H. fulva	early summer
H. middendorfii	early summer
H. lilioasphodelus	summer
H. citrina	late summer
H. altissima	early autumn

In China the daylily buds (rehydrated and flower stalks removed) are essential in hot-and-sour soup (there are typically about 5-6 daylily buds/person used in these recipes). They are also usually used

283: Double orange flowered **Hemerocallis fulva** *'Kwanso double' is one of Ken Fern's favourites (*Plants For A Future, *1997).*

284: I often use daylily buds in a simple Chinese stir-fry dish with noodles or rice, often mixed with other available vegetables, here with Malva moschata leaves and Scorzonera flower buds and stems.

in the well-known Buddhist Chinese vegetarian meal Buddha's Delight, which may contain up to 40 ingredients! Now, there's my next challenge...

Elsewhere in the Far East, Pemberton and Lee (1996) refer to *Hemerocallis fulva* (*wonchurri*) being wild-foraged and cultivated on a small scale in Korea for the spring shoots (the main product) and the flower buds. Baranov (1967) says that *H. minor*, *H. lilioasphodelus* and *H. middendorfii* flower buds are collected by the Chinese in Manchuria. Khasbaghan (2000) says that the Mongolian herdsmen use *H. minor* (*shira checheg*).

I most often use daylily buds fresh in simple Chinese stir-fry dishes with other available vegetables. In the picture from mid-summer, I have picked daylily buds, musk mallow leaves, Scorzonera flower buds and stems and these were stir-fried with green onions, rehydrated winter chantarelles (alternatively Chinese black mushrooms), *mitsuba* (this chapter), ginger, chilli and soy sauce. Served with noodles or rice, this is simple, nutritious 'fast *slow food*'! You will also see a few flowers or a bud or two decorating my summer salads (see front cover). The raw buds are very tasty and most people really like them, likening them most often to spicy beans.

In North America, the orange daylily, *Hemerocallis fulva*, persists widely from earlier cultivation in old gardens and in other habitats where root fragments have established. It is essentially a self-sterile clone called 'Europa'. In addition, the earlier mentioned double flowered cultivar 'Kwanso' is also commonly found. Thanks to Gibbons (1962), Gail's (1989) book devoted to the daylily and Brill (1994), all of whom give this novel food a good write-up, it has become a popular 'semi-wild' foraged food in North America.

I have obtained seed of various species daylilies through alpine gardening seed lists, but it can take five or more years from seed to first flowering. You should also be aware that seed might not be pure as daylilies readily cross with one another in a garden. Therefore, in order to be sure what you are getting it's better to invest in plants from a reputable nursery. The RHS Plant Finder currently lists several sources for all the species listed above in the UK and the same is probably also true in the US (otherwise try the American Hemerocallis Society). Daylilies are best propagated by dividing the roots in spring and autumn.

Malva moschata

FAMILY: Malvaceae
ENGLISH: Musk Mallow
FRENCH: *Mauve Musquée*
GERMAN: *Moschus-Malve*
ITALIAN: *Malva Moscata*
SPANISH: *Malva Moschata*

Malva alcea

ENGLISH: Greater Musk Mallow, Cut-Leaved
  Mallow, Hollyhock Mallow
FRENCH: *La Mauve Alcée*
GERMAN: *Rosen-Malve*

Malva sylvestris

ENGLISH: Common Mallow
FRENCH: *Grande Mauve*
GERMAN: *Wilde Malve*
ITALIAN: *Malva Selvatica, Nalba, Riondell*
SPANISH: *Malva Común, Malva Silvestre*

Malva verticillata

CHINESE: Dong Kui, Dong Han Cai, Pinyin
ENGLISH: Chinese Mallow, Salad Mallow
FRENCH: *Mauve Verticillée*
JAPANESE: *Zeniaoi*

I wouldn't be without the perennial mallows in my garden. During the summer months this is probably the perennial I use most along with various Alliums, but it is also available in early spring. Unlike other perennials that reach peak production during a few short spring weeks, the mallows are available in smaller quantities throughout the summer. They have a mild, neutral taste and are therefore usually mixed with other greens in salads and cooked dishes.

When eating mallows, we are actually taking part in a tradition that can be traced back thousands of years. In ancient China, mallows were probably the most important leafy vegetable (Li, 1969). As brassicas arrived in China from the West the importance of mallows in the diet declined, but were still important up to about AD10. Both the Greeks and the Romans used the common mallow, *Malva sylvestris* in the classical period, a tradition that has survived to the present day in remote mountain villages. For example, the Roman poet, Horace, wrote, '*Me pascunt olivae, me cichorea, me malvae*' ('as for me, olives, endives and mallows provide sustenance', c. 30 BC). According to Sturtevant (Hedrick, 1919), the Egyptians extensively cultivated mallow along the banks of the Nile. This may be the same source as the following quote from Mrs. Grieve's *Modern Herbal* (1931): 'Prosper Alpinus stated (in 1592) that a plant of the mallow kind was eaten by the Egyptians'. However, this may well alternatively have been *Corchorus olitorius* (Jew's mallow or *mulukhiya*), another member of the mallow family that remains a popular green today. *Mulukhiya* has been grown since antiquity in the Middle East as a food crop. It is better known as the fibre plant jute, a short-lived perennial, but not very hardy and difficult to grow in colder areas.

There are around 15 *Malva* species with a distribution roughly centred on the Mediterranean and temperate Europe, but extending to China and northern India. Mallows are nowadays to be found naturalised in all the inhabited continents.

285: Common mallow, seen here in Norway in spring, is quite a large floriferous plant. It often dies after such a display, but self-seeds and so can be classed as a semi-permanent vegetable.

286: Malva sylvestris ssp. mauritanica *is a taller plant.*

They are annual, biennial or perennial herbs. *Malva sylvestris* or common mallow has the widest natural distribution from western Europe including the UK, the Mediterranean countries, the Caucasus and east towards the Himalayas and is possibly also native in China. This species ranges from having an annual habit in Egypt and the Middle East (growing in the winter time) to biennial in the Mediterranean countries and a short-lived perennial further north in Europe. In my garden, they live 2-3 years and usually die after flowering. There are a number of garden cultivars with larger flowers in various colour schemes, but these tend to be even shorter-lived.

Musk mallow, *Malva moschata*, is on the other hand reliably perennial in my garden and the one I would recommend if you were only to have one. I have both pink and white flowered forms and both of them self-sow, but not in a bad way. I've had the

287 & 288: Malva moschata *is in my experience a long-lived perennial (left). White flowered cultivar (above).*

standard pink-flowered form for at least 15 years in the same location. The white-flowered form died once about nine years ago, but rebounded from a self-sown plant. Musk mallow is a bit smaller than common mallow, reaching about 30-50cm. It is a native mainly in western and central Europe, including Italy and is also widely naturalised in North America and Australasia.

I have less experience with *Malva alcea*, greater musk mallow, which is, as the English name suggests, a larger plant. It has a similar range to musk mallow, except that it isn't found in the UK. I've only grown the form 'Fastigiata' which is long-lived and a nice ornamental, needing staking up during the summer. My plant was sterile and is thought possibly to be a hybrid between *M. alcea* and *M. moschata*. The flowers are also good in salads.

With its wide distribution, *Malva sylvestris* has probably been one of the most popular wild-foraged plants in the Mediterranean area since antiquity, a tradition which still survives in some parts. Amongst certain repressed communities such as in Palestine, wild foraging traditions are still very much alive in the 21st century. Ali-Shtayeh (2008) found that *Malva sylvestris* (*kubbaizeh*) was the most popular leafy green amongst the Palestinians on the West Bank. The Israelis are also known to have utilised this plant during World War II (as *hubeza*). In Italy, it has also been widely used and is one of the 45 documented wild herbs used in the Italian wild edible soup, *minestrella* (see Chapter 2).

Elsewhere, it was also an important traditional edible in Spain and Egypt. In Egypt, a study shows that it was used (wild-collected) as much as *Corchorus*. This suggests it

could be used in a similar way. The mucil-aginous leaves of both species act as both a flavouring and thickening agent.

In Italy, mallow leaves are also used in risotto. Simply sauté a couple of handfuls of leaves with onions, add some stock, herbs, salt and pepper and rice (and a multitude of other ingredients of your choice in the spirit of risotto, i.e., whatever else happens to be available). Serve with strong tasting grated mature cheese such as Parmesan. Another easy wholesome meal is to steam (or boil) a few potatoes, adding some mallow leaves. Mash, fry in oil, adding beaten eggs to finish. In Palestine, they simply fry the leaves in olive oil as a vegetable.

289: Malva alcea 'Fastigiata' is an attractive plant.

Egyptian Mallow Soup (inspired by *Molokhia* / Jew's Mallow Soup)

Fresh *Molokhia* (*Corchorus*) leaves are most often used in soup (also very popular in Syria and Jordan). You can simply replace the *Molokhia* leaves with whatever mallow leaves you have at hand.

Several cups of stock (in the Middle East they use chicken stock, just replace with a vegetable stock or add miso)

500g fresh mallow leaves, finely cut (if you don't have enough mallow leaves, add some other perennial spinach leaves such as Hosta, Hablitzia etc. or just spinach or Swiss chard)

One or more dried chillies, chopped (optional)

One or more bay leaves (optional)

A handful of perennial or standard onions, as available (optional)

Black pepper

Several garlic cloves, minced

2 tbsp olive oil (or butter)

Ground coriander

Salt

Chopped fresh coriander leaves (cilantro) if in season or fresh parsley or *mitsuba*, finely chopped (optional)

Lemon juice or vinegar (optional)

Boil up the stock; add the greens, chillies, bay leaf and onion and black pepper, stirring as you do. Simmer for about 20 minutes. Meanwhile, fry the garlic, onion, coriander and salt in the oil for a few minutes. Add to the soup and add any other optional ingredients and simmer a minute more before serving. The Egyptians often serve this thick soup over rice (I prefer a mix of brown rice and whole barley which have about the same cooking time), but it could also be served with wholegrain bread and garlic butter.

(A mallow soup, known as *molochosoupa*, is also known from Cyprus; Della et al, 2006.)

290: Annual curly mallow (Malva verticillata crispa) can grow to gigantic proportions, dwarfing my friend, Frank van Kiersbilck, in his Belgian garden.

291: The attractive curly edged leaves of Malva verticillata crispa in my garden.

292: Selection of ingredients collected for a mixed summer salad including various leafy greens, fruit and flowers. The pink flowers are Malva moschata; daylily flowers can also be seen.

So what has all this to do with the Far East? Well, as mentioned earlier, it is believed that the mallows were the most important leafy vegetables in Ancient China. According to Li (1969), it was annual *Malva verticillata* that was cultivated in Ancient China. It is still cultivated today, both the species and curly mallow, *Malva verticillata crispa*. However, when discussing *M. verticillata* he refers to it as a perennial. I believe that perennial mallows were also cultivated in ancient times in China. The most likely candidate then is *M. sylvestris* that is found in some places in the wild in China today, perhaps a relic from cultivation in the past?

Facciola (1989) informs us that a whole range of cultivars of *Malva verticillata* were available in China in the past, but, sadly, have not survived. *M. verticillata* reliably self-sows in my garden, so that it easily becomes a 'permanent fixture vegetable' and the *crispa* variant also comes true from seed.

Although a bit fiddly, the green immature fruits or mallow cheeses are crisp and sweetish. So, if you're out in the garden and peckish, you'll just be doing what generations of children have done across Europe in the past (e.g. Mabey, 1997). The flowers are also an attractive addition to your summer salads (see front cover).

For everything you wanted to know about the mallow family and were afraid to ask, I'd direct you to Stewart Robert Hinsley's 'The Malva Pages'.*

* www.malvaceae.info/Genera/Malva/Malva.html

Medicago sativa
(syn. *M. sativa* ssp. *sativa*)

FAMILY: Fabaceae
CHINESE: *Zi-Mu-Xu*
ENGLISH: Alfalfa, Lucerne
FRENCH: *Luzerne*
GERMAN: *Luzerne*
ITALIAN: *L'Erba Medica*
JAPANESE: *Arufarufa*
SPANISH: *Alfalfa*

Medicago falcata
(syn. *M. sativa* ssp. *falcata*)

ENGLISH: Wild Alfalfa, Sickle Medick, Wild Lucerne

Most of us will be familiar with alfalfa sprouts as they are readily available from most supermarkets nowadays, often touted as a super food. However, few realise that this is the same plant as the perennial lucerne, *Medicago sativa*, one of the world's most important forage plants (i.e. grown as animal feed). Even fewer have let their alfalfa sprouts grow on and eaten the spring shoots of the resulting plant which can reach 1m high and live for over 20 years. I've learnt to 'forage my forage' since I first read that it could be eaten in Joy Larkcom's *Oriental Vegetables* from 1991. A productive, tasty, protein and mineral rich spring green it is too!

I grow both *Medicago sativa* and *M. falcata* in my garden and haven't noticed any difference food wise, being quite similar plants. The most noticeable difference is the colour of the flowers. In fact, many of the cultivated varieties of lucerne have *falcata* blood in them as the two species readily hybridise. Lucerne is nowadays found escaped from cultivation more or less worldwide. However, the range of the wild species *M. falcata* is from western Europe (Spain, Portugal, south and east England) eastwards through South and Central Europe into West Asia.

293 & 294 (above): Medicago falcata *(left) and* M. sativa *(right) have different coloured flowers and are quite attractive edimentals when in bloom, although the plants tend to need support, becoming straggly as they age.*

295 (right): The spring shoots of lucerne (alfalfa) are ready to harvest at the time that primroses are in full flower here.

In China, use of lucerne as human food goes back to the early centuries AD, having been introduced quite early on as a forage crop. In China (5th century AD), a whole chapter is devoted to this plant as a vegetable (Li, 1969). It was said, 'young growths in early spring can be used, raw or cooked, as a vegetable, and when older it is suitable for feeding horses'. In Bretschneider's (1882) *Botanicon Sinicum*, various other references are given to this plant being used in the 15th, 16th and 17th centuries along with other perennial vegetables such as perennial sow-thistle (*Sonchus arvensis*, next profile), victory

296: If you get good seed set on your plants, you can save the seed and sprout your own alfalfa in the winter months.

onion (*Allium victorialis*, Chapter 6) and dandelion (*Taraxacum officinale*, Chapter 1). Its use has in fact survived to modern times and Hu in *Food Plants of China* from 2005 notes that the tender shoots of Zi-mu-xu are eaten in Shaanxi. An annual species, *Medicago polymorpha* (syn. *M. hispida* or *M. denticulata*), called Chinese Clover (*nan-mu-xu*) by Larkcom (1991), is a common vegetable in parts of China. This latter species has also been introduced from the West and is in fact a widespread native in Europe including the UK where it is found on coastal grasslands and is known as spotted medick. I've never seen seed offered of this or seen references to it being used in its native range. I presume there are improved forms available in China. Let me know if you find a source.

Larkcom recommends growing the perennial lucerne for the spring shoots and suggests growing it as a regularly trimmed low hedge around a vegetable or herb garden. Trimming or cutting right back will encourage new edible shoots to appear but you won't then get flowers. As a forage plant, lucerne is cut up to 12 times a year in warmer climates where growth can continue through the winter.

Elsewhere, I noticed this species growing in the wild edible garden in Firenze, Italy (see Chapter 2, page 59), the sign noting that the young shoots were used in salads, the leaves raw or cooked, and the flowers to decorate food, in addition to the best-known alfalfa sprouts. It is not impossible that the traditions of eating this forage plant followed it on its journey to China from its home range that is believed to have been the eastern Mediterranean.

I have usually used the spring shoots in Chinese style stir-fry dishes. My plants are now over 10 years old and have shown no sign yet of becoming less productive and haven't required additional fertiliser. I also haven't noticed any pests on my plants (lucerne does however have a wide range of pests where grown commercially). Apart from staking the plants, as older plants get untidy as the season develops, they are trouble free for me.

297: Lucerne is also often recommended as a quick growing nitrogen-fixing green mulch.

Lucerne is sometimes sold in nurseries as a medicinal, but why not just try carefully planting a few shop bought alfalfa sprouts in soil and grow them on to large plants? Seeds for sprouting can also be used as starters. There are numerous cultivars that have been developed commercially, but not readily available in amounts suitable to the home gardener. For example, 'Ranger' is a very hardy, prolific variety. Please be aware that if you are in the US, large acreage of Roundup-ready (GMO) lucerne has been planted in recent years ... so be sure your seed source is GMO-free.

Cultivation is relatively easy. Prepare the ground, adding manure or compost before planting. Lucerne grows better with relatively high pH, so you may want to correct for that. I had noticed that although my plants flowered prolifically, hardly any seed set at all in some years. A possible reason for this is that efficient pollinating insects are not present. Under commercial seed production, pollinating insects are introduced.

The last profile in this chapter takes us on a short trip over the equator to New Zealand and Australia before we cross the Pacific to South America in the next chapter.

Sonchus arvensis

FAMILY: Asteraceae
CHINESE: *Shan-Ku-Mai, Ye-Ku-Mai*
ENGLISH: Perennial or Field Sow-thistle
FRENCH: *Laiteron des Champs*
GERMAN: *Acker-Gänsedistel*
ITALIAN: *Grespino di Campi*

Sonchus palustris

ENGLISH: Marsh Sow-thistle
FRENCH: *Laiteron des marais*
GERMAN: *Sumpf-Gänsedistel*
ITALIAN: *Grespino dei campi*

Sonchus oleraceus and *S. asper*

ENGLISH: Common Sow-thistle Prickly Sow-thistle

In late 1991, I was working in Fiji on a Norwegian funded ocean wave energy project, mapping the enormous quantities of renewable energy arriving onto beaches throughout the South Pacific. On the way home I took a few days off in the North Island of New Zealand and stumbled over the book *Native Edible Plants of New Zealand* by Andrew Crowe. Browsing, there were a few wild food plants that I recognised from home: hairy bittercress (*Cardamine hirsuta*), cuckoo flower (*Cardamine pratensis*), dandelion (*Taraxacum officinale*), stinging nettle (*Urtica dioica*), annual nettle (*Urtica urens*) and fat hen (*Chenopodium album*). All of these are associated with agriculture and horticulture, and had arrived in New Zealand with the Europeans. In addition, there is one cosmopolitan species, bracken fern (*Pteridium aquilinum* var. *esculentum*), also used in Japan and other countries, but considered by some to be carcinogenic if used in large quantities. It is nevertheless a very important traditional food plant for the indigenous population, the Maori. What I found the most interesting was that various *Sonchus* (sow-thistle) species had always been extremely important vegetables for the Maori, even today. Both common sow-thistle (*Sonchus oleraceus*) and prickly sow-thistle (*Sonchus asper*), collectively known as *puwha*, both annuals, are used. Crowe informs us that these 'weeds' were even cultivated commercially and sold on markets in Auckland and Wellington both fresh and frozen. Perennial sow-thistle (*Sonchus arvensis*) is also used, but is much less common. Crowe writes, 'I eat the plant almost daily, in salads, in soups, or as a spinach.'

The sow-thistles (*Sonchus* spp.) are relatively large plants belonging to the Aster family (*Asteraceae*). As with the conventional vegetables endive, Scorzonera and lettuce, foraged plants such as alpine sow-thistle (Chapter 6) and dandelion (Chapter 1), they belong to the subfamily *Cichorioidae*. Common to these species is that they contain white latex. There are five *Sonchus* species in Western Europe.

The sow-thistles are foraged by peoples literally worldwide and the perennial and annual (but often overwintering) species are used in more or less the same way. I therefore discuss all four of the most common European species here, both the annuals (*Sonchus oleraceus* and *S. asper*) and the perennials (*S. arvense* and *S. palustris*). All sow-thistle species have hollow stems and shiny, kale-green leaves and yellow flowers. The English name sow-thistle describes a thistle-like plant which was fed to pigs. All of these species apart from *S. palustris* have spread to all six continents with human activity, and can be found as weeds in gardens, waste ground and farm fields.

Common Sow-thistle (*Sonchus oleraceus*)

This annual species is about 50cm tall and has broad leaves, usually triangular at the end. The leaves are not prickly, softly spined, clasping the stems with arrow shaped ends to the lobes. *Oleraceus* just means edible, the name given to it by Linnaeus in 1753. The seeds are able to germinate in a wide range of temperatures from 7 to 35°C so that it can also be encountered in tropical climates.

Prickly Sow-thistle (*Sonchus asper*)

This is also an annual and is a similar size to *S. oleraceus*, but its leaves have sharper spines, usually undivided with rounded stem clasping lobes. The species name *asper* means rough.

Perennial Sow-thistle (*Sonchus arvensis*)

This is a larger spreading perennial plant, reaching 1.5m. The leaves are lobed and toothed, with rounded lobes clasping the stem. The species name *arvensis* refers to the fact that the plant is found in cultivated fields. It is a troublesome weed of agriculture, but is also found on the upper part of beaches and edges of marshes.

Marsh Sow-thistle (*Sonchus palustris*)

This is the tallest of the group, reaching over 3m in good conditions. The leaves are deeply lobed with soft spiny teeth, clasping the stems with arrow-like lobes. *Palustris* describes the plant's marshy habitat.

Already in 1637, Englishman John Josselyn (1674) wrote that several *Sonchus* species could be found in pilgrim gardens in North America. We also know that common sow-thistle was in New Zealand quite early on and botanist Joseph Banks, who accompanied James Cook to New Zealand in 1769-70, wrote in his diary that a *Sonchus* species that grew there was identical with the common sow-thistle in England.

One can find sow-thistles anywhere where the natural vegetation has been removed, also in areas that have been burnt, either controlled or caused by lightning or volcanic activity. Common sow-thistle is a common weed plant on burnt land in France, and the same species is one of the first colonists of lava fields after volcanic eruptions in New Zealand. The latter species is quoted as one of the world's worst weed plants and is said to be a pest in at least 55 countries. But to me, this is just about the most useful vegetable in my garden from late spring when the perennials are finished to late autumn. Do as I do, FEST ON PESTS!

Prickly sow-thistle has a more bitter taste than its common relation. Both plants are stronger flavoured in very hot weather. My experience from our cool Norwegian summers and in the spring in New Zealand is that the taste of common sow-thistle is mild and only slightly bitter. Note that the spines on *Sonchus asper* must be removed before cooking. The perennial sow-thistles, *S. arvensis* and *S. palustris*, are however quite bitter and I always blanch the spring shoots (see photos 301 and 302) for a milder vegetable.

When I revisited New Zealand in September 2003, I decided to try to find a Maori 'weed' market. Some scientist friends at the conference I was attending advised me that the Otara Market, about 30 minutes by bus from downtown Auckland, is the most authentic Polynesian market in the city. Already on the first stall, I found *puwha* for sale and in fact a quarter of all the stalls were selling this plant.

I asked one of the stall-owners whether it was correct, as reported by Crowe, that they cultivated the plant. No, he had not heard that it was cultivated in the traditional sense, the plants just grew as encouraged 'weeds' on the edge of vegetable plots or between other vegetables being cultivated (see the discussion on what is known as cryptocropping in the Introduction, page xv). He told me that availability was somewhat seasonal, as the plants bolted in the summer. Further, he said that the stems were reddish when the temperature was low. The plants looked to be harvested just before flowering (not only the young leaves, as is often recommended in the literature). He recommended that I wash the plants I had bought in water to remove the slightly bitter taste. Maoris eat this plant usually with pork. Later that day I cooked it up for dinner in my apartment hotel. The flavour was fairly strong (in the way kale is strong), but not bitter.

In summer 2004, I decided to grow a small area of common sow-thistle in my garden as it had surprisingly not found its own way here! I had even sourced an edimental cultivar, *Sonchus oleraceus* 'Custard 'n' Green' from a seed trader, so called as the leaves are yellow variegated. That summer my brassicas were badly damaged by field slugs, but common sow-thistle was completely left alone! Since then, every year I use more and more of this excellent vegetable, managing it, like I imagine the Maoris do, so that it is allowed to seed itself, but in a modest way and leaving plants on the edges of my traditional veggie beds. It now gives me a significant part of my total yield of greens and like Andrew Crowe I now use it almost every day from mid-summer to late autumn. In warmer climates, the annual sow-thistles will also overwinter or in Mediterranean climates germinate during winter.

One word of warning that, although I haven't had any problems here, *Sonchus* can suffer from diseases and pests affecting lettuce and if one stops growing lettuce for a year to get rid of the problems, you will also need to remove all sow-thistle plants that appear. There follows a review of how sow-thistles have been used in different parts of the world.

Round the world sow-thistles

Mediterranean countries

The first references to the use of sow-thistle in Europe come from Pliny the Elder. In his *Naturalis Historia* (AD 23-29), he mentions that the Romans used the plant in salads and as a vegetable. We can get inspiration from the Greek hero Thesevs who enjoyed a dish of sow-thistle before he overcame the Minotaur in the labyrinth of Crete. The Greek physician Pedianos Dioscorides also mentions sow-thistle as a vegetable in *Materia Medica* (1st century AD). *Apicius*, a Roman cookbook from the 1st century AD, includes a salad recipe where *Sonchus* species are included along with lettuce, borage, mint, calamint, parsley, wild thyme, chervil, oregano, nightshade and fennel flowers.

Sow-thistles are still used in several Mediterranean countries. A report published by the Food and Agriculture Organization (United Nations) in 1999 gives *Sonchus asper* and *S. oleraceus* as two of 200 species that are still wild-foraged in Crete.

*299 (right): Three edible cryptocrops (or encouraged weeds) harvested on my vegetables beds: common sow-thistle, shepherd's needle (*Scandix pecten-veneris) and perennial rocket (Diplotaxis tenuifolia).*

300 (above): Sonchus oleraceus, showing the shiny young leaves just ready to harvest.

301 & 302 (far left): Sonchus arvensis in the author's garden is blanched to reduce the bitterness; (left) with Allium senescens, blanched Silene vulgaris, Rumex acetosa, Maianthemum racemosum and Cirsium oleraceum.

In Italy, sow-thistle species are used along with many other plants in salads and soups, especially in springtime. An example is *minestrella*, a traditional local soup in Garfagnana (Chapter 2). In an ethnobotanical study among Arbëreshë-people (ethnic Albanians) in southern Italy, extensive use of edible wild plants was documented, including *rrëshëd*, the Arbëreshë name for common and prickly sow-thistle (Pieroni et al., 2002). *Sonchus oleraceus* was one of the 10 most commonly used herbs. In some of the most isolated of Ponziane islands in the Tyrrhenian Sea west of Naples, Laghetti et al. (2002) recorded that the use of common sow-thistle was still common. Further east in the Mediterranean, in Israel, there is a different tradition. This plant is included in the traditional Passover Seder meal commemorating the Jews' escape from Egypt. In the Talmud, herbs which one has a duty to eat that day are listed and include: lettuce, chicory, *Eryngium creticum* and *maror* (*Sonchus oleraceus*). *Maror* represent the bitterness of slavery.

303 (left): Marsh sow-thistle, growing here on boggy ground next to the author's pond, will also grow well on ordinary garden soil as long as it doesn't dry out.

304 (above): Perennial sow-thistle growing at the high tide line on the beach below the author's house.

305 (right): Marsh sow-thistle can be of giant proportions, here seen in the Oslo Botanical Gardens in June and seeding.

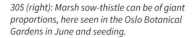

Britain

It also seems that the use of *Sonchus* species in Britain is traditional, but not very common over the last few hundred years. Johnson (1862) mentions that it was also used in Germany and that '...the young leaves are put into salads, and this common weed is exceedingly wholesome'. Richard Mabey in *Food for Free* from 1972 thought that perennial sow-thistle (surprisingly, the only species in this genus mentioned) was 'the best of all wild plants in the Asteraceae family', and that it was more fleshy and milder in taste than dandelions (this is contrary to my experience of quite a bitter plant...). In Roger Phillips' *Wild Food* from 1983, he mentions only *Sonchus oleraceus*. Phillips recommends a simple salad made with the leaves and a French dressing, so that the good taste of the plant is preserved.

Scandinavia

In the comprehensive tome about Danish ethnobotany (Brøndegaard, 1978-1980), it is curious that *Sonchus* species are not mentioned. Neither does Swedish Stefan Källman find any reason to mention it in his book from 1997. In Norway, Holmboe (1941) gives all three species as edible when they are young. In Nyttevekstboka (1979), in Nilsson (1976) and Blekastad (1979) it is included but only noted as being edible. The most positive review I've found from Scandinavia is in Mehus and Vorren (1978), who state, 'perennial sow-thistle is one of the really good food plants', and 'it doesn't have the strong flavour of many plants in the Aster family'. So, we have two authors that disagree with my experience of it being very strong tasting. Other famous Norwegian authors do not mention the genus *Sonchus* at all and the most important ethnobotanical work records it only as pig feed (Høeg, 1976).

America

US based forager Arthur Lee Jacobson says, 'bitterness is relative, and for anyone unaccustomed to it, Sow Thistle is revoltingly horrible. In defence, really foul flavour resides in wild chicory and teasel (*Dipsacus*) leaves. Compared to them, almost painful in their repulsiveness, sow thistle is merely a strong-flavored lettuce.' He goes on to say that a selection programme would result in milder forms, as was done to get from wild chicories (*Cichorium* species) to milder vegetable chicories and endives. Elias and Dykeman (1990) say that perennial sow-thistle should be picked in very early spring when the plant is still only a few centimetres high, the leaves becoming stronger later on. They also recommend boiling the leaves twice to reduce bitterness. Charlotte Clarke's book, *Edible and Useful Plants of California*, actually has a picture of common sow-thistle on the cover. She says that the Indians quickly learned to appreciate the plant after it was introduced to California.

Nelson Coon (1974) also finds that the plant is bitter, but says that it is good as a salad plant when mixed with milder plants. Wildman Steve Brill's book, *Identifying and Harvesting Edible and Medicinal Plants in Wild (and not so wild) Places* (1994), is full of information and funny anecdotes from Brill's foraging trips. For sow-thistle, he says that all species have mild taste in chilly conditions. Therefore, plants are best in spring and autumn. Brill holds a 'wild' party in New York every year in December and he says that common sow-thistle is a plant he can rely on at this party and suggests that the plant is well suited to his guests who often eat like pigs, referring to the meaning of the English name sow-thistle.

Further south, Diaz Betancourt et al. (1999) registered edible weeds in Coatapec, Mexico (tropical) and Bariloche, Argentina (temperate) and found respectively 43 and 32 edible weeds that were used by the local populations. There were four species common to both areas: field mustard (*Brassica rapa*), dandelion (*Taraxacum officinale*), white clover (*Trifolium repens*) and common sow-thistle (*Sonchus oleraceus*).

Asia

In Siberia, *osot polyevoy* (perennial sow-thistle) is a common weed of disturbed ground, steppe and forest areas ('Edible Wild Plants of Siberia', www.sibrast.ru). It is recommended to pre-soak the young leaves and stems in salty water. They are then used raw in salads, and cooked in soups and purées.

Crowe (1990) says that all three cosmopolitan *Sonchus* species are used for food in Indonesia and that common sow-thistle is considered to be the best, since it is the least bitter. Facciola (1998) has an interesting piece of information that in Indonesia improved varieties of perennial sow-thistle are cultivated for food. *In Food Plants of China*, Hu (2005), the young leaves of perennial sow-thistle (hillside bitter wheat or wild bitter-lettuce) are used by people living in the Nanling mountains in southern China). Another closely related perennial species, *S. brachyotus*, is used by farmers in northern Jiangsu. The young rosettes are washed, mixed with wheat flour, steamed, cooled, seasoned with mashed garlic, chopped onion, salt, vinegar and soy sauce (no doubt disguising the bitter taste suggested by the name, Bitter Wheat-field Herb, in the process). In Nepal, Manandhar (2002) records both of the annual species as edible and another 1m tall perennial, *Sonchus wightianus*, is also used.

Australia

Tim Low (1988 and 1989) mentions that Aboriginal people in the states of Victoria and South Australia are very fond of the bitter leaves of common sow-thistle and says that they are a good substitute for endive. He also relates a funny story: 'E. Stephens, an early settler who lived near Adelaide witnessed a "Thistle Feast". Some Aborigines noticed that Stephens had an acre of luxuriant common sow-thistle on his land. They asked if they could have them, and Stephens replied that they could take everything.

They had soon climbed over the fence and the plot was soon "one seething mass of men, women and children". Within 10 minutes everything was picked, and the tribe moved on gratefully devouring the juicy weed.' Today it is a very common plant in gardens and fields in southern and eastern Australia.

In New Zealand, several plants were used against scurvy during Captain Cook's stay there, sow-thistle being one of these. Forster (1786) wrote, 'Its delicate stems and young leaves made a salad for our enjoyment.' The crew of Cook's HMS *Resolution* used sow-thistle both in salad, cooked with peas and in soup.

The Maori used both common (*pororua*) and prickly sow-thistle (*raurorua*) as food, the former being preferred. An endangered endemic perennial species in New Zealand, *Sonchus kirkii* (syn. *S. asper* ssp. *littoralis*), was possibly the original *puwha* or *rauroroa* (Crowe, 1990). *S. kirkii* grows slower than the other two species and is eventually out-competed. The stems, young leaves and unopened flowers were boiled in an earth oven with other food, such as fish. This is a must for the permaculture inspired garden in New Zealand. Plants are available from native plant nurseries.

According to Crowe (1990) sow-thistles were also used as food plants in some of the Pacific Islands, and particularly in New Caledonia. During World War II, New Zealanders were recommended to eat it, as it was rich in vitamin C. Cooper and

306: Sonchus kirkii *is an endangered endemic in New Zealand and was perhaps the species originally used by the Maoris when they first came to the country. This picture is taken in 'The Threatened Garden' in the Auckland Botanical Garden.*

Cambie (1991) report that the authorities in the city of Marlborough (in the north of the South Island) started a project for the commercial cultivation of *puwha* in 1983.

Africa

In South Africa, *Sonchus oleraceus* is one of the commonly used pot herbs known as *imifino* or *morogo*, used as a spinach and cooked and eaten with corn porridge. Fat hen, annual nettle and dandelion are three other *imifino* plants. *Ugadugadu* are vegetable cakes made of *imifino* spinach and corn flour.

Concluding, wherever you might find yourself in the world, you're unlikely to go completely hungry, as you will easily find members of this plant family and others such as the nettles. These plants may also be super healthy as Thomson and Shaw (2002) suggest that sow-thistle (and/or watercress) in the diet may play a role in the lower incidence of colorectal cancer among the Maori in New Zealand, compared with non-Maori people. The diet of the Maoris would otherwise point to a higher incidence. It can also be mentioned that Trichopoulou et al. (2000) found a remarkably high content of flavanol antioxidants in some of the wild plants that are in use on Crete, in particular corn poppy (*Papaver rhoeas*), fennel (*Foeniculum vulgare*), Roman pimpernel (*Tordylium apulum*) and common sow-thistle (*Sonchus oleraceus*). Flavonoid content of these crops far exceeds that found in red wine, black tea and onions.

Otherwise, you will want to know that sow-thistle was the Viagra of the 13th century! A herbalist in the 1200s recommended eating the plant 'in order to prolong the virility of gentlemen' and Culpeper, herbalist from the 1600s, recommended the use of this herb for ladies as a cosmetic, wonderfully good to wash their faces with, to clear the skin and give it lustre. Finally, the Maori of New Zealand believed that a flower essence from the flowers of *Sonchus asper* could solve problems from the previous life. What are you waiting for, sow-thistles offer something for everyone, transgressing time and space – they are truly remarkable plants!

Of course it is the perennial species that are of most interest here and I note above very different opinions on the bitterness of the perennial sow-thistle. As I have discussed elsewhere, people can have very different perceptions of bitterness, but as some authors say it is less bitter than other members of the same family it could point to there being real differences between different populations. So, please report back your experience, as it is a productive perennial vegetable. Be aware that as it does spread vegetatively it should therefore be planted somewhere where it can roam relatively freely in a sunny spot.

307: The Jerusalem artichoke is probably the best-known wild-foraged North American native vegetable. The most productive Norwegian variety is Dagnøytral (literally, 'day-neutral'). We believe it is identical to the Russian variety 'Bianca' and the North American variety 'Stampede', originally selected by the Indians of northern Ontario for earliness and tuber size (Facciola, 1998).

chapter 5

THE AMERICAS

Arriving in South America on the coast of Chile's largest island, Chiloe, a spectacular giant herb covering an extensive area greets us on the coastal dunes. The locals call it *nalca* and we're told that it's a popular vegetable that is wild-foraged and also sold on markets. However, this first glimpse of the native flora gives us a false impression of the importance of native green vegetables in the diet. Although the mountainous areas of the Andes are extremely rich in perennial root crops such as oca, mashua, ulluco, achira, ahipa, arracacha, maca, mauka, yacon and not forgetting the humble potato, there doesn't seem to be a similar richness amongst endemic leafy greens. The best reference to these wonderful colourful root vegetables is the freely downloadable *Lost Crops of the Incas* (Anon, 1989). Strangely, there are no species used primarily as a leafy vegetable included in that book, although there are some root vegetables for which the leaves are also sometimes eaten (e.g. ulluco, *Ullucus tuberosus* and mauka, *Mirabilis expansa*). There are also annual seed crops for which use as a leafy vegetable is a secondary use (e.g. amaranth, *Amaranthus* spp. and quinoa, *Chenopodium quinoa*). It is, however, possible that part of the reason for lack of South American native perennial vegetables is that this area has been understudied.

However, in a recent study of the edible wild plants of a community of the indigenous Mapuche people (Ladio, 2001), 14 leafy vegetables are documented. Eight of these, including dandelion and watercress (Chapter 1) and perennial wall-rocket (*Diplotaxis tenuifolia*; Chapter 2) are introduced plants, the other six natives include a species of bamboo (*Chusquea culeou*, colihue), *Oxalis adenophylla* (Chilean oxalis), *Apium australe* (southern wild celery) and *Sanicula graveolens* (*Cilantro silvestre*). The latter would be very interesting to try as a perennial cilantro or leaf coriander.

308: Some of the myriad of colourful perennial Andean root crops harvested in my garden, ready for the pot for Christmas dinner: ulluco (Ullucus tuberosus), mashua (Tropaeolum tuberosum) and oca (Oxalis tuberosa); sadly there isn't the same diversity in leafy vegetables.

309 & 310: Two other South American perennial vegetables (left) a bamboo, Chusquea culeou, *here thriving in the Hillier Arboretum in Hampshire, UK and* Oxalis adenophylla, *hardy in my garden (right).*

On the other hand, the foraging traditions of the native North American peoples have been well documented by numerous authors and are summarised in the comprehensive book *Native American Ethnobotany* (Moerman, 1998), which can also be browsed online. Of the over 20,000 species in North America, excluding Mexico, Moerman notes 1,649 species having been used by the indigenous peoples. Three of the most important wild leafy food plants of the Native Americans are included in this book. These are cow parsnip and common cattail (this chapter) and stinging nettle (Chapter 1). One of the best-known perennial Native American food plants is the root crop Jerusalem artichoke (*Helianthus tuberosus*), although young shoots have also been used and are very tasty. Jerusalem artichokes arrived in Europe well before the potato.

Of the species documented by Moerman (1998) as used as green vegetables, I have estimated that about 80% are perennials, 8% biennials and only 12% annuals.

The European colonists often adopted these wild food traditions and also inadvertently brought with them numerous weedy edibles. Over the last 50 years, since arguably the greatest modern day American foraging writer, Euell Gibbons, wrote *Stalking the Wild Asparagus*, numerous foraging books have been published. The best of these have appeared in just the last few years, penned by foragers like Steve Brill and Leda Meredith (in New York), Peter Gail, John Kallas (in Oregon) and the best of the lot, Samuel Thayer in Wisconsin. All of these great foragers write from first-hand experience of their subject and Thayer's work is particularly thorough, innovative and inspirational.

Over half of the leafy edibles described by Gibbons (1962) are European introductions, including asparagus. Similarly, half of Brill's (1994) wild vegetables are foreigners. However, Thayer's *Forager's Harvest* has over 80% indigenous edible greens. Although there are only 10 North American natives described in this chapter, they are really some of the best!

Gunnera tinctoria (syn. *G. chilensis*)

FAMILY: Gunneraceae
DUTCH: *Mammoetblad*
ENGLISH: Chilean Gunnera,
   Prickly Rhubarb, Chilean
   Rhubarb
FRENCH: *La Nalca*
SPANISH: *Nalca, Pangue*

In December 2004, I attended a conference in Chile. I took advantage of this and had a short holiday afterwards with the main aim of seeing the old growth Andean monkey puzzle (*Araucaria araucana*) forests (edible nuts). I remember making a list of Chilean edibles that I wanted to see in the wild using the Plants For A Future Database and on that list was *Gunnera tinctoria*. This is a giant rhubarb-like species that I was already familiar with, as it is commonly planted in botanical gardens in milder parts of northwest Europe along with the even *gianter* species, Brazilian *Gunnera manicata* and *G. masafuerae* from Chile's Juan Fernandez Islands. Although the leaves superficially resemble rhubarb, it's not even a distant relation. Easy to spot due to its size, I found this species in a wide range of habitats from the mountains to the coast and from heavily shaded locations around mountain waterfalls to completely open locations. It is often planted in gardens in wetland habitats, so it was therefore a big surprise to find it growing en masse on the west coast of Chiloe Island on sand dunes and cliffs near to Cucao, perhaps the last plant before the vast expanse of the Pacific. In one area, it had colonised an open area as far as the eye could see, forming an apparent vast 'monoculture'. However, at ground level in the partial shade of the Gunnera 'forest' was another familiar edible, the beach strawberry, *Fragaria chiloensis*, one of the two wild species of strawberry that were hybridised in France to create the modern garden strawberry. One of the most impressive natural forest gardens I have ever seen, even though there were rather too few species for my liking. However, this garden was not very old as it turns out that it was growing on an area that had been wiped out by one of the strongest earthquakes and tsunamis of the 20th century that occurred off the coast of Chile in 1960.

170 years before me, Charles Darwin had explored Chile and was clearly as impressed as I was when he wrote:

> *'On the large island of Tanqui there was scarcely one cleared spot, the trees on every side extending their branches over the sea-beach. I one day noticed, growing on the sandstone cliffs, some very fine plants of the panke (Gunnera scabra), which somewhat resembles the rhubarb on a gigantic scale. The inhabitants eat the stalks, which are subacid, and tan leather with the roots, and prepare a black dye from them. The leaf is nearly circular, but deeply indented on its margin. I measured one that was nearly eight feet in diameter, and therefore no less than twenty-four in circumference. The stalk is rather more than a yard high, and each plant sends out four or five of these enormous leaves, presenting together a very noble appearance.'*
>
> *Voyage of the Beagle*

Chilean Gunnera is native to the southern and western parts of Chile and Argentina, but has naturalised in some countries, escaped from cultivation, and has been declared a noxious unwanted weed in several countries including New Zealand, the UK, Ireland and the Azores.

This plant is very important to the indigenous Mapuche people. I had stopped off in Temuco on my way to the Andes and had found it for sale on the Mapuche market there. They call it either *nalca*, which is the Mapudungun (Mapuche language) word for the leaf stalk (petiole), or *pangue*, meaning the leaf, the two parts used for food. These Mapuche words have been adopted for general use throughout the country, the two names often also referring to the whole plant. Ladio (2001) simply notes that the Mapuche use the shoots (young leaf petioles) raw in salads. Older stems apparently do not taste good.

Back to Chile and on my second day, I went on a trip into the interior of the park to see some impressive old Alerce trees (*Fitzroya cupressoides*) and I had a guide with me the whole day. As we passed a Gunnera, I asked him how they ate it and he demonstrated how they peeled the stem to remove the prickles (which aren't sharp) and just ate it raw. The taste was not remotely astringent and not anything like as acid as rhubarb, a faint lemony acid taste and very pleasant and refreshing. He also told me that they made a kind of marmalade with it, but when I visited the local market to source the product, they claimed that they didn't make marmalade with *nalca* and tried to sell me rhubarb jam instead. I think there is a certain amount of confusion between rhubarb and *nalca* in Chile, perhaps mainly amongst city dwellers who haven't grown up with the plant. I've seen pictures on the web purporting to be *nalca* and the picture clearly shows rhubarb. In fact, there are numerous commercial *nalca* products including jams, marmalade and chutneys, e.g. *chutney de nalca y murta* (Murta is the fruit of *Ugni molinae*, Chilean Guava, sometimes grown in the UK).

The most common way of eating the peeled *nalca* is either raw (some people swear that this is the only way to eat it), dipped in salt (like the British do with celery) or salt with *merken* (this is a ground mix of dried, smoked chilli with various seasonings such as cumin, coriander and salt). It is also prepared in salads such as *nalca* with apple, lemon and a little salt or alternatively with *merken*, onion, lemon and cilantro. It is also served with a local South American fungus *dihueñes* (*Cyttaria* spp.) seasoned with salt, olive oil, chives and cilantro. Petzold et al. (2006) have carried out a nutritional analysis of the plant as part of a push to increase its use and develop new products. The spring leaves are best, becoming a bit fibrous later in the year.

Pangue, which is the large leaf of the plant, is used in the preparation of the traditional dish *curanto* that originates from Chiloe Island, but has spread to much of the country. It is basically a mix of fish, meat and vegetables cooked over hot stones in an earth oven. The leaves are used to separate the different ingredients during cooking.

311 & 312: I have seen Gunnera tinctoria *planted both in woodland settings with a fair amount of shade as (left) in RHS Garden Wisley, UK and on the edge of a pond, here in Hortus Botanicus Leiden in the Netherlands (right).*

Elsewhere, one enterprising blogger on the Scottish west coast island of Harris, has pointed out that rather than fighting a losing battle against this plant, one should recognise it as a resource. Knowing of its edibility, he suggested a new slogan for the island: 'Harris – Scotland's Gunnera Cuisine Island'.

Plants are readily available in European and North American nurseries as is seed that germinate readily if fresh. Note that there is some confusion in the trade between *G. tinctoria* and *G. manicata*, so it's worthwhile knowing how to tell them apart, although it's more likely that *G. manicata* is wrong than *tinctoria*. The inflorescences of *manicata* are longer, thinner and stay green, whereas those of *tinctoria* are shorter, thicker and are a red-brown colour. Although *tinctoria* is a large plant, it is still relatively small compared to *manicata* and therefore more suitable for the smaller garden.

Gunnera tinctoria is not that hardy, surviving down to maybe -15°C for shorter spells. Gardeners go to great lengths to overwinter this species in marginal areas. Keeping off winter rainfall helps as does mulching the roots with ferns and the plant's own huge leaves. In the Bergen Botanical Garden at Milde in Norway, polystyrene boxes, used by the fish industry, are placed over the roots during winter with success. I have a couple of plants growing in large pots that I overwinter cold and dark in my cellar.

Allium validum

FAMILY: Amaryllidaceae
ENGLISH: Swamp Onion, Tall Swamp Onion, Pacific Onion, Pacific Mountain Onion

It is said that the swamp onion prefers soils with good drainage. It is a common species in this kind of habitat from 1,200-3,400m in California and is otherwise found north into the Cascade Mountains and southern British Columbia. *Allium brevistylum* (shortstyle onion) is similar but smaller (and less productive).

313 (above): Spring shoots of Allium validum.

314 (right): The shoots of Allium validum *can be harvested and used in a wide range of dishes raw and cooked, here with* Tradescantia ohiensis *(right), see later in this chapter.*

Dilys Davies (1992) writes that it is 'Odd rather than beautiful, the umbel rather too small for the length of the stem,' adding, 'If the plants do not please they can be eaten.' Perhaps I just like odd plants, but maybe it's rather that we have been spoilt by the myriad of large spherical ornamental onions that have *swamped* (sic!) the market in recent years. Anyway, I find it a very attractive plant, both the spring shoots and when in flower. It is a large vigorous species reaching about 70cm (*validum* actually means vigorous). The flowers are purple, sometimes almost white. The bulbs form on iris-like rhizomes that produce new bulbs in succeeding years.

Not knowing that it doesn't grow in swamps, I planted seedlings from the Sierra Nevada in a marginal area that's damp all year next to my pond. The plants have actually thrived there for several years now. However, Davies (1992) says that as this species is adapted to relatively dry winter conditions due to snow cover (water is above rather than at the roots), it therefore needs good drainage in winter to succeed in areas with damp milder winters. Therefore, it is probably not advisable to plant in a bog like I did. On the other hand it mustn't dry out in summer. I've never seen it in the numerous botanical gardens I've visited whilst researching this book, so perhaps it is difficult in gardens (in which case, sorry for wasting your time). There is one nursery that sells it in the UK and they claim on their website that it is easy … It probably needs cold treatment to germinate. Otherwise it is a plant that prefers a sunny open location, although it will tolerate some shade.

Swamp onion is a favourite wild-gathered onion for the Native American Cahuilla tribe in California and they use it both raw and cooked as flavouring for other food. The shoots can be harvested until the flower shoots appear in late spring to early summer. It will subsequently regrow after harvesting. The flowers are a good summer addition to mixed salads. If you have enough, how about making Onion Swamp (onion soup made with swamp onion, invent your own recipe and ... enjoy).

Heracleum maximum
(syn *H. lanatum*, *Heracleum sphondylium* var. *lanatum*)
and other *Heracleum* spp.

FAMILY: Apiaceae
ENGLISH: Cow Parsnip, Indian Celery, Indian Rhubarb, Pushki
RUSSIAN: *Luk Ponikaiushchii, Luk Sklonennyi*

I bought Roger Phillips' wonderful book *Wild Food* in 1983 soon after it was published. A picture of the shoots of common hogweed (*Heracleum sphondylium*), cooked and served with a knob of butter, attracted my attention. Phillips writes: 'This is unequivocally one of the best vegetables I have eaten,' and, 'hogweed shoots will surprise even the most conservative of your friends.' This didn't exactly decrease my enthusiasm to try it! Why then did it take me 25 years to have a go? Here in the part of Norway where I live, a very similar species, *Heracleum sibiricum* replaces common hogweed, which is mainly found further south. In Norwegian literature I'd read that it was considered to be poisonous and that you should quickly drink a lot of water if you happened to ingest some ... I found this confusing as this seemed to apply to all hogweeds. I therefore contacted the Norwegian Useful Plants Society and they passed on my enquiry to a professor who advised me strongly against eating it, as it was probably toxic, he said. I therefore left it alone. I did find numerous references though to the plant containing furanocoumarins and, in sensitive people, when absorbed by the skin in sunlight, it may cause an irritating rash. However, this also applies to various other umbellifers such as parsnip (*Pastinaca sativa*), a commonly grown vegetable. I did however miss a reference to *Heracleum sibiricum* being recommended as a vegetable in soups in the Norwegian wartime book on free food from wild plants (Holmboe, 1941). However, he doesn't exactly encourage the reader when he says that it is questionable whether most people wouldn't find the taste too strong.

I've chosen to profile the North American species, *Heracleum maximum*, due to its size (higher yield), the fact that its edibility is very well documented both in Native American ethnobotanical and modern day foraging literature, and also that it seems to be reliably perennial. Some *Heracleum* species die after flowering. However, this is a genus that has been highly prized as a wild gathered food plant by indigenous cultures throughout the northern hemisphere, to which it is restricted. I will therefore also mention some of the numerous other species used, as local species will probably be better adapted to your locality.

315: Heracleum maximum *grows well in my garden on no more than 15cm of soil on the edge of a vegetable plot which is watered in dry weather. It has typical carrot family flower umbels and large leaves.*

Cow parsnip is the only native species of the genus in North America and is widely distributed across the US and Canada except the very far south. This is one of the largest herbaceous plants of the region and can reach 3m under ideal conditions each summer. It is found in a wide range of habitats, growing best in damp shady places such as along stream banks from sea level to sub-alpine habitats. It forms an interesting natural plant community in North America as an understorey with *Crataegus douglasii* (black hawthorn). This might be a combination that would be worth emulating in your forest garden as black hawthorn has tasty berries. Alternatively other tasty hawthorns could be used.

Also known as Indian celery, it was used by native tribes across its range, but it was particularly in the northwest that it was the most important wild vegetable and enjoyed by almost everybody (Kuhnlein and Turner, 1986 and Moerman, 1998). People were fully aware of the photosensitive nature of this plant and handled it with care. The young leaf and flower bud stalks were used as greens until the bud of the inflorescence appeared (this signalled that it would be too tough and bitter). As it was mainly eaten raw (like we would eat celery), the stalks were first peeled, as the furanocoumarins were concentrated in the skin. Sometimes, the stems were roasted over a fire before peeling. This was a vegetable that was often eaten in large quantities in season and it was also sun-dried or stored in seal and/or whale oil or grease for later use. Foraging expeditions could involve journeys of up to 50 miles to favourite locations. Plants growing in shady conditions were said to remain edible longer and were then also more tender.

Cow parsnip could also have been called 'grizzly bear parsnip' as this wasn't only food for *Homo sapiens*, but is also an important spring delicacy for bear, deer, elk and moose.

Unless you live within cow parsley's wild range, you will probably have to start from seed but seed companies seldom offer this species. My seed came from two different internet seed traders in North America. Before trying this plant, please be absolutely sure that what you have is cow parsnip and not one of the poisonous look-alikes found across its wild range (you can't be sure that whoever sent you the seed hasn't made a mistake). I've also come across one ornamental cultivar 'Washington Limes' which is described as having attractive bright lime-green spring growth. Seed should be sown outdoors preferably in the autumn as it will need cold stratification to germinate. It will probably quickly lose its viability as with other umbellifers such as parsnip. Note that the seed may take two years to germinate, so don't give up if it doesn't appear in the first spring. Plants don't seem to be particularly fussy and will tolerate shady places as long as they have sufficient moisture during the spring/early summer growth period.

The taste of the raw plant is mild and sweet and could be described as celery with a dash of lemon, but it also has a taste of its own. As Sam Thayer says in his *Nature's Garden*, 'These sweet, aromatic stalks are one of the many intense food experiences that only foragers get to enjoy...' Well, not anymore, for if you follow my recommendation here, you can also enjoy this at home.

If you cut the plants down to the ground in early to mid-summer, new leaves will emerge, although these are less vigorous. Again the taste is good and mild.

There are several parallels here with the way Angelica or *kvann* was used in Scandinavia (see Chapter 6). One could imagine improving the hogweeds by selecting for filled petioles/stems as was done in Norway with Vossakvann. It would be interesting to know if there is much variation in this characteristic in wild populations.

The wild range of *Heracleum maximum* also includes the Kamchatka Peninsula in the Russian Far East. Captain Cook (1824) documents the former use of probably this species as a principal ingredient in cookery by the local peoples in that area. In the online Edible Wild Plants of Siberia (Anon, 2011), *Heracleum dissectum*, a species with a wide range in eastern and West Asia, is noted for its edible peeled shoots used raw and it is also used in *borsch*. Although nowadays synonymous with beetroot soup, the original *borsch* and the word itself has origins in the original wild-foraged hogweed soup that was once widespread (a good review of the history of *borsch* can be found in Turner et al., 2011). The plant was also lactofermented for winter use in soups. A simple

316 & 317: Blanched cow parsnip petioles are genuinely one of the tastiest foods on the planet.

318 & 319: Taking 'Tromsø palm' seed to Norway is akin to taking coals to Newcastle, but unknown to most people the Iranian community in Norway had been importing the seed from Iran (left) to make a spice (ground on the right).

hogweed stew is also described comprising layers of potatoes and hogweed, sprinkled with caraway seeds and simmered in water until tender.

My own local species *Heracleum sibiricum* is also prominent on Russian foraging and survival sites, used in much the same way, raw, cooked and also sometimes candied. In the Caucasus, young shoots of *Heracleum pubescens* are reported to be used raw (Hedrick, 1919). From Turkey, both *H. persicum* and *H. pubescens* shoots are used. There are also older accounts from the UK of hogweed shoots being used, this tradition being revived by Phillips' glowing recommendation.

Whilst writing this account I held an open day in my garden organised by the local Useful Plants Society. While discussing a rather fine flowering *Angelica gigas* (Korean angelica), an Iranian woman, Saideh Salamati, who had lived in Norway for many years, suddenly spoke up. She told us that she used the seed of a plant popularly known here as Tromsøpalme (literally Tromsø palm after the city in northern Norway) as a spice. After much discussion, botanists had recently identified this plant to be *Heracleum persicum*. This large hogweed, which resembles and is very closely related to giant hogweed (*Heracleum mantegazzianum*), was introduced originally to the region as a garden ornamental. It has escaped in many places in northern Norway and it is a characteristic plant of the city of Tromsø. It is blacklisted in Norway as an unwanted invasive species, particularly because of its reputation, as with giant hogweed, for causing nasty blisters on the skin of those who get too near. Thus it was a big surprise to those gathered in my garden that anyone would actually eat a plant that we had been taught was quite dangerous! However, it turns out that this use is well documented in the literature.

Facciola (1998) states that *golpar* (*H. persicum*) seeds are ground into a powder and are sprinkled over potatoes, cooked fava/broad beans (purportedly also reducing gas) and roasted watermelon seeds. It is also one of the ingredients in the variable Iranian spice mix *advieh*, which can also include cinnamon, nutmeg, rose petals, cardamom, cumin, turmeric, cloves and ginger etc. Whole seeds are added to soups, stews and some types of pickles.

The use of *Heracleum* seed as a spice is also found in other cultures. In Nepal, *Heracleum nepalense* seed are ground and used in dal and other dishes (Manandhar, 2002). In Sikkim, the seeds of *H. wallichii* are used as a spice in pickles.

I've since found *golpar* seed for sale locally in Iranian supermarkets. I've also collected seed myself from different species and use it regularly on various dishes with success – as a curry spice and as a replacement for cumin in other dishes. All the *Heracleum* species I've tried have very similar taste.

It is also very likely that cooked young shoots of both Tromsø palm and giant hogweed are perfectly safe to eat, BUT BE VERY CAREFUL HANDLING THESE PLANTS IF YOU DO DECIDE TO TRY! *Heracleum persicum* shoots are, for example, known to be boiled and eaten as a breakfast food in Turkey (Facciola, 1998). Both species grow in Norway and botanists thought for many years that the plants here in Trondheim were in fact giant hogweed. It is unlikely that non-specialists could tell the difference. My friend Jan Erik Kofoed in the Useful Plant Society volunteered to try the shoots during spring 2012. He harvested them and simply cooked them quickly in lightly salted water. He found the leaf stems to be mild and aromatic but the leaves were a bit on the strong side. He joked that he took a chance eating them in the evening despite the fact that they are breakfast food, but that if he survived to morning he would finish the rest for breakfast in the traditional way! He survived and so did I when I also tried them. I wonder if Holmboe (1941), who states that Tromsø palm is so acrid that it's definitely not to be recommended as a food plant, actually tasted it?

Hogweed Recipes from Iran

Thanks to Saideh Salamati

To be authentic, one should use *Heracleum persicum*, but any species will do.

Candied Hogweed

About 1kg hogweed shoots
Approximately 0.5 litre white wine vinegar
About 1 litre of water
3 tbsp sugar
2 tbsp salt
1-2 cloves of garlic

Cut the shoots into 5cm bits and cover with water for 24 hours. Rinse in a sieve. Boil the brine composed of all the ingredients apart from the shoots (you can adjust the salt and sugar to your own taste). Fill sterilised jars with the uncooked shoots. Pour the boiling brine over the shoots and close tight immediately. Can be used in about 2 weeks. Should be kept in a cool place.

Olive Salad with herbs

Can 200g olives
100g walnuts
150g redcurrants (originally pomegranate would be used in Iran)
100g chopped mint
1-2 cloves garlic
A little pepper
50ml olive oil
Juice of 1 lime
1tbsp ground *golpar* (hogweed seed)

Fry the minced garlic in olive oil. Grind or chop walnuts. Mix all the ingredients. Add the fruit at the end. Can be eaten as an appetiser with bread or with other dishes such as fish.

Maianthemum racemosum (syn. *Smilacina racemosa*)

FAMILY: Asparagaceae
ENGLISH: False Solomon's Seal, Solomon's Plume, False Spikenard, Treacle Berry
FRENCH: *Maïanthème à Grappes*

Many of the perennials in my garden are thanks to the generosity of various gardening friends and serve to continuously remind me of those people. Most generous of them all was an English woman, Marie Gaden, now in her 80s, who married a Norwegian and moved here during the last war. She had a fantastic perennial ornamental garden and I always came away with more plants than I had space for. One of these was *Maianthemum racemosum*, and I think of it therefore as *Marieanthemum* whenever I see it. It thrives in an almost completely shaded place under an old birch tree, quite a dry spot from mid-summer.

False Solomon's seal is a widespread species found across North America from east to west coasts and from Canada down into Mexico and is the largest and best known of the five North American *Maianthemums* as it is also often cultivated. Otherwise, representatives of this genus are found in Europe, Asia and the Himalayas. False Solomon's seal is a woodland plant, tolerating shady conditions. Two subspecies are recognised, *Maianthemum racemosum* ssp. *racemosum* in eastern North America and ssp. *amplexicaule* (western false Solomon's seal). The latter is found in more open woods than the eastern form. The most obvious difference between the two is that *amplexicaule* is a more robust, erect plant with leaves that clasp the stem. Unlike *Maianthemum stellatum* (Starry False Lily of the Valley) which can be an invasive species in a garden situation, spreading with rhizomes, *Maianthemum racemosum* spreads gradually into a dense clump and keeps to where you put it.

320: Eastern false Solomon's seal (Maianthemum racemosum ssp. racemosum) has stems that arch downwards. Seen here in the woodland garden at RHS Wisley in the UK on 16th April, well past the edible stage.

In mid-summer the plants are covered with racemes of attractive hanging small white flowers at the stem tips, this characteristic separating the *Maianthemums* from their cousins the *Polygonatums*, the real Solomon's seals, also incidentally with edible spring shoots. The latter have larger groups of individual hanging flowers along the stems. In autumn, the bad tasting red berries are also attractive.

The shoots are harvested in early spring until the leaves start unfurling. They have a slightly unpleasant aftertaste both cooked and raw, although the initial taste is pleasant. I therefore don't normally serve them on their own. In mixed salads, mixed spring vegetable stir-fries and pasta sauces, the aftertaste isn't noticeable. The leaves at the top of the shoot are also stronger tasting so you may prefer to discard them before use, just using the stem. Interestingly, Thayer (2010) notes that both the spring shoots and berries of plants in the Pacific Northwest lack this aftertaste. Nevertheless, he agrees that the eastern form makes a good asparagus-like vegetable. He also uses the rhizomes. Forms of this plant found in our gardens have only been selected for good looks so far, so selection for good taste and higher yield is a good project waiting for somebody ... I have also tried blanching. This both forces the plants on more quickly due to the higher temperature under the bucket, the shoots now lack the characteristic reddish base to the stem, and the taste *is* milder, although I can still detect a slight aftertaste.

Traditionally, Moerman (1998) reports that the Nlaka'pamux or Thompson people of British Columbia used the spring shoots, but doesn't record shoots of the eastern

*321 (right): Western false Solomon's seal (*Maianthemum racemosum *ssp.* amplexicaule*) has stems that are much more erect than its eastern counterpart. Seen here in the Oxford Botanical Garden on 21st April.*

322 (below): Maianthemum racemosum *can be grown in the forest garden and is a well adapted edimental for a range of climates! Ringve Botanical Garden, Trondheim, Norway.*

323: The red autumn berries are also attractive but are not pleasant tasting.

form having been used. Elsewhere in the world, *Maianthemum purpureum* shoots are recorded as being used for food in Nepal (Manandhar, 2002) and *Maianthemum japonicum* (*pulsomdae*) is wild-foraged in Korea (Pemberton and Lee, 1996).

This plant is readily available in UK nurseries at present and will also be easy to source in its homeland. The RHS Plant Finder lists, at the time of writing, as many as 52 nurseries offering the species, but only one nursery offers the western form, ssp. *amplexicaule*. There are also a few cultivars available, notably 'Emily Moody' with larger more fragrant flower heads. It is also described as a bigger plant (to 1m). A combination of greater yield and higher ornamental value sounds worth investigating! If you're not in so much of a hurry and would like to propagate several plants cheaply, then you may want to start from seed, which will need cold treatment to germinate, so ideally sow in autumn outside or as soon as you can. This plant will not tolerate very limey soil, but my experience is that it isn't necessary with acid conditions either. It will need sufficient moisture early in the season when it is in growth, tolerating drier conditions later in the summer.

324: The spring shoots are harvested from late March to mid-May, according to your location, before the leaves unfurl. Blanching by covering with a large bucket, or just a pile of leaves, gives a milder tasting vegetable (the blanched and unblanched shoots are shown together here). Note that the shoot density is quite high.

325 & 326: Harvested and steamed blanched false Solomon's seal shoots.

Laportea canadensis

FAMILY: Urticaceae
ENGLISH: Canadian Wood Nettle, Wood Nettle, Itchweed

A few years ago, I was surprised to find several pages in Sam Thayer's *The Forager's Harvest* from 2006 devoted to this species and he opens with, 'Wood nettle doesn't get even one tenth the coverage of stinging nettle in the wild food literature, despite the fact that, in the opinions of most who have tried both plants, it is the superior vegetable by a wide margin'. Praise indeed and hardly believable to someone like me who already rates stinging nettle very highly (see Chapter 1). Wood nettle doesn't get a mention in *Sturtevant's Edible Plants of the World* (Hedrick, 1919) nor does *Cornucopia II* (Facciola, 1998) include it. There are also, surprisingly, no records of its use for food in the comprehensive *Native American Ethnobotany* (Moerman, 1998). Thayer believes that many people often mistake wood for stinging nettle and refers to the fact that one of the best-known North American foraging books, Elias and Dykeman's *Field Guide to North American Edible Wild Plants*, has a picture purporting to be stinging nettle which is actually wood nettle. Wood nettle's use is therefore probably vastly under-reported.

327: Sign in the Linnaeus botanical garden in Uppsala, Sweden, warning the public that Laportea canadensis *stings.*

The genus *Laportea* consists of some 22 species found almost worldwide. Apart from the West Indian wood nettle (*L. aestuans*) found in southern Florida, *L. canadensis* is the only species found in the US and Canada. Its range is in the east of the continent reaching northwards into southern Canada. Its habitat is rich, moist deciduous forests and it is often associated with ostrich fern (this chapter) in lowland floodplain forests as the dominant herbs, most often under silver maple (*Acer saccharinum*). Under ideal conditions, it may form large colonies by way of its creeping rhizomes. Wood nettle is then an ideal species for a damp forest garden, growing better than stinging nettle (*Urtica dioica*) in shady conditions. In my garden, plants grow to 70-90cm tall and can reportedly reach 1.5m in good but not too shady conditions. Like stinging nettle, wood nettle is armed with stinging hairs, but the initial more painful sting wears off quite quickly.

Unfortunately, plants and seed of the wood nettle are currently hard to come by. I was lucky to get hold of a plant via my local botanical garden; otherwise I've never come across seed or plants offered in Europe. Plants can be easily propagated vegetatively. In North America, it is available from some native plant nurseries.

By far the best account of the edibility of *Laportea canadensis* can be found in Sam Thayer's *Forager's Harvest*. His is an account based on first-hand experience with this plant and I unashamedly repeat some of his experiences here.

Thayer rates the stingless spring shoots as one of his favourite cooked vegetables, likening both the sweetish taste and texture to asparagus and he serves it simply

328: Spring shoots of Laportea canadensis *in my garden appear about a month later than stinging nettles, in mid-to-late May.*

329: Laportea canadensis *in early June; at this time the top 10-15cm of the plant can be used.*

with salt and butter. He also likes to eat the shoots raw after rubbing off the stinging hairs. Later on, the lower shoots become tough and at this stage he recommends using the top 10-15cm of the plants down to where the stem still breaks easily. I wholeheartedly agree with this assessment. This is a prime perennial vegetable, the leaves similar in taste to stinging nettle but with the added benefit of the delicate stems. I'm now trying to increase the number of plants in different parts of my garden.

Having easy access to large quantities of this plant, Thayer tells us that it is an important part of his diet and he preserves and freezes large amounts for later use. Drying is also worth trying if you ever have large enough quantities. Thayer also harvests the seed and uses it in the same way as flax (*Linum usitassimum*) seed is used on bread and in hot cereal.

Other *Laportea* species are reported to be used around the world. For example, in China, young shoots of various species are eaten (ref. the online Flora of China[*]) and Mansfeld's World Database of Agricultural and Horticultural Crops reports that *Laportea aestuans* is cultivated for its edible leaves.

To various Native American tribes, wood nettle is both a medicinal and, like stinging nettle, fibre plant. In the 1800s, it was actually identified as a promising commercial fibre plant and it was trialled in Europe. Interestingly, its perennial nature was seen to be an advantage as, unlike flax and hemp (*Cannabis sativa*), it wasn't necessary to sow seed every year.

[*] www.efloras.org/flora_page.aspx?flora_id=2

Allium cernuum

FAMILY: Amaryllidaceae
ENGLISH: Nodding Onion,
   Chicago Onion
FRENCH: *Ail Penché*
GERMAN: *Nickender Lauch*
RUSSIAN: *Luk Ponikaiushchii,*
   Luk Sklonennyi

Nodding onion is a must for both the edible and ornamental garden. Not only is it one of the easiest plants to grow, it is also for many the most attractive of the 90 or so recognised North American Allium species. It also has quite a long flowering period. It is therefore not uncommonly seen in gardens, particularly in the north, as it is very hardy, but rarely seen grown as an edible. This is certainly also one of my favourite Alliums that I frequently use in the spring 'hungry gap'. Nodding onion and other spring-harvested onions allow me to be self-sufficient in onions. *Allium cernuum* remains green all winter and as long as the soil isn't frozen, bulbs and greens can also be dug at any time. They have a strong onion taste not unlike bulb onion.

The 'onion that nods' is also the most widely distributed species in North America, found both in Canada, in the mountains in the south and from east to west coasts, although there are large areas from which it is missing, particularly in the centre of

330-333: Allium cernuum *is a very attractive plant, available in a wide range of forms with varying flower colour and some forms reaching almost 50cm. The flower scapes or stems remain drooping although the individual flowers turn upwards once pollinated.*

334 & 335: Attractive red-based spring shoots of Allium cernuum (top), with Hablitzia, lovage and sweet cicely, can be used until the flowers start to appear. The flowers are a tasty and appealing addition to a summer salad (bottom).

the continent. This species is distinguished from other similar species such as *Allium stellatum* (prairie onion) by the fact that the flower scape remains nodding through to seed forming. It is also unusual in having two flower stems arising from each bulb.

Nodding onion can be propagated vegetatively by simply separating and replanting as many bulbs as you like. Alternatively, cold stratify seed over winter for several months and seedlings should then appear in the spring. If not, be patient, as they will germinate in the second year. In good conditions, plants can flower already in the second year! They will then spread vegetatively quite quickly supplemented by self-sown plants, if allowed to seed.

There are numerous cultivars available and it's wise to seek out one of the larger types for food. The cultivars 'Pink Giant', 'Major' and 'Hidcote', the latter having won the RHS Award of Garden Merit, are all good-sized similar plants. I have learnt from Allium guru Mark McDonough in the US that *A. cernuum* readily crosses in gardens with some other European and Asian species such as *Allium senescens* and *A. nutans* (see Chapter 4) and for this reason a number of hybrids are doing the rounds!

Nodding onion is found mostly in open sunny spots, but will tolerate some shade, and can also handle periodically dry, shallow soils. In trials carried out by Michigan State University on plants suitable for growing on the increasingly popular green roofs, this species was preferred together with *Tradescantia ohiensis* (this chapter), *Coreopsis lanceolata* and various *Sedum* spp. Therefore, *Allium cernuum* and *Tradescantia* are worth considering for your perennial edible roof garden along with *Allium fistulosum* (see Chapter 6).

There's a park in Chicago called Marquette Park where a remnant of the original prairie on which the city was built thrives. *Allium cernuum* is one of the original plants that grows there and it was once abundant in this area. The name Chicago was in fact a local Indian tribe's name for an onion, although there doesn't seem to be a consensus as to whether it was the nodding onion or *Allium tricoccum* (wild leek or ramps), briefly discussed in Chapter 1. I was originally inspired to try this species when I read in *Sturtevant's Edible Plants of the World* that *Allium cernuum* and *A. canadense* had formed almost the entire source of food for the French missionary (Jacques) Marquette and his party on their way from Green Bay to the present site of Chicago in 1674.

Being such a widespread, abundant and tasty species, it is not surprising to learn that nodding onions form an important food source to numerous Native American tribes, including the Apache, Blackfoot and Cherokee (Moerman, 1998). So important was it that it was considered to be a staple for several tribes. Both the leaves and bulbs were eaten raw in salads and as an accompaniment to other food (e.g. corn-meal dumplings). It was used to flavour sauces, soups, fish and meat dishes and bulbs were also cooked with other food in pit or earth ovens. Bulbs were also often dried or stored for later use.

Tradescantia ohiensis

FAMILY: Commelinaceae
ENGLISH: Bluejacket, Ohio Spiderwort

Tradescantia occidentalis

ENGLISH: Western or Prairie Spiderwort

Tradescantia virginiana

ENGLISH: Virginia Spiderwort

Some years ago I happened upon the website of the Wild Food Foragers of America, who don't seem to exist anymore. I found a glowing report of an edible plant genus I'd seen only scant mention of previously. This was *Tradescantia*, commonly known as the spiderworts. I had up to then grown plants from the diverse group of garden hybrids, known as *Tradescantia* (Andersoniana Group), but not terribly successfully, surviving but not really thriving like the vigorous plants I'd seen in gardens in the UK.

The author of the article (written in 2003) had taken part in a local foraging walk on which a sprightly 87-year-old, Jane Dunn, had told the assembled group how she had been eating this weed for years and it had clearly not harmed her, rather the contrary. The author also relates that his garden was covered with spiderwort and that they wouldn't mow until the beautiful

336: Tradescantia *(Andersoniana Group) 'Leonora' in RHS Wisley Gardens, UK.*

sea of blue flowers, attractive to bees and butterflies, was over. However, the author hadn't been aware of its edibility until meeting Jane Dunn and strangely had found little to encourage trying it in foraging books and searching the internet. After much searching I sourced seed of two native species, *Tradescantia ohiensis* and *T. occidentalis* from a native seed company in the US, both species readily germinated and were planted in my garden by 2004.

The perennial genus *Tradescantia* is native to the Americas from Canada to Argentina and some 70 species are recognised, some 30 of which are found in the US and Canada. *Tradescantia ohiensis* (Bluejacket) is a larger plant reaching 1m and is the most common and widespread species found throughout the Eastern US and Canada. *Tradescantia occidentalis* (western spiderwort) grows further to the west and to the untrained eye is identical to the former. They are both found in a wide range of open and partly shaded habitats. *Tradescantia subaspera* (zigzag spiderwort) is another large species up to 1m found in rich damp and, sometimes, dry woods in the Eastern US. *Tradescantia virginiana* is a smaller eastern species under which name the garden hybrids were formerly incorrectly known. Another commonly grown genus of ornamentals in the same family as *Tradescantia*, is *Commelina* or the dayflowers some of which are also perennials. They can be used in exactly the same way. For example, try *Commelina coelestis*, from Mexico and California or *C. cyanea* from southeast Australia (known locally as scurvy grass). *Commelinas* are less hardy however (I've grown them in pots which overwinter without water in a cold room inside).

Various species of *Tradescantia*, notably *virginiana*, *ohiensis* and *subaspera* were introduced into Europe from the 17th century and the genus was named after the father and son naturalist/gardener team John Tradescant (the elder and the younger). They were head gardeners for Charles I of England. The different species readily cross and today's Andersoniana hybrids have resulted in the 50 or so cultivars offered by UK nurseries in recent years!

337 & 338: Tradescantia occidentalis *(left) and* T. ohiensis *(right) flowers make a colourful addition to summer salads; flowers have three petals contrasting with the six yellow stamens.*

339: Tradescantia ohiensis *spreads slowly outwards forming a clump.*

340 (above): **Tradescantia subaspera** *tolerates deeper shade than the other species (here in the Oxford Botanic Garden in mid-April).*

341 & 342 (right): End of May mixed salad 'foraged' from my garden including 'Ragged Jack' kale, white flowered Allium zebdanense *and* A. humile, Viola canadensis, Tradescantia ohiensis, *chervil, sorrel,* Primula veris *'Red Strain', mustard greens and honewort,* Cryptotaenia canadensis.

The use of Tradescantia as an edible plant can be traced back to various native American tribes who wild-gathered this plant. Moerman in *Native American Ethnobotany* (1998) documents various tribes using *T. occidentalis* both raw and cooked. The Cherokee used the young growth of *T. virginiana* first parboiled then fried and frequently mixed with other greens.

African-American botanist George Washington Carver (1864-1943) is best known for his research into and promotion of alternative crops that could benefit poor farmers and this included wild plants. Fernald and Kinsey (1958) quote Carver as 'highly commending them (Tradescantias) as *rich flavoured* and that the one most highly prized ... is *T. virginica* (*virginiana*).'

Twentieth century compilations of edible plants such as *Sturtevant's Edible Plants of the World*, Plants For A Future and *Cornucopia II* only mention *Tradescantia virginiana*, and being a smaller plant this species is probably less productive. Whatever species you have, the stems become fibrous as they approach flowering stage, so it is best to harvest them while they are still young. Leaves, however, remain good throughout most of the season. The tasty flowers appear from mid-summer and continue to be produced over a couple of months. They can be used to decorate salads and other food, like a perennial version of borage (*Borago officinalis*). Cutting back a part of a Tradescantia clump for the leaves will also give a prolonged flowering period. The taste of spiderwort is distinctive, mild and crisp, it tastes ... well ... just like Tradescantia, so you'll have to try it yourself (its taste is somewhat reminiscent of Typha, this chapter). The leaves and stems can be used raw in salads, in soups, sautéed with omelette and is particularly good in Chinese stir-fried dishes.

Tradescantia ohiensis is available currently from three nurseries in the UK and seed can be sourced from seed companies in the US specialising in native plants. The seed should be autumn/winter sown and given cold treatment. Seedlings will appear irregularly over the next two springs, so be patient! Established plants are easy to multiply by division or just dig up seedlings as Tradescantia readily self-sows. Plants prefer soils that do not dry out in spring, but can tolerate drought later in the season. You should find a place in your garden where it is free to spread, but also select a site where it can be appreciated as an ornamental. This is, for example, an ideal ground cover plant for the open forest garden, tolerating some shade. *Tradescantia subaspera* can be used for deeper shade.

Matteuccia struthiopteris (syn. *M. pensylvanica*)

FAMILY: Woodsiaceae
CHINESE: *Jiaguojueshu*
ENGLISH: Ostrich Fern,
    Shuttlecock Fern
FINNISH: *Kotkansiipi*
FRENCH / CANADIAN: *Crosse de
    Fougère à l'Autruche,
    Tête de Violon*
GERMAN: *Straußenfarn*
JAPANESE: *Kogomi*
NORWEGIAN: *Strutseving*
RUSSIAN: *Strausnik Obyknovennyi*
SWEDISH: *Strutbräke*

For many who have tried, ostrich fern fiddleheads are simply the most delicious vegetable they've ever eaten. I'm not sure I would go that far, but they are certainly near the top of my list. In the late 1990s, I joined an email discussion group based in North America called Wild Forager. The first spring, there was a lot of discussion about the use of ostrich fern for food. It was evident that this was one of the most important wild-collected food plants in parts of the US and Canada. Although absent from the UK, but sometimes naturalising, this is an extremely common fern just across the North Sea here in Norway. However, I had never heard of it being used for food. Was perhaps North Europe's best wild edible plant undiscovered?

Up to then, my only experience of using ferns for food was one day in the 1980s. Our local group of the Norwegian Useful Plants Society (see box on page 210) had a stand at an open day at a traditional museum, Sverresborg, a wonderful collection of old wooden buildings and related household traditions. We were serving nettle soup and we'd organised a guided walk to show the public some of the interesting useful plants to be found in the grounds of the museum. A Japanese tourist was on one of these walks and, at one point, he suddenly shouted something in Japanese and disappeared into the woods. He returned smiling, clutching several young fern fiddleheads and gestured that he intended to eat this delicacy later that day!

Ostrich fern is found naturally in a belt of the mid-to-high latitudes from parts of China, Japan, Kamchatka, Sakhalin and North Korea in the east, westwards to western Siberia, the Caucasus, and in Eastern Europe, the Alps and northwest Europe (Norway, Sweden and Finland). This species is also common in the northeast of the US and Canada as well as parts of western Canada and Alaska. There are relatively minor differences in *Matteuccia struthiopteris* var. *struthiopteris* in Europe and var. *pensylvanica* in North America. It is found throughout Norway and is most common along rivers, streams and on rich, fertile land. It needs a constant supply of moisture to thrive and forms large colonies, particularly in open rich woodland. It is our largest

fern and can reach a height of 2m. It has two types of leaf. First, the conspicuous (in summer) long sterile leaves that are green, hairless, widest near the tip and tapering abruptly upwards. These are the ostrich feather-like fronds that give the plant its common name in most languages. The fertile spore-bearing leaves are most conspicuous in winter, and are much shorter and brown in colour.

Ferns have traditionally been important vegetables for native peoples, particularly in southeast Asia, Australia, New Zealand and North America. In New Zealand, for example, bracken (*Pteridium aquilinum* ssp. *esculentum*) was the most important wild food plant for the Maoris. Both the rhizomes and spring shoots were used. Young spring shoots of bracken are also used in Japan on quite a large scale, but there are studies possibly linking bracken consumption to cancer. Ostrich fern is also wild-

343: Ostrich fern can be found along rivers and in rich, open woodlands with constant supply of water, often associated with nitrogen-fixing alder (Alnus *spp.*).

Phots 344 & 345: Ostrich fern has two very different leaves; the dark fertile spore-bearing fronds stand proud all winter (above) releasing spores in mid-winter to spring. The infertile green fronds are much longer (right).

foraged locally in Japan. In Ussuria in the far east of Russia where both ostrich fern and bracken are found, it is mainly bracken that is used, probably because it is more readily accessible.

346: Ostrich fern gives almost a tropical magical feel to a shady woodland in summer. Dokka, Norway.

The use of ostrich fern for food is best known from the northeastern parts of North America, in particular in Maine and the Maritime provinces in Canada. The edible part of this fern is known as fiddleheads, due to their resemblance to the scroll at the top of a fiddle. In Canada, the French population call them crosier (as in Bishop's crosier). They are harvested early in spring before the fiddleheads unfold and are cut with several centimetres of the stem (as long as they snap off, they can be eaten, later becoming too fibrous). The harvesting period doesn't last long (2-3 weeks), very much depending on the weather conditions.

347 & 348: The fiddleheads are best harvested as soon as they appear in the spring with a few centimetres of stalk.

The use of ostrich fern for food is a Native American tradition that was adopted by Europeans. Today as much as 500,000kg of fiddleheads are harvested from the wild every spring. Traditionally, they would be packed in snow and transported to market. Nowadays, the market for fiddleheads has spread across North America due to refrigerated transport. Some of the harvest is also tinned. With such a large harvest there has been some concern about its sustainability. For this reason there has been an increasing interest in its cultivation and Norcliff Farms in Ontario is the first sizeable operation, with some 300,000 plants in a naturalistic swampy area, located near Port Colborne on the north shore of Lake Erie.

Was the ostrich fern ever used for food in Europe? Norway has enormous quantities of this fern, which remain practically unharvested. There is only one account of it having been used for food in Norway, and this is the only one I know of from Europe. In 1774, it was written that '...farmers prepared a vegetable dish by cooking the young fiddleheads of ostrich fern', so perhaps this is a very old tradition after all that has simply just died out?

It is difficult to describe the taste of fiddleheads, but most people like or even love it. It can be described variously as a cross between spinach and asparagus or green beans and artichokes. One group of Italians on a course I held were so impressed that they asked, 'Why on earth import asparagus when you have ostrich fern?' There are lots of ways to cook with fiddleheads. Get inspiration from the many recipes on the Internet or just improvise. Most people simply steam or boil the fiddleheads and serve in butter or with some garlic. I also use cooked fiddleheads in salads. There's even a cookbook out there, if you can find it, devoted to fiddlehead cookery, Melvin Nash's *Cooking North America's Finest Gourmet Fiddleheads*.

Finally, I should add a warning to make sure you cook your fiddleheads properly. Although potential dangerous chemicals haven't been found in this fern, in 1994 there were several reports of people who became ill after consuming the fern either raw or cooked only briefly. Although the toxin involved has never been identified, it was probably a water-borne pathogen from winter flood waters which can easily lodge in the emerging fiddleheads which are difficult to wash thoroughly. This is not likely to be a problem in gardens, but I nevertheless recommend washing thoroughly in water and cooking (boil or steam) them for 10 minutes.

Ostrich fern is also a surprisingly nutritious and healthy plant as can be seen from the results of various studies: 'Twice as much protein as in other vegetables', 'Rich in unsaturated fatty acids', 'Low levels of sodium', 'Comparable to spinach', 'Equivalent to blueberries in phenolic compound content', 'A good source of Omega 3' etc.

I count myself lucky living near a steep-sided canyon-like river valley packed with ostrich fern. The river (the Homla) is also a salmon river, so what better accompaniment to the fiddleheads (just omit the salmon/ seafood for a vegetarian dish). The recipe I used is given below. Just improvise if you don't have all the ingredients.

349: Ostrich fern is grown as an ornamental in many botanical woodland gardens in Europe and has won the Royal Horticultural Society's Award of Garden Merit (AGM).

Ostrich fern is an excellent choice for the woodland or edible forest garden, thriving in shady conditions. They prefer moist humus-rich soil, but as long as the soil isn't allowed to dry out they will be perfectly happy. They will also not object to quite swampy land. Once planted, they will spread slowly on lateral rhizomes on which new plants are formed. In nature, huge areas can in this way actually be the same plant. They are often planted as ornamentals and for me are one of the most beautiful sights of our Norwegian nature when seen en masse in dappled light growing in deciduous woodland along a fast flowing river. They are readily available from nurseries in Europe. For example, at the time of writing there are 84 nurseries offering *Matteuccia struthiopteris* in the online RHS Plant Finder in the UK. In North America it is often available under the synonym *Matteuccia pensylvanica*. Established plants are easily divided in the winter and spring. They more or less look after themselves as long as they get sufficient water and there are no known pests or diseases. A number of cultivars are also available in a limited number of nurseries: 'Bedraggled Feathers', 'Depauperata', 'Erosa' and 'Jumbo'. The latter is potentially a higher yielding variety, emerging later in my garden than the local plants.

Wild Ostrich Fern and Salmon Pasta

125g fiddleheads, wash thoroughly to remove the small brown scales and steam for 10 minutes

Italian *porcini* pasta (if you can get or make your own), cooked until tender (*porcini* is the cep or penny bun mushroom, *Boletus edulis*)

250g cooked wild (not farmed) salmon (or other seafood), cut into small pieces

Olive oil

⅔ cup wild onions (I used *Allium oleraceum*, see Chapter 6)

½ cup green and red pepper

A handful of dried winter chantarelle, soaked in water for 5 minutes, or just replace with any other mushroom

1 tsp wild (or garden) thyme

¼ tsp black pepper

Pinch of salt

⅛ tsp celery seed (easily home grown from second year celery plants)

1 lemon

Sunflower seeds or pine nuts

Alpine bistort bulbils, roasted in a dry frying pan for a couple of minutes (see Chapter 6)

Parmesan or other strong tasting cheese

Winter chantarelle (Cantharellus infundibuli-formis) and related species can be found in large quantities in late autumn over much of the temperate northern hemisphere and are easily dried for later use.

Fry the onions, pepper and chantarelle in the olive oil for 5 minutes, add the various flavourings, cooked fish and ostrich fern and fry for another 10 minutes. Serve over the cooked pasta. Finish off with sunflower seeds, alpine bistort bulbils and cheese.

Hydrophyllum virginianum
H. canadense
H. appendiculatum
and others

FAMILY: Hydrophyllaceae
ENGLISH: Waterleaf, Indian Salad

Looking for a useful ground cover for the forest garden or other shady places, then look no further than the genus *Hydrophyllum* which translates directly to the English common name waterleaf due to the fact that the young leaves often have pale patches like a water stain.

There are eight or nine species in this genus in North America, half of which are restricted to the east and half at higher elevations in the west. I only have experience so far with *Hydrophyllum virginianum* (Eastern waterleaf) and *H. appendiculatum* (great waterleaf), both from the eastern US and Canada. Unfortunately, *Hydrophyllum appendiculatum* turned out to be a biennial, although it self-seeds in my garden. In Ohio, this species grows in woods with an assemblage of interesting perennial edibles including *Claytonia virginica* (spring beauty), *Dentaria laciniata* (cutleaf toothwort) and *Podophyllum peltatum* (mayapple), all of which I have in my garden, so perhaps I will plant up a replica edible Ohio woodland.

Unfortunately, *Hydrophyllums* never became popular as woodland garden plants even though various authors have recommended them as an ornamental ground cover. Therefore, they can be difficult to get hold of, although there are a handful of UK nurseries offering them at present. *Hydrophyllum capitatum* (ballhead waterleaf) is sometimes grown in rock gardens, in particular compact forms from montane areas. I've also seen plants in various botanical gardens including Oxford, Oslo, Ghent, Kew and the Chelsea Physic Garden in London, where *H. virginianum* was grown as early as 1739. My experience is that it is easily grown and seeds itself lightly around without becoming a problem. Sam Thayer in *The Forager's Harvest* says that it sometimes 'conquers backyards, but it is usually left alone as it doesn't get in anyone's way'. However, it is sometimes referred to as an invasive, no doubt depending on your climate and growing conditions. So, keep an eye out...

350: The early spring leaves of Hydrophyllum *species often have pale 'watermarks' on the leaves, hence the common name waterleaf; here* Hydrophyllum appendiculatum *in the author's garden.*

351 & 352: A mass ground-cover planting of Hydrophyllums can be a pleasant sight when in flower (above) H. appendiculatum; *(right)* H. virginianum.

355: Mass ground cover planting of a waterleaf at Kew Gardens in London.

353 & 354: Older spring leaves of the waterleafs are good cooked; (top) H. appendiculatum; *(bottom)* H. virginianum.

Various alternative common English names exist for the waterleafs, reflecting their importance in Native American cuisine; *H. virginianum* and *H. canadense* are often referred to as Indian salad or Shawanese/Shawnee salad and west coast *H. occidentale* is known as squaw lettuce. The name John's cabbage is also used in the east, vouching for the fact that white settlers also learned to use this spring vegetable. In 1818, William Barton wrote that, 'The Indian Salad and Shawnee Salad of Kentucky and Ohio are praised by the white settlers', and, 'The young shoots are praised by all who eat them'.

The young leaves and the tips of stems are best in salads; the older leaves usually being cooked (boiled or steamed). I usually use them mixed with other seasonal greens in salads and vegetarian dishes. Thayer (2006) describes the flower stalks well as 'sweet, juicy and crunchy' before the flowers open and says that the unopened clusters of flower buds can be enjoyed cooked. Some species such as *H. appendiculatum* have taproots and these were also important Indian food (*H. fendleri* and *H. tenuipes* are also documented used as a root vegetable by Moerman, 1998). In California, Vizgirdas and Rey-Vizgirdas (2009) consider that *H. capitatum* and *H. occidentale* are 'exceptionally good in salads or eaten as a trail nibble'.

Typha latifolia

FAMILY: Typhaceae
ENGLISH: Great Reedmace, Bulrush, Broadleaf Cattail, Common Cattail
FRENCH: *La Massette à Larges Feuilles*, *Roseau à Massette*, *Rauche*
GERMAN: *Breitblättriger Rohrkolben*
RUSSIAN: *Rogos Sirokolistnyj*
SPANISH: *Totora, Junco de Esteras, Espadaña*

Again and again we come across plants that are massively important food plants in some parts of the world whilst being completely ignored in others. Known as common cattails in North America, *Typha latifolia* was so important to some native tribes that the whole community was based around this abundant shallow water plant, supplying not only food through the carbohydrate-rich rhizomes, but also several green vegetables from different parts of the plant. In addition, the pollen was used as flour, oil was obtained from the seed, and it was also an important source of fibre for weaving, stuffing and insulation, tinder and torches as well as medicine. Yet, on the other side of the Atlantic in the UK where it is a common aquatic, all that Richard Mabey can muster up in his 480 page ethnobotanical work *Flora Britannica* (1996) is that it is occasionally used in flower arranging.

Legendary 1960s American forager Euell Gibbons, who advocated nutritious but neglected plants, described cattails as the 'supermarket of the swamps' (this would be hypermarket or even mall of the swamps nowadays, judging by the number of uses...). He comments in *Stalking the Wild Asparagus*, his first book from 1962, that, 'For the number of different kinds of foods it produces, there is no plant, wild or domesticated, which tops the common Cattail'. This plant should be in any permaculturist's garden as a symbol of a plant representing the absolute minimum transport/food mile requirements, as so many of our basic needs are found in exactly the same place/plant ... As Ken Fern stated in his book (Fern, 1997), "I cannot understand why the reedmaces aren't exploited more and we drain their habitat to grow high-energy input cereals instead..."

The genus name comes from the Greek *typhos*, meaning marsh. There are about a dozen species found literally worldwide and whether you are in Europe, North or South America, Australasia, Africa or Asia it is likely that you will be familiar with one of these plants or other closely related *Typha* species. You therefore needn't go hungry in a foreign land. Its cigar-like seed heads, which contain the female flowers in summer, persist through the winter making the extensive stands of this plant instantly identified and it is therefore probably one of the world's best-known plants. The male flowers are located directly above the 'cigars' but, having done their business, quickly wither away in summer. This plant forms large dominant stands, spreading by horizontal rhizomes (underground stems). The common cattail

356: The familiar cigar-shaped flower heads of bulrushes that appear in summer and persist through the winter.

or greater reedmace (*Typha latifolia*) has an extensive natural range throughout North America and parts of Central and South America, in Europe, apart from the far north, the Mediterranean countries, North Africa, some African countries, in West Asia, the Caucasus, western Russia, Siberia, Pakistan, the Russian Far East, Korea, Japan and China. It has also been introduced into Australasia and some tropical countries in Asia.

Typhas thrive over a wide range of climates from tropical to sub-arctic! It is clearly a robust and adaptable plant ... However, it grows most successfully in very wet places in shallow water, in ponds, lakes and ditches. It can reach 3m each summer in ideal conditions. The narrowleaf cattail or lesser reedmace (*Typha angustifolia*) has a similar range. These two species are most easily separated by the fact that the male and female flower spikes are clearly separated on their stalk in *T. angustifolia* and the leaf tips are not higher than the male flowers. The opposite is true for *T. latifolia*.

Again, the best account of the varied vegetables provided by *Typha latifolia* (and *T. angustifolia*) can be found in Sam Thayer's *The Forager's Harvest* from 2006 and I would thoroughly recommend that you get yourself a copy as there are many more details than I have space for here! I quote, 'This amazing plant produces four delicious vegetables, plus a rhizome that is packed with nutritious, edible starch; finally its beautiful pollen provides an interesting, protein-rich flour.'

The most commonly used vegetable from the plant is what Thayer refers to as the 'Leaf Hearts' or 'Shoot Cores'. This is also the vegetable you will probably want to harvest from your garden pond. Yields are highest from late spring to mid-summer or until the flower stalks begin to show and the plants are maybe up to half of full size. They are also simple to harvest, as you just have to grab the leaves and pull firmly upwards. The shoots should then come free from the rhizome. It really is as easy as

357: The spring shoots of the common cattail (Typha latifolia) are truly a gourmet vegetable and are easily harvested to mid-summer by simply pulling the shoot firmly upwards.

that! You then just peel away the coarser outer leaves until the crisp inner core or heart is revealed. This can be up to 20-30cm long. It is an important spring vegetable for numerous Native American tribes (Moerman, 1998), who ate them raw, cooked and roasted. Thayer warns, however, that he reacts to the *raw* shoots with an itchy, irritated throat.

A second vegetable can be had from the immature flowers that will at this stage still be hidden behind a leafy sheath. As noted above, the flowers are divided into an upper male and lower female part. It is the male part that is used and it is also easy to simply break it off without any tools. Euell Gibbons (1962) recommended boiling them for a few minutes and rated it as one of the finest wild vegetables, eaten like corn on the cob and likened to that vegetable by some. This part is also enjoyed by various Native American tribes. Thayer also uses the immature rhizomes (laterals) and the buds at the end of the rhizomes as vegetables.

I've already commented how strange it is that there are apparently no traditions of using bulrushes for food in Western Europe. This also applies to the Mediterranean countries where it is widespread, and this is perhaps even stranger given the high number of edible species documented from that region (see Chapter 2). Nevertheless, archaeological finds show that it was probably an important carbohydrate source in Europe in the Stone Age.

It was, however, used in the past further east in western Russia. In the early 1800s, English naturalist, Edward Daniel Clarke, travelled along the lower Don River in Russia and recorded the following (Clarke and Walpole, 1811):

> 'In the shallows of the Don, a sort of flag, Typha palustris, flourishes most luxuriantly. We found the inhabitants of the Oxai (Aksaj), and afterwards of Tscherchaskoy (Novocherkassk), devouring the plant raw, with a degree of avidity as though it had been a religious observance. It was to be seen in all the streets, and in every house, bound into

faggots, about three feet in length, as we tie up asparagus, which were hawked about, or sold in the shops. The season for eating it had just commenced. They peel off the outer rind, and find near the root a tender white part of the stem, which, for about the length of eighteen inches, affords a crisp, cooling, and very pleasant article of food. I have not noticed this sort of vegetable diet in any other country. We eat of it heartily, and were as fond of it as the Cossacks, with whom, young or old, rich or poor, it is a most favourite repast.'

(For this reason, the spring shoots are sometimes referred to as Cossack asparagus.)

In the Far East, we find the only known record of large scale Typha cultivation for food, a tradition which, according to the Chinese Online Encyclopaedia (zwbk.org in Chinese), goes back at least 3,000 years! The spring shoots are known as *pu cai* or *po* shoots and are described as a delicious vegetable. It seems to be *Typha latifolia* that is cultivated both in northeast China and in Yunnan in the northwest. Before discovering this, I had suspected that this mild crispy vegetable would go well with

358 & 359: Peeled cattail shoots have the perfect texture and mild taste for stir-fry dishes.

360 (above): The pollen from the male flowers of the bulrushes or cattails is produced in such large quantities that it was used by aboriginal peoples in several parts of the world as a protein-rich flour.

361 (right): Welsh onion (Allium fistulosum), peeled Typha shoots and blanched sea kale harvested in my garden in late May.

Chinese cuisine. Hu (2005) includes *Typha latifolia* and suggests that this is a delicacy for special occasions: 'The yellow tender centre portion taken off from younger plants sold in large cities of northern Jiangsu for banquets, not a vegetable for the public'. Otherwise, the spring harvested young shoots were also pickled in China in the past (Li et al., 2003). The young shoots were sometimes used by the Aborigines in Australia, who also ate the immature flower stalks in great quantity (Low, 1989), and the shoot hearts were also sometimes used by the New Zealand Maori (Crowe, 1990).

The value of pollen as a nutrient rich food is particularly interesting and has evolved in all continents. Pollen of *Typha elephantina* was used in India in bread. It has also been recorded used in China (mixed with honey and sold as a sweetmeat, Li et al., 2003); by the Maoris in New Zealand where the pollen of *Typha orientalis* was known as *pungapunga* or *pua* (Crowe, 1990) and was either mixed with water into a porridge with a taste similar to sweetcorn, was formed into cakes and cooked in the earth oven, reminding one European author of the taste of gingerbread, or, for the extreme food fan, mixed with large quantities of a crushed beetle and steamed in the earth oven; Native American tribes use the pollen in cakes and porridge (Moerman, 1998); in South Africa, the pollen of widespread *Typha capensis* was used (van Wyck and Gericke, 2000); and in South America, Arenas and Scarpa (2003) describe numerous ways that ethnic groups of the Gran Chaco used the pollen of *Typha domingensis*, in small cakes or biscuits fried in oil, and simply toasted and eaten. The latter authors also refer to the pollen being used in Iraq.

In a garden, you are unlikely to have a sufficient number of plants to try out bulrush pollen and you will have to find an extensive wild stand of this plant to satisfy your

362: Bulrushes will quickly invade a pond if unrestrained and are therefore usually planted in large tubs. They also grow well in pots as long as they are kept moist.

363 & 364: *Starting a trend in mini-permaveggies?* Typha minima *(top) could be what you are looking for.* Typha laxmanii, *graceful cattail, (bottom) is a medium-sized species with stunted 'cigars'.*

curiosity. A pond is a must in any permaculturist's garden and if I had to choose one plant to provide maximum yield it would certainly be *Typha latifolia*. It is often stated that this species is too vigorous in ornamental ponds and unless restricted in a large solid tub (the rhizomes can puncture tubs made of more flimsy material), they may take over the whole pond and the surrounding boggy ground. However, from the viewpoint of cultivating for food, you may actually want it to take over (even at the expense of diversity) for maximum pond yield. Even on its own, it is an ornamental plant. Less vigorous is *Typha latifolia variegata*, a variegated selection frequently offered by suppliers of aquatic plants. If you live outside the range of *T. latifolia* you may wish to source the species that is native to your own area.

This plant will grow well in water depths of 40cm or more. Indeed, experience from China is that the yield or length of usable stem increases with the water depth. In colder areas, deeper water also offers frost protection. In fact in a recent very cold winter, I lost my *Typha latifolia* in a relatively shallow pond. Bulrushes do not grow wild this far north. Propagation is easily done by dividing the rootstock in spring.

Various Typha species are also invasive species in the wrong place and are a hated weed of rice paddy fields in some areas and the species *Typha australis* has invaded shallow Lake Chad in Africa on such a large scale that it is accelerating the evaporation of the lake (it has decreased dramatically in size since the 1960s). However, various authors have suggested that a part solution is to utilise this enormous resource, e.g.:

> 'There appears to be enough Typha australis in the Lake Chad basin to feed the entire population of Africa (were it all fit for consumption and harvestable). Picture my horror at a picture of a dozen starving refugees hiding in a Typha stand that would feed and clothe a small town. These people are starving in the midst of plenty. And, unused and unchecked, that cornucopia of food is killing them with thirst.'
>
> Steve Klaber, 2009. Africa Project 2020; http://africaproject2020.com

We leave North America with that thought…

chapter 6

NORWAY
(AND SCANDINAVIA)

The final leg of our journey takes us from North America back across the Atlantic via Greenland, Iceland and the Faroe Islands to Norway. We retrace the voyages of the Vikings and on the way we find a plant that they almost certainly took with them, Angelica. We also find an onion growing in one small area of Iceland, taken there almost 1,000 years ago from an island that I can see from my house.

A few of the plants in this chapter are wild plants that have actually been cultivated in gardens as vegetables, and improved forms have been selected (e.g. Angelica); one (rhubarb) is normally cultivated as a fruit (sweetened); a few are grown in our gardens but only as ornamentals (giant bellflower and alpine sow-thistle); one is normally cultivated for its seed, but few are aware that it doubles as a vegetable (caraway); two were introduced from abroad probably originally as vegetables, and only relic and naturalised populations are found today (rocambole and victory onion); one, Welsh onion, has long been cultivated both as food and on traditional turf roofs as a succulent edible fire-proofing; one was introduced into gardens as a curiosity and vegetable (*Allium* x *proliferum*); others are considered by most people as garden weeds although originally introduced as vegetables (ground elder); one is a native, unknown as an edible in Norway, but is now actually being commercialised abroad (sea aster); and finally we have plants from the wild flora not so far domesticated, but with a potential (e.g. alpine bistort).

Norwegians ate surprisingly few greens in the past. Particularly in the countryside, vegetable food was not very important. It seems that people in some areas had to be almost starving before vegetables became an important part of the diet and then the most important wild (perennial) species used were *Campanula latifolia*, *Cicerbita alpina*, *Rumex acetosa*, *Rumex longifolius* and *Angelica archangelica*.

The Sámi people (also known as Laplanders) inhabit northern and highland Norway, Finland and Sweden and the Kola Peninsula in northwest Russia. As most other Arctic peoples, they did eat quantities of wild-collected (mainly) perennial vegetables (Eidlitz, 1969). Several of the plants were also definitely or probably cultivated during the Viking era. The Vikings cultivated the country's first known vegetable gardens, fenced off from farm animals.

During the Second World War, when the Germans occupied Norway, the government published literature, educating people to utilise the wild edible resources. The comprehensive book by Professor Jens Holmboe from 1941 literally translates as 'free food from wild plants'. It became an important reference when interest for wild food became popular again in the 1970s. Ove Arbo Høeg, Professor of Botany at the University of Oslo, spent 45 years gathering ethnobotanical information around the country, mainly through interviewing people. This culminated in Norway's most important ethnobotanical work, the 750 page long *Planter og Tradisjon* (*Plants and Tradition*) from 1976. From about the same time, the Norwegian Useful Plants Society (see box to the right) began organising spring wild edible foraging excursions. This was instrumental in increasing the popularity of foraging. I believe that the relative popularity of wild edibles in Norway has prepared people for the concept of perennial vegetables, now being championed by the young Norwegian Permaculture Society (Norsk Permakulturforening).

Nyttevekstforeningen – The Norwegian Useful Plants Society

(Now Norges sopp- og nyttevekstforbund, Norway's fungi and useful plants society)

I know of no other country with a society dedicated to useful wild plants. The society was founded over 100 years ago in 1902. It was known initially as the National Society for the Exploitation of our Useful Plants. The main objectives were initially two-fold. First, to encourage the cultivation of the many plant products that were at that time being imported to Norway. Secondly, to help poor people to help themselves through education on wild useful plants. By the 1930s, crops which were actively promoted were flax, hemp, willow (for basketmaking), caraway, hops, nut trees, herbs, various berries, Timothy grass and clover. During the Second World War, the society's work and information material were very important in raising the awareness of the people to the importance of wild food resources. The increased interest in green values in the 1970s led to increased membership numbers and many courses and projects started up. People's interest in wild edibles and medicinals also increased and one course in particular, Food of Spring Wild Plants, was a success.

Website, in Norwegian: www.soppognyttevekster.no

Angelica archangelica ssp. *archangelica* var. *maiorum*

FAMILY: Apiaceae
ENGLISH: Voss Angelica, Norwegian Angelica (US)
FAROESE: *Hvonn*
FINNISH: *Väinönputki*
FRENCH: *L'Angélique Vraie, L'Archangélique*
GERMAN: *Arznei-Engelwurz*
ICELANDIC: *Hvönn*
NORWEGIAN: *Vossakvann*
RUSSIAN: *Dyagil Lekarstvennyj*
SÁMI / LAPP: *Fadnu, Faatna*
SPANISH: *Hierba del Espiritu Santo*
SWEDISH: *Kvanne*

365: Angelica archangelica at Narsarsuaq in Greenland is a monster, almost alien-looking herb compared to other plants in its natural arctic environment. On the opposite side of this ice-infested fjord is the site Brattahlid settled by Norseman Erik the Red. Perhaps Erik brought Angelica with him?

Arriving at the airport Narsarsuaq in Greenland where I was attending a conference some years ago, I was greeted along the road to the hotel by a familiar plant. It looked totally out of place, dwarfing the other vegetation, as so often umbellifers do.

It was *Angelica archangelica*, quite possibly originally introduced by the Vikings who settled this area.

Angelica is well known from herb gardens and the herbal literature. However, until recently, the unique heritage Norwegian cultivar 'Vossakvann' was almost unknown outside of Scandinavia (Fosså, 2006). Botanists described it as a variety (var. *maiorum*) of the common wild Norwegian mountain angelica (*fjellkvann*). Angelica is actually one of the oldest cultivated plants in Norway, going back to the time of the Vikings. A very hardy wild plant, it was traditionally grown on farms in the mountains, so-called *kvanngard*, or Angelica enclosures.

366: 'Vossakvann' leaf stems are more solid than the hollow stems of the wild plant.

The variety 'Vossakvann' differs from the wild plant in that its leaf stems are not hollow or are only partly so (thereby increasing its food value). The variety also tastes sweeter, characteristics that were probably selected over the years by the farmers. This variety is named after the small mountain town of Voss. By the 16th century, Angelica had become an important trading article from Norway to other parts of Europe, mainly for its medicinal uses.

At one time, almost every farm around Voss cultivated Angelica. The plants were mulched to suppress weeds with manure, ashes and/or charcoal. These traditional *kvanngard* have luckily just about survived around Voss into the 21st century. With increased focus on heritage plants in Norway over just the last few years, this special variety has now been rescued from extinction by the Norwegian Genetic Resource Centre. It has also been adopted by the *Slow Food Ark of Taste* (an international catalogue of threatened traditional food products). Angelica cultivation was replaced in some areas by two other hardy crops: redcurrant (*Ribes sativum*) and rhubarb (*Rheum* x *rhabarbarum*). Similar Angelica gardens were also earlier found in both Iceland and the Faroe Islands, but there is no surviving evidence of cultivars like 'Vossakvann' having been developed.

Angelica is a wild member of the carrot family, found mainly in damp places, and is widespread in the Norwegian mountains. Due to over-harvesting in the wild and increased grazing pressure, *kvann* has in the past been locally eradicated in Norway and has been slow to return to its former haunts. It is also found elsewhere in Scandinavia, including the Faroe Islands, Iceland and as we have seen, southern Greenland. Its range also includes Central and Eastern Europe and eastward to western Siberia. Further east, the subspecies *decurrens* takes over, ranging towards eastern Siberia and also in the Himalayas. It has naturalised in parts of the UK and other countries.

There are long traditions of Norwegians eating *kvann*, mostly wild collected. This often involved a long strenuous walk into the mountains. It was mainly the young flower stems that were harvested from wild plants, as the leaf stalks were considered to be too bitter. As Angelica only produces one flower stalk, this led to the plants dying without producing seed and populations of this plant went into serious decline and those walks became more strenuous. However, from the sweeter, milder tasting cultivated 'Vossakvann', it was rather the leaf stalks that were used and this also prolonged the life of the plants as removing leaves delayed flowering. Both leaf stalks and flower stems were prepared by first peeling the outer layer that could be a bit fibrous and stronger tasting. My experience is that the peeled flower stems are tasty and not bitter right up to the flower's opening (see the notes on page 42 on preparing stronger tasting herbs).

The most common use of garden Angelica nowadays is candied, in ice cream and cakes. Most of the angelica grown for this purpose is cultivated in the Marais-Poitevin wetland area to the west of the French town Niort. This is a tradition going back a couple of hundred years. Angelica is sometimes known as French rhubarb in the US.

I grew up being force-fed cod liver oil, and it's difficult for me conceiving anything with this in it as a delicacy. However, in coastal areas of Norway, *kvann* stems were dipped raw in the stuff as, just that, a delicacy (this would also have disguised the strong taste of the herb although it is debatable which is the worse evil!).

Another exotic but rather advanced dish one could try comes from Lapland. Two of the Sámi people's most important vegetables were *fatnu* (angelica) and *juopmu* (*Rumex acetosa*). All you need is a reindeer stomach, reindeer milk and Angelica flower umbels just before they have opened! Cut up the Angelica and cook up in the reindeer milk until porridge-like. Then hang up in the reindeer stomach to dry. The result is a kind of cheese that could be stored over the winter. Nevertheless, just eating the Angelica raw was probably the commonest way of eating it.

The Sámi actually had separate names for the first year plant, called *faatnoe*, and the second year growth with flower stalk and flowers, *batske*. Linné described *batske* as being eaten like we would eat an apple, i.e. as a delicacy. It must be harvested before the flowers open. Peel the outer layer with a knife; the inner part is fruity and tasty. The unripe seeds were not suitable for eating raw, but were cooked together with sorrel and milk (*syrebladmelk* or *jåamoemielkie*). Incidentally, seeds of another member of the carrot family, *Heracleum persicum* (see Chapter 5) are sometimes wrongly labelled as Angelica seeds. *Batske* was also divided into thin strips and

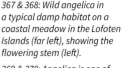

367 & 368: Wild angelica in a typical damp habitat on a coastal meadow in the Lofoten Islands (far left), showing the flowering stem (left).

369 & 370: Angelica is one of the earliest spring veggies to emerge. If one covers the plant in spring one can harvest milder tasting shoots that resemble leaf celery (below left). Faroese angelica in my garden at the end of April (below right).

dried either in the sun or over the fire. Later when sugar became available it was candied. The upper part of the leaf stalk where it divides into three was considered to be the best bit or *bestibiti* (see, Sámi isn't so difficult after all) (Fosså, 2006). The Inuit in Greenland used this plant in a similar way to the Sámi people (Moerman, 1998).

Planning a trip to Mount Everest or just trekking in Nepal? Well, you might well see *Angelica archangelica* ssp. *decurrens* on the wayside as this was found to be the second most important wild-foraged food of the Rolwaling Sherpas (Sacherer, 1979). *Gumdang* as it is known locally is eaten both raw and cooked during May and June and was eaten almost every day.

The special characteristic of 'Vossakvann' of solid stems and stalks is unfortunately not stable and only a proportion of seed propagated plants will have this property. It is therefore important to select the best plants at each generation (keep plants with leaf stalks that feel hard when you pinch them). Angelica is a large plant that under good conditions can easily reach 1-2m. It will grow well in an open sunny location, but prefers damp conditions with lots of organic matter incorporated. The plants should be about 0.5-1m apart. In the Norwegian mountains it can take 2-7 years before the plants flower, but it is shorter in the lowlands (2-3 years). The plant usually dies after flowering and it will normally self-seed. If the flowering stems are removed as they appear, it is possible to prolong its life, although this doesn't always work, so don't do this on your last plant. The seed of Angelica like its cousin parsnip, *Pastinaca sativa*, needs to be sown fresh as it quickly loses its viability.

371: View of my edimental gardens with Korean angelica, Angelica gigas *(top left), three types of* Monarda *and* Lilium lancifolium *var.* flaviflorum *(yellow tiger lily).*

For your edimental garden, you might also like to try the variegated leaved cultivar 'Corinne Tremaine', available at a few nurseries in Europe, although it's not as vigorous as the species.

Other species of Angelica have been used in similar ways in other parts of the world, e.g. Korean angelica (*Angelica gigas*) is a wonderful edimental, brightening up the garden with its dark purple stems and flowers. Seacoast angelica (*Angelica lucida*) was also used, for example, by the Eskimos in Alaska (served with seal oil). Purplestem angelica (*Angelica atropurpurea*) from eastern North America is another one worth trying. Eurasian wild angelica (*Angelica sylvestris*) is also, in my opinion, better than its reputation, particularly the immature flower umbel broccolis!

Allium oleraceum

FAMILY: Amaryllidaceae
ENGLISH: Field Garlic
FRENCH: *L'ail des Jardins, L'Ail des Champs*
GERMAN: *Kohl-Lauch, Gemüse-Lauch*
ITALIAN: *Aglio Selvatico*
NORWEGIAN: *Vill-Løk*
SWEDISH: *Backlök*

Moving on to Iceland, we unearth a 1,000-year-old onion story which starts from where I live. In the middle of the Trondheimsfjord, I can see the island Tautra in the distance from my house. The island has a long history stretching back to the time of the Vikings and is best known for the ruins of a medieval monastery. Around 2006, I heard of a special onion that grew on the island. The local people called it *geirlauk*, but they didn't know more of its identity. *Geirlauk* is an old name that the Vikings used for an onion that they grew in their vegetable gardens. It is also the origin of the word garlic (*geir* means spear and *lauk* is onion). Later, on an open day in my garden two youngsters, Lars and Jørn, turned up. It turned out that they were mostly interested in my collection of hops and herbs that could be used in brewing. Jørn's dad owns a restaurant specialising in local food located next to the monastery ruins and also works as a gardener at the rebuilt monastery herb gardens nearby.

Jørn knew about the local onion on Tautra through his dad and promised to bring me a sample. I wondered if it could be rocambole, (*Allium scorodoprasum*), an onion associated with the Vikings elsewhere in Scandinavia. This onion survives, for example, naturalised near old Viking era farms on the Swedish island Gotland in the Baltic. On Gotland, this onion has a local name, *kajp*, and a local soup, *kajpsoppa*, made from it, has had a renaissance in recent years (see box on page 217) and it is said that there are as many recipes as there are farms on Gotland.

372 & 373: From my local wild population of field garlic, Allium oleraceum, *(top) in very shallow dry soil over rock where only moss has otherwise found a foothold. In the shade of hazel woodland (bottom). Even though the individual plants are small, there are tens of thousands of plants in a relatively small area.*

I didn't have to wait long as Jørn delivered some onions the following day. I was disappointed, however, when I saw that it was field garlic (*Allium oleraceum*), a relatively common but local species along most of the Norwegian coast. I was confused as to why this species should command the respect it had on Tautra.

My story continued in Denmark later the same year when I attended a Nordic seminar called 'Plants that Tell Stories'. Just before the meeting I had been in touch with the Botanical Gardens in Reykjavik as part of a project investigating old Scandinavian onions. They had offered me, among other things, bulbils of *Allium oleraceum* collected wild at its only Icelandic locality at Bær in Borgarfjörður. At the seminar, I was chatting with a Danish researcher and he told me a remarkable story about how the Icelandic field garlic had arrived there. In old documents, it was written that it had been introduced to Iceland by an English missionary bishop who had lived in Borgarfjörður for at least 20 years in the 11th century and it had been suggested that it had managed to survive there for such a long time as the area has

374: **Allium oleraceum** *flowers and bulbils from the monastery ruins on the island of Tautra.*

375: **Allium scorodoprasum** *(sand leek or rocambole) is perhaps the onion which most resembles a spear and is therefore probably the hottest candidate as the spear onion cultivated by the Vikings.*

a local climate due to geothermic activity. There was more, however, as it was also known that the bishop in question had taken the onion from Nidaros (now called Trondheim) only 10 miles from my home! The documents also informed us that our onion was collected from an island nearby Trondheim. There are only two islands nearby and *Allium oleraceum* only grows on one of them today, Tautra! The circle was made complete a few weeks later when I received bulbils in the post from Reykjavik. I now had in my hands plants of probably the same origin, but growing isolated from one another for about 1,000 years. This story certainly seems to indicate that field garlic was more important 1,000 years ago than it is today. It also gives credence to suggestions that this was one of the onions cultivated by the Vikings and may well have been their original Geirlauk simply moved from local wild populations for easier access.

Many years before this I had picked up some bulbils in the UK and regretted later planting them in one of my beds as it quickly spread and took several years of systematic weeding to remove again. Having said that, a weed is just a plant in the wrong place and I think it could be a useful perennial onion for the shady conditions of the wilder kind of forest garden, on green roofs and edible lawns. After many years of missing it completely I discovered that I actually had a large population of field garlic only a few hundred metres from my house. It is difficult to see in the spring as it looks just like grass and doesn't smell from afar as ramsons (*Allium ursinum*) does.

In the wild, field garlic ranges through most of central and eastern Europe, parts of northern Europe, Italy and east to western Russia and the Caucasus. In the UK, it has a patchy distribution and is rare or absent in the north and west. It has been introduced in North America where it is found in a few states and has also become naturalised in Victoria in Australia. It is most often found on dry, thin calcareous soils in both sunny and shady locations.

Kajp Soup from Gotland

400ml green *kajp* onions (or other
  green onions such as field garlic)
1tbsp butter
1 small bulb onion
100ml finely grated carrot
2 medium mealy potatoes
1 litre water and vegetable stock or
  miso
150ml cream

Fry the onions in butter in a saucepan
in the butter until soft. Grate the
carrot, slice the potatoes and add to
the pan. Add water and stock. Cook
until the potatoes are soft. Mix with a
hand blender, adding cream, salt and
pepper.

376: *Norwegian botanist Per Arvid Åsen at the* Allium oleraceum *site on Iceland at Bær,
June 2011. (courtesy of Per Arvid Åsen)*

In Norway, Høeg (1976) found that field garlic leaves and bulbs were eaten in the
past by children in the springtime and were also sometimes used in the kitchen.
In Kvæfjord, in northern Norway, it was used like chives in fish soups. It was also
sometimes planted in home gardens. In Sweden, Nyman (1868) says that it was used
in country areas, the young shoots being gathered in spring and added to kale. The
German common name *kohl-lauch* just means cabbage onion. In the UK, it has also
been used for food in the past (Johnson, 1862).

The field garlic can owe its success and sometimes invasive nature to the fact that
rather than setting seed, it sets masses of small bulbils. These fall to the soil and
each one can quickly sprout into a new plant. I use the leaves in all kinds of cooking
and salads as mild garlic. Along with many other Alliums, leaves will often sprout in
the autumn and in mild winters can be harvested most of the winter. These winter
shoots are hardy enough to stand very low winter temperatures.

The reader should be aware that there are a number of other Alliums that produce
small bulbils in Europe. *Allium vineale* (crow garlic) is, for example, more common
than *Allium oleraceum* in the UK; *Allium carinatum* (keeled garlic), some large garden
forms of this species lacking bulbils are worth growing as edimentals (e.g. var.
pulchellum and *pulchellum* var. *album*); *Allium paradoxum* (few-flowered leek) and
the aforementioned *Allium scorodoprasum*.

In North America, several of these bulbiliferous species have naturalised and the
native *Allium canadense* is another widespread bulbil producing species. As long as
you are sure that it's an Allium you have in front of you then it's safe to eat (N.B. there
are poisonous wild Allium look-alikes, but not smell-a-likes in North America).

Allium victorialis

FAMILY: Amaryllidaceae
ENGLISH: Alpine Leek, Victory Onion, Korean
  Long-rooted Garlic
GERMAN: *Allermannsharnisch, Siegwurz-Lauch*
ITALIAN: *Aglio Serpentino*
JAPANESE: *Gyoja-Ninniku, Kitopiro*
KOREAN: *Sanmanul, Makino*
NORWEGIAN: *Alpeløk, Seiersløk*
RUSSIAN: *Luk Cheremsha, Luk Pobednyi*

Arriving in northern Norway in the Lofoten Islands, we find another onion associated with the Vikings. It is strange that victory onion is seldom mentioned in the gardening literature in the West. It is in my opinion one of the best, both as an edible and an ornamental. Like ramsons (*Allium ursinum*), this is a broad-leaved onion, but an altogether larger plant.

My interest in this species was aroused when I received an interesting email from a Dane called Søren Holt, who found seed of this species on my Internet trading list around 2002. He wrote:

'I'd really love to have Allium victorialis in my garden. From this species they make a fantastic delicacy in Siberia. The leaves are clipped and pressed in brine. They ferment and develop a fantastic aroma. It's eaten with sour cream. I've had it served when visiting my family there, and I must agree with them that it's a delicacy on a level with caviar. Now and again we've brought a glass back with us to Denmark. Unfortunately, there's a serious tick-borne disease which has become common in the woods of the Irkutsk area where they live. They call both the onion species itself and the lactofermented product Tjeremsha (or Cheremsha). I'm dreaming of growing and making Tjeremsha myself, so that we can enjoy this delicacy on special occasions. Tjeremsha is served as a side dish with many Russian dishes, e.g. Pelmeni (meat dumplings similar to ravioli), or simply as a starter with masses of crème fraîche.'

Søren's *Tjeremsha* recipe

Chop leaves and stalks, weigh them and add 2-3% salt by weight. Crush the leaves and salt until juices appear. Put into a Kilner jar or similar making sure the rubber seal is in good condition (it needs to be airtight). Press down so that no air remains and top up with water so that the juice covers the leaves. Put the lid on loosely in a warm place at 16-22°C. It should start to bubble. After 2-3 days when the juice ceases to run over the edge, put the lid on properly. After 1-2 weeks, keep the jars in a cool dark place or fridge for another three weeks or so. The finished *Tjeremsha* smells very strong. However, mixed with crème fraîche it tastes fantastic. This is a very healthy dish in part due to the lactic acid bacteria in the finished product. Ramsons (*Allium ursinum*) and, in North America, Ramps (*Allium tricoccum*) can also be used.

On a visit to Søren Holt in Copenhagen in 2008, he was kind enough to prepare a Tjeremsha and caviar starter for me.

377 (top left): Victory onion has beautiful shoots in the early spring; here in the author's garden in mid-April when the soil is still frozen about 10cm below.

378 (top right): Victory onion in a graveyard in the Lofoten Islands.

379 (above): Victory onion ornamental allées are a common sight on the island Vestvågøy in the Lofoten Islands, but people are often not aware that they are edimental allées.

380 (right): Judith and Christoph gathering victory onion shoots in the Lofoten Islands for their locally produced pesto; there couldn't be a more beautiful work place!

Allium victorialis ranges in the wild over a large area from the mountains of southwest Europe, the Carpathian Mountains, the Caucasus, Siberia, Japan and is even found in Alaska on Attu Island in the far west of the Aleutian Islands. In the north and west of its range it is found west to the Kola Peninsula in northern Russia on the edge of the Barents Sea. Whilst in Europe it is a plant mostly growing in alpine habitats, it is also a woodland plant in the east of its range in Siberia and Japan. It prefers damp conditions in spring as do ramsons (*Allium ursinum*).

Norwegian ethnobotanist Brynhild Mørkved, from the Arctic-alpine Botanical Garden in Tromsø, had on a visit to the Lofoten Islands in the 1970s, found naturalised *Allium victorialis* in a graveyard on the second largest island, Vestvågøy. It was subsequently discovered in many gardens on the island. It had also naturalised in a big way in several places, but almost exclusively on this one island. Interviews with old folk revealed that this plant had been there at least before 1920. A few people used the spring leaves in salads, but most people were not even aware that it was edible or even that it was an onion. It was mainly encouraged as an attractive ornamental as I found when I visited the area in 2009. It can be seen in many gardens planted along driveways.

Judith van Koesveld is Dutch and has started up production of a specialist pesto made from locally harvested victory onion. She also has a small nursery from which she sells victory onion plants. My visit in early June 2009 coincided with Judith and partner Christoph's harvesting day on the west side of the island, where they had been given permission to collect leaves from a large naturalised population. It was impressive to see how well this onion has adapted to its new environment.

Scientists in Tromsø are currently using genetic fingerprinting to hopefully find the wild origin of the Lofoten onions. The hottest theory is that they are in fact relics originating from plants that the Vikings originally introduced and grew in the area. It seems too much of a coincidence that this onion is commonest in the area around the Lofotr Viking Museum at Borg, which has been built on the site of an important Viking settlement. I like to think that the Vikings brought this onion back from as far away as the Caucasus, where it is still cultivated in vegetable gardens. We should maybe change its name from victory to Viking onion.

381: **Allium victorialis** *has naturalised at one location in southwest Norway, at Granvin in Hardanger. It has probably originally escaped from a nearby garden and has found its niche on a small wooded island in the river.*

382-384: From harvest to victory pesto. Ingredients: Victory onion, pine nuts or sunflower seeds, parmesan cheese or other strong-tasting cheese, olive oil and basil (optional).

Elsewhere over its range, in Mongolia, where it is known as *haliyar*, Khasbagan et al (2000) report the leaves being used by Mongol herdsmen. In Manchuria, which is in the far northeast of China the leaves are also eaten (Baranov, 1967).

In Japan, *Allium victorialis* (*gyoja-ninniku*) is also an important wild collected vegetable, and is cultivated in gardens. Some selection of better cultivars and work on best cultivation practices is ongoing in response to increasing demand and commercial field grown production has started. It is the local wide-leaved subspecies *platyphyllum* that is being studied. This is apparently the most important edible plant of the Ainu people who are indigenous to Hokkaido, the Kuril Islands and Sakhalin. The leaves are today sold in supermarkets throughout Hokkaido. The first Ainu restaurant was opened in 2003 in Sapporo and *gyoja-ninniku* is, of course, on the menu.

385: Allium victorialis. *The creamy-white flowers brighten up the edible garden in season.*

As long as the soil is damp in spring this plant will tolerate anything from full sun to shady conditions. As a result of its cultural history in Norway and press and internet coverage, *Allium victorialis* is now available from several nurseries in Norway. It is also available from a few nurseries elsewhere in Europe. As it takes several years from seed to harvest, it is best to purchase plants or perhaps both seed and plants. The seeds should preferably be sown fresh as they germinate normally in autumn, overwintering as an embryo. If not sown at the ideal time, they may hop over a year before germinating and emerge the following spring. Mature plants are easy to divide. A couple of cultivars are also available. 'Kemorovo' is small with red bases to the flower stalks and 'Cantabria' is a larger upright form. In North America, it is rarely offered, but is sometimes seen in the seed list of the North American Rock Garden Society (NARGS).

Rumex acetosa

FAMILY: Polygonaceae
CHINESE: *Suan Mo*
ENGLISH: Sorrel, Common Sorrel, Garden Sorrel
FINNISH: *Niittysuolaheinä*
FRENCH: *Oseille Sauvage*
GERMAN: *Auerampfer*
ICELANDIC: *Túnsúra*
ITALIAN: *Acetosa*, *Erba Brusca*
JAPANESE: *Suiba*
NEPALESE: *Hali*
NORWEGIAN: *Matsyre, Engsyre*
RUSSIAN: *Shchavel Obyknovennyi*
SWEDISH: *Ängssyra*
TIBETAN: *Sho-Mang-Ri-Sho*

In Scandinavia, common sorrel (*Rumex acetosa*) was one of the most important vegetables used by the Sámi people. Being the only vegetables eaten during the long, cold, dark winter, these greens were also very important preventive medicine against scurvy.

Famous Swedish botanist, Carl Linnaeus (Carl von Linné), travelled in Swedish Lapland in 1732 and recorded the use of plants. Sorrel was the most important plant used alongside mountain sorrel (*Oxyria digyna*), alpine sow-thistle (*Cicerbita alpina*) and Angelica. Rosebay willowherb (*Epilobium angustifolium*) and lady's mantle (*Alchemilla* spp.) were also sometimes used. They were first cooked in water to a pulp-like mass that was drained and then fermented in milk. This coagulated into a kind of thick green yogurt called *g* . It could be stored in this form in a reindeer stomach right through to the following spring in a cool place like a cold river spring (Dunfjeld, 2011).

It's very interesting that an abundance of sorrel was found in places where the reindeer had been gathered (*reingjerder,* literally reindeer compounds) as these areas were heavily fertilised. People would return to these abandoned sites to gather the sorrel, a kind of primitive gardening. Johansson (1947), writing about the Sámi people in Frostviken in Sweden, tells us that they '...had the same importance to the Sámi as the grain or potato field had for the farmers'.

Rumex acetosa is found throughout Europe, even in alpine habitats up to 2,100m in the Alps and 1,900m in Norway. It ranges eastwards as far as Japan and is also found in the Himalayas and mountains of China. It has also naturalised in North America, New Zealand and Australia. It grows in open woodlands and meadows. In Norway, a subspecies *Rumex acetosa* ssp. *lapponicus*, Lapland sorrel, has broader leaves and is also a larger, more productive plant.

You will probably already have a relationship to sorrel. Throughout much of this plant's extensive range, this is probably the most widely foraged plant, along with nettles (*Urtica* spp.). In particular, sorrel is widely eaten by children raw. In the UK, Mabey (1997) states, 'sorrel leaves are still nibbled by children across Britain'. Here in Norway, it has traditionally been at the top of the list of children's favourite wild plants, the thirst-quenching refreshingly sour taste being appealing to the juvenile palate. The leaves and young flower stems are the parts eaten. Isn't it strange then that supermarkets, at least in the UK and Norway, rarely sell the stuff? You would have thought that a vegetable that children naturally like the taste of would be very popular with parents. Sheep sorrel (*Rumex acetosella*), mountain sorrel (*Oxyria digyna*) and its namesake wood sorrel (*Oxalis acetosella*) were also used in a similar way.

Wild and cultivated sorrels have been used in numerous dishes including the following: mixed salads; egg dishes including omelettes and quiches; sorrel soup, often served with hard-boiled egg in the Baltic countries and Eastern Europe; in the Polish *zupa szczawiowa* (with flour, cream, eggs, buckwheat or potatoes); cooked as a traditional Norwegian thick soup with flour and in the French *soupe aux herbes*; in stews (particularly French fricassée and ragouts); used in the Middle Ages in Pease (pea) porridge (it is also a good accompaniment to other pulses such as lentils); it goes well with fish, often used in stuffed fish recipes including the old English greensauce which is sorrel ground to a paste with vinegar; the Sámi people in Scandinavia would also cook fish (e.g. trout) with sorrel stems; sorrel was also one of the ingredients in traditional Italian spring ritualistic dishes such as *minestrella* (wild herb soup in the Garfagnana) and in *pistic*, a mix of up to 56 wild plants cooked and sautéed together

386 (left): Spring shoots of **Rumex acetosa** ssp. lapponicus in my garden ready to harvest. This sub-species is found in the Norwegian mountains and has broader more useful leaves than lowland plants.

387 (below left): Common sorrel, Rumex acetosa ssp. acetosa, in early spring growing wild in lowland Norway.

388 (below right): True French sorrel in my garden. This plant is over 25 years old and has never flowered and can therefore only be propagated vegetatively.

(see Chapter 2); in Palestine, it is also wild gathered and used as a filling in *sambosek*, a traditional pie (Ali-Shtayeh, M.S. et al., 2008). It has also been used sweetened in the same way as rhubarb. In Kashmir, *kakutari* was used as an acid vegetable (Lawrence, 1884) and leaves of other *Rumex* species were dried for winter use.

Young leaves of both *Rumex longifolius* (northern dock) and *Rumex crispus* (curled dock) have also been used in Norway, particularly in famine years. A number of other species associated with the Mediterranean countries, including *Rumex scutatus*, were discussed in Chapter 2.

Sorrel has long been cultivated in gardens as a vegetable, at least from the Middle Ages. There are today a number of cultivars offered as seed or plants. The most useful are the large-leaved true French sorrels. These are non-flowering selections of *Rumex acetosa* ssp. *ambiguus*. I've grown one of these for over 25 years and it still produces every year. William Woys Weaver writes in his excellent little book *100 Vegetables and Where They Came From* (2000), that the variety 'Profusion' was sent by a French customer to Richters Herbs in the late 1980s. 'Prolific' and 'Abundance' are

389: Spring salad greens collected from my garden on 8th May, a mix of annuals and perennials: Claytonia perfoliata, *pak choi, mustard greens 'Giant Red', 'Ragged Jack' kale,* Allium ramosum, Mentha *spp., red garden orach (*Atriplex hortensis rubra*), rocket, sorrel non-flowering (centre), Purple mitsuba (*Cryptotaenia japonica atropurpurea*), chives (*Allium schoenoprasum*) and wild dandelion (*Taraxacum *spp.*).*

other cultivar names that are sometimes seen, but I have no experience with them, but I do grow at least two forms and they are not the same. Unlike wild sorrel plants, which once they have bolted are less useful, one can continue harvesting from French sorrel throughout the summer. Other cultivars of note are 'Blonde de Lyon', its leaves adding a splash of acid yellow to spring salads, and, more as a curiosity, the variegated form 'Saucy', with irregular splashes of white on the leaves.

390: Rumex acetosa *'Blonde de Lyon' has attractive yellow-green leaves in springtime.*

There are also a number of other cultivars that I've yet to find, including 'Belleville', a productive French form, 'Nobel', with more succulent leaves and there is also a low oxalic acid cultivar developed in Holland. Wine sorrel (ssp. *vinealis*) has beautiful deep red leaves

Common sorrel is easy to source from garden centres and seed companies in most parts of the world. Seed can be either spring or autumn sown. Plants are best divided during winter or early spring.

Oxyria digyna

FAMILY: Polygonaceae
ENGLISH: Mountain Sorrel
FINNISH: *Hapro*
FRENCH: *Oxyrie de Montagne*
GERMAN: *Alpen-Säuerling*
ICELANDIC: *Ólafssúra*
NEPALESE: *Banbare*
NORWEGIAN: *Fjellsyre*
SÁMI / LAPP: *Juopmu*
SWEDISH: *Fjällsyra*
TIBETAN: *Kyurba*
....

Ever thought of constructing an edible rock garden? I could argue that my whole garden is actually a rock garden as the soil is thin more or less everywhere (10-20cm) over bedrock and the old name of my house is Bergstua which translates as cottage on the rock. I have constructed a rock garden. This is basically a large pile of sand with rocks randomly decorating it. Here I've planted mostly low growing edibles from the mountains of the world. One of them is mountain sorrel. This plant is a common trail snack that my kids also loved to nibble on when walking in the mountains.

Mountain sorrel is a widespread mountain plant throughout much of the northern hemisphere, occurring also at lower elevations and even at sea level on coasts in the far north and west (Ireland, Scotland, Norway and on the Norwegian Arctic islands). It is found in damp places throughout, along rivers and associated with seabird cliffs in the lowlands.

It is quite an attractive plant with its kidney-shaped leaves. Like its close relative common sorrel, it has pleasant tasting slightly sour leaves, which are excellent in mixed salads. Local peoples throughout its range, including the high Arctic Inuit people, have prized it. They would eat it traditionally raw or cooked in seal oil; in Greenland it was used like stewed rhubarb, sweetened and with a little potato flour to thicken. Alternatively, it was lactofermented with, for example, dandelion, roseroot (*Rhodiola rosea*) and black crowberry (*Empetrum nigrum*). The Sámi people in Scandinavia also ate it raw or cooked it with other greens in reindeer milk. Native Americans in the Rocky Mountains used it in salads and preserved this and other plants by fermentation. It is also found in the Sierra Nevada in California, known there as backpacker's salad, and is also frequently found around old mining camps. It was even used as far away as Sikkim and Nepal.

*391: Mountain sorrel (*Oxyria digyna*) in my garden produces a useful amount of leaf in the early spring.*

Unless you are near to a wild population, it is not easy to get hold of seed or plants (currently only one nursery is selling plants in the UK). The best bet otherwise is one of the rock gardening clubs such as NARGS, SRGC or the AGS[*] who frequently offer seed on their seed lists. Sow the seed and cold stratify outside and it will germinate in the spring. It grows well on dampish sand in my garden. Unless you want a lot of seedlings, it is best to remove the flowering shoots before the seed is ripe.

Allium schoenoprasum ssp. *sibiricum*

FAMILY: Amaryllidaceae
ENGLISH: Giant Chives, Siberian Chives
NORWEGIAN: *Sibirgressløk*
SWEDISH: *Jättegräslök*

Most people picking up this book will be familiar with chives, possibly the most commonly grown perennial vegetable. Here in Norway, garden chives (*Allium schoenoprasum* ssp. *schoenoprasum*) are still common in gardens and it is often also found naturalised in and around old gardens. In the very far north of Norway, from the Lofoten Islands northwards, large populations of giant chives, similar in appearance to the common chives of gardens but larger, can be found growing wild in coastal meadows. In fact, in some places this can be the dominant plant, and a fantastic sight in mid-summer when it is in flower, particularly with the midnight sun illuminating it. Although earlier reckoned to be a separate species, it is now considered to be a subspecies, *Allium schoenoprasum* ssp. *sibiricum*. Apart from its larger stature, it also has thicker and broader leaves and, although normally up to 60cm high in the wild, it can reach 1m when nurtured in a garden. The flower petals are also larger at about 1.5cm, against 0.5-1cm for standard chives.

Although Norwegian botanists separate giant and common chives into two distinct subspecies which grow in different geographical areas, differences are less clear-cut elsewhere in the plant's extensive range which encompasses Siberia, Mongolia, Japan, China and North America.

Leaves of giant chives were wild-gathered and also planted in home gardens in northern Norway. It was particularly used with fish, including fish stews, fishcakes and fish ball soup. The leaves were also preserved in brine for winter use in wooden barrels. Giant chives can otherwise be used in salads, egg dishes, etc. At least one company in the north of Norway markets a salad oil flavoured by this plant (*sibirgressløk olje*). In Siberia, it is a widespread species of the tundra and alpine areas and is eaten fresh and preserved by lactofermentation. Moerman (1998) documents this plant as having been used by several Native American tribes, both fresh and salted for winter use. The Eskimos in Alaska used this plant traditionally with fish and seal meat.

[*] NARGS: North American Rock Garden Society. SRGC: Scottish Rock Garden Club. AGS: Alpine Garden Society.

392 (top left): A diversity of chives from my garden.

393 (bottom left): A good clump of the emerging flowers of giant chives in Gothenburg Botanical Garden, Sweden.

394 (above): Giant chives and victory onion planted in the reconstructed Viking onion garden at the Borg Viking Museum in the Lofoten Islands.

Giant chives are not often seen in gardens in Europe, but it is available from a few nurseries and seed can also be obtained. It is possible that some of the larger forms of common chives such as cultivar 'Major' are actually Siberian chives.

Cicerbita alpina (syn. *Mulgedium alpinum*; *Lactuca alpina*)

FAMILY: Asteraceae
ENGLISH: Alpine Sow-Thistle,
  Blue Sow-thistle, Tall Blue
  Thistle
FRENCH: *Laitue des Alpes*
GERMAN: *Alpen-Milchlattich*
NORWEGIAN: *Turt*
SÁMI / LAPP: *Jarja*

Alpine sow-thistle was another very important vegetable of the Sámi people in Scandinavia. It is a very abundant plant of the Arctic areas inhabited by the Laplanders. This plant is quite bitter raw. I nevertheless decided to include it as (a) it is one of the best known wild edibles in Norway; (b) we are very different in our experience of bitterness; (c) it is perennial, very hardy and a large plant

395 (left): Alpine sow-thistle at home in northern Norway where it grows in open rich woodland, often forming extensive stands.

396 (below): The alpine sow-thistle is also a garden-worthy ornamental.

which is productive; (d) with some work, perhaps a milder variant could be selected (this would certainly be repaid by making this plant one of the best perennial edimentals, also suitable for the forest garden); (e) lactofermentation, a preservation technique showing a revival at the moment, would make for a milder product; (f) finally, even if you do find the taste too strong, it is a very attractive garden-worthy ornamental.

Cicerbita alpina is found in the wild both in Scandinavia, mainly in the north and west, and also in the Alps. In the UK, it only remains in four sites in Scotland on mountain ledges free from grazing pressure and it is a protected species. It is a tall perennial that can reach 2m under favourable conditions and has non-invasive creeping rhizomes. After some years it can form large clumps, often forming large old growth stands in the wild. The leaves are dandelion-like and have a large triangular terminal leaflet. In summer a tall flowering spike is produced, bedecked with numerous blue flowers. This can remind one of chicory (*Cichorium intybus*), to which it is closely related. It is mainly found in the wild in moist, fertile, humus-rich and open woodlands often growing with other tall herbs.

Apart from the traditional use of this plant as a fermented vegetable with reindeer milk, the flower stems were also peeled and eaten raw, the core being less bitter. In fact, I find the peeled stems to have a very pleasant taste. There are also many accounts of Norwegians eating this plant (Høeg, 1976). Both the young shoots in the spring and the stem were consumed. Most note, however, that the stems are either peeled or divided in two lengthways and the pith scraped out. Children in particular seemed to have liked this plant, referring to it as wild rhubarb and for many it was clearly a delicacy. It is also noted that the plants are not as strong tasting at flowering time, similar to several other plants in the Aster family covered by this book. Some also left the stems to wilt before eating, this also apparently reducing the bitterness.

There are however also people who did find it too bitter and amongst them was the famous Swedish botanist Carl Linnaeus who named the plant *Sonchus alpinus* and considered it inedible. In 1762, the Norwegian botanical priest Hans Strøm wrote that farmers would chew on *turt* stems in church in order not to fall asleep during the service!

I prefer to blanch this plant by covering with a large bucket or a heap of leaves[*] in early spring before the shoots appear and this makes for an excellent spring vegetable. Later on, I use the peeled flower shoots and flowers in summer salads.

There are currently a few suppliers of this plant in the UK. Seed is not readily available and my one clone does not produce seed. B and T World Seeds is probably your best bet at present.

Campanula latifolia

FAMILY: Campanulaceae
ENGLISH: Giant Bellflower
GERMAN: *Breitblättrige Glockenblume*
NORWEGIAN: *Storklokke*
SWEDISH: *Hässleklocka*

When I first moved to my present garden, there was one weed that I struggled to eradicate from my cultivated beds, *Campanula latifolia* or giant bellflower. The roots in particular were almost impossible to dig out, having a knack of germinating in the most difficult places. Then, one day I was reading the Norwegian book *Free Food from Wild Plants* (Holmboe, 1941). I learnt that my worst weed had been wild-gathered for food by farmers in my area in the 17th century, a tradition which probably died out soon afterwards. The leaves and stems were collected in springtime and made into a soup. Similar stories have also survived from other parts of Norway and Sweden. *Storklokke* (literally large bell) is considered to be one of the most commonly used wild food plants in the past in Norway. Both the leaves and roots were used, the latter also ground and added to bread. Since this revelation, I've treated it with more respect and nowadays use it regularly in all sorts of cooked dishes and salads in the springtime.

This bellflower is quite a common herb in my area, found in the wild in open rich woodlands, where it can in places be the dominant plant. It is also commonly seen in open areas on roadsides, railway embankments as well as in gardens, often escaped as it was used as an ornamental in the past. Its wild range is from the Alps in the

---

[*] It is best to use dry leaves so that the shoots aren't dirtied as they grow through the mulch and I put hessian over the leaves to keep them from blowing away.

south and west to the Caucasus as well as northern Britain, southern Sweden and the lowlands in North Norway to the Lofoten Islands.

If growing in favourable conditions, giant bellflower can reach 2m. In mid-summer, the plants are covered with tubular bell-shaped edible flowers in leafy spikes. Both purple to blue and white flowered plants are often seen growing side-by-side in nature. It is not surprising that such an attractive plant should have been moved as an ornamental into gardens. There are currently at least 12 cultivars available in the UK. This includes the smaller hairier and perhaps even more showy subspecies *macrantha* that hails from the Caucasus.

The taste of the raw leaves is mild and slightly sweet. The roots are a good size and have a good flavour. One year, I accidentally blanched some leaves. Not only were the blanched bellflower leaves attractive in a spring salad, but the blanching had also sweetened them further.

397: Giant bellflower is one of the best and most productive garden edimentals, here in purple and white as commonly seen in wild populations.

This species was also a favourite of the Sámi people but only in the south as the plant isn't found in the far north. Dunfjeld (2011) believes that *kåle* or *kåle-kræsie* as it's known in Sámi language, found at isolated inland sites, had been introduced by the Sámi for food. As late as the mid-1900s, this plant was still being used both as cabbage and carrots.

There are a number of other large edible perennial *Campanula* and closely related *Adenophora* (Lady Bells) species (see Chapter 4), most of the latter from Asia. Campanula-fan Ken Fern lists a number of his personal favourites in his book *Plants For A Future*, but strangely not giant bellflower. Another good one is the nettle-leaved bellflower, *Campanula trachelium* (see Chapter 2), found in similar habitats to *C. latifolia* in southern Britain. This species is one of many wild plants used traditionally in Italian ritualistic spring dishes, such as *pistic*, and elsewhere, such as Turkey (see Chapter 2).

398: The roots of the giant bellflower are of a reasonable size (much bigger in my garden than biennial rampion, Campanula rapunculus, earlier cultivated as a root vegetable) and are sweet and crisp and are excellent eaten raw or cooked.

399 (above): Giant bellflower can dominate the ground layer in open rich woodland as here in a local nature reserve in Norway. It is therefore an excellent candidate for the forest garden.

400 (right): Blanched giant bellflower leaves are both an attractive addition to spring salads and are also sweeter.

401: I use giant bellflower leaves in a wide range of dishes, including the Spanish/Portuguese dish Bacalao, made with Norwegian dried/salted cod. The ingredients in this bellflower Bacalao are: Dry salted cod soaked for two days, Jerusalem artichokes, potatoes, bellflower and prairie onion, Allium cernuum.

Aegopodium podograria

FAMILY: Apiaceae
ENGLISH: Ground Elder, Bishop's Weed, Goutweed
FRENCH: *L'Égopode Podagraire, Herbe aux Goutteux*
GERMAN: *Giersch*
ITALIAN: *Girardina Silvestre*
NORWEGIAN: *Skvallerkål*
RUSSIAN: *Snyt Obyknovennaja*

When I started cultivating my garden, ground elder was absolutely everywhere. Ten years after I stop cultivating my garden, it will once again have spread everywhere with its underground rhizomes. In the meantime I have systematically removed this plant from all my cultivated beds, without giving any support to Monsanto, by a mixture of eating it, burying it alive by the age-old technique of bastard digging and suffocating it by mulching with newspaper for a year. Bastard digging is a wonderful technique whereby the top spit (or length of your spade) of soil ends up upside down two spits down. Although it is probably the most invasive widespread introduced plant in gardens in Europe it really isn't difficult to control if you tame it in a systematic way and have plenty of patience.

Nevertheless, I wouldn't do without it as a vegetable and I use it frequently in spring over a 6-8 week period when the fresh young growth is available. I also use it later in the summer where it regenerates after I scythe the areas where it still grows in my forest garden. However, you must be absolutely sure that it is ground elder that you are picking as there are some poisonous look-alikes. I've decided that the persecution of *Aegopodium podograria* has now gone far enough and have formed the Friends of the Ground Elder support group (Facebook) campaigning to stop the chemical warfare and show this wonderful plant in a new light.

> ## Danish *skærtorsdagssuppen* / *kål* (Maundy Thursday Soup / Greens)
>
> This soup was eaten at Easter and should ensure one's good health for the following year. It was important that there should be seven vegetables in this dish, but unless you are superstitious, don't feel that it has to be as few as seven!
>
> 400g kale
> 100g white cabbage
> 100g of the following vegetables: leek, chervil, caraway, sorrel, dandelion, nettles and ground elder
> 125g fine pearl barley
> 1kg potatoes

Ground elder is actually one of eight species in the genus *Aegopodium* and by far the best known. It is widely introduced outside of its wild range making the true boundaries difficult to be sure of. However, it inhabits Eurasian continental open deciduous forests including parts of Europe, the Caucasus, western Russia, and southwest Siberia (including Novosibirsk and the Altai Krai). It is doubtful whether it was ever a native in northwest Europe. In North America it has been widely introduced and is mainly found in the north and east, including the Pacific Northwest.

It is often stated that ground elder was introduced to Britain by the Romans and otherwise spread to northern Europe by monks in the Middle Ages, who cultivated it as a medicinal and possibly edible plant. The Romans spread ground elder in Britain (Campbell and Hall, 2006), but it was certainly already in Scandinavia when the monks started cultivating it. In fact, archaeologists in Denmark have found it at pre-Roman and Viking sites (Sørensen, 1994).

Ground elder comes into its own when mixed with other spring vegetables giving a subtle celery-like taste to mixed salads, stir-fries, curries, omelettes, quiches etc. I don't have any fixed recipes, I just improvise. I've even used it in a mixed vegetarian pizza. Use the young leaves and stems whilst still shiny. Members of our local branch of the Norwegian Useful Plants Society have regularly in the past made ground elder soup for members of the public, popular at outdoor events. I particularly liked a recipe for a pie called Gardener's Revenge on an Estonian forager's blog. Danish cook Claus Meyer has used ground elder on his TV cooking series, resurrecting an old tradition as Paulli documents in 1648 that it was common in Denmark, eaten in the springtime. In Denmark's major ethnobotanical work, *Brøndegaard* (1978-80), *skvalderkål* is one of seven different greens used in a once common health-bringing springtime dish, *skærtorsdagssuppen* (see box on page 232).

This dish is related to the northern England dish Dock Pudding, which has very similar ingredients (see the end of this chapter). Sørensen (1994) also gives a reference to ground elder being added to cabbage in the springtime in the early 20th century, giving the cabbage a more interesting taste.

In its wild range in western Siberia, Edible Wild Plants of Siberia[*] informs us that ground elder was a favourite wild green of various peoples including the Bashkirs, Tatars, Chuvash and Mordovians. The leaves were used in salads, cooked like cabbage,

402: Young ground elder leaves appear in the very early spring. The fresh, glossy, lighter green leaves are best for eating raw.

403: Variegated ground elder is available from some nurseries, planted as a woodland ground cover and foliage plant. Although less aggressive than the species, it's still wise to keep an eye on it!

404: Choice spring perennial vegetables from top left and clockwise: Turkish rocket (Bunias orientalis), giant bellflower (Campanula latifolia), cabbage thistle (Cirsium oleraceum), sorrel (Rumex acetosa), garlic mustard (Alliaria petiolata), Hosta sieboldiana, stinging nettle (Urtica dioica) and ground elder (Aegopodium podograria).

in *borsch* (soup) and cooked with eggs. It was also lactofermented. Ground elder was also used in spring time in *botvinya*. This special cold soup was made from the leaves of root vegetables, often sorrel and beetroot, in addition to onion greens, dill, cucumber, horseradish, garlic, mustard and *kvass* (a drink made from lactofermentation of rye bread, sometimes sweetened in springtime with tapped birch sap). In the *Flora of the USSR* (1968, Vol 16) it is stated that all parts of the plant are suitable for making *borsch* and the young leaves are eaten as a salad green.

[*] http://sibrast.ru

Another species, mountain goutweed, *Aegopodium alpestre*, found as the name suggests at higher elevations in montane forests and alpine meadows is used in a similar way in west and central Siberia[*] and in Manchuria (Baranov, 1967). I'd be very curious to try this if I could only get my hands on seed or a plant.

A variegated, less aggressive form of ground elder is not uncommonly cultivated as a ground cover in woodland gardens. There's also a cultivar that goes by the wonderfully descriptive name 'Dangerous' (listed by two nurseries in the UK RHS Plant Finder in 2008). Try it if you dare! I haven't seen it, but it apparently has intermediate foliage between the species and variegata.

Chances are that you already have this in your garden. If you do deliberately plant ground elder on this extreme gardener's recommendation I take no responsibility for your actions.

Aster tripolium (syn. *Tripolium pannonicum*)

FAMILY: Asteraceae
DUTCH: *Lamsoor, Zeeaster, Zulte*
ENGLISH: Sea Aster
FRENCH: *L'Aster Maritime*
GERMAN: *Strand-Aster*
JAPANESE: *Ura-Giku*
NORWEGIAN: *Strandstjerne*

Some years ago, I was contacted by a journalist who worked in the local newspaper where I live. He wanted to know what I thought about the choice of the sea aster (*strandstjerne*, or beach star in Norwegian) as our municipality flower. This plant's showy pale violet daisy-like flowers brighten up the shoreline during its extended flowering period from mid-summer into autumn. It is particularly floriferous here forming an extended violet border between land and sea in summer. An excellent choice I thought. Knowing my interest in edibles, he joked, 'You'll be telling me it's edible next'. I replied that I'd read that it had been used as survival food somewhere, but I had never heard of it being used in Norway. I was right about the latter, but I was in for a surprise when I did a search for the edibility of this species that night on the internet.

First though, I checked my Norwegian books on wild food and also the bible, Stephen Facciola's comprehensive *Cornucopia II*. There was no mention in any of these books. On the online Plants For A Future database it is given only a brief mention as an edible. It states that the somewhat fleshy leaves are used to make pickles or are cooked and this seems to be taken from *Sturtevant's Edible Plants of the World* (1919), which in turn refers to a paper from 1870. Nor is this plant mentioned in Britain's major ethnobotanical work *Flora Brittanica* (Mabey, 1996), despite the plant being found along all coasts in the UK.

A quick search on the net and five minutes later I had learnt that our humble municipality flower was actually the centre of attention in a number of research projects in Europe as a potential future vegetable. More than that, field trials had

[*] http://sibrast.ru

405: Wild Aster tripolium *in its natural habitat.*

already started in Belgium, Portugal and Morocco. In the Netherlands, commercial cultivation was already underway and *Aster tripolium* was on sale as a specialty vegetable in one of the leading supermarket chains!

The reason for this research is in short that in many countries, in particular in warmer climates, salt concentrations on agricultural land have been increasing due to irrigation from groundwater sources and subsequent evaporation (salinisation). This in turn has reduced yields of conventional crops. In the Netherlands, salt is a problem for another reason, due to seawater influx in coastal areas. Researchers had been looking at alternative crops and here halophytic plants (see box above) are a good place to look. By using seawater irrigation, even barren dry lands can be greened using halophytes. In my other life, I'm an ocean wave researcher. An interesting idea is that one could potentially pump salt water on to the land using the energy in the waves or the wind to drive biosaline agriculture and using seaweed as fertiliser.

Sea aster is one of these halophytic plants, adapted to a life with high concentrations

> ## Ready-salted vegetables
>
> If you are lucky enough to live next to the sea, why not try your hand at growing halophytic (ready-salted) vegetables? Halophytes are plants which have adapted to thrive in soil with high concentrations of salt, either in wetlands inundated by seawater or in dry, inland saltpans. If you don't have your own personal saltmarsh, you could try mulching your patch with seaweed. Some better-known halophytes are sea kale (*Crambe maritima*) and sea beet (*Beta vulgaris* ssp. *maritima*), ancestor of domesticated beets (both are covered in Chapter 1) as well as glasswort or marsh samphire (*Salicornia* spp.).

406: Aster tripolium album *turned up locally near where I live in Norway.*

of salt, and thriving where the sea regularly floods. The leaves are relatively thick and succulent and the flower stems can reach up to 50cm. It belongs to the daisy family (*Asteraceae*) along with other better known vegetables such as lettuce, endive, chicory, artichoke, Jerusalem artichoke, Scorzonera, burdock and dandelion. There are in fact probably more edible species of plant in the daisy family that any other family. In a study of wild gathered plants in Spain and Portugal, Pardo-de-Santayana et al. (2007) found 92 wild edible species belonging to the daisy family, with the next largest family being the mint family represented by 52 species. In Chapter 4, another little known perennial relation of the sea aster, *Aster scaber*, from Japan was discussed. The flowers are typical for the aster family, many of which are popular ornamentals.

The wild range of sea aster covers saltmarshes, coastal meadows and pebbly seashores. It is found along most of the coasts of northern Europe, although becoming rare in the north of Norway, and south to Portugal and on the Mediterranean coasts of France, Italy and the Adriatic coasts of the Balkans. It is also found in association with inland saltpans from Europe through Asia to the Pacific where also isolated coastal populations are found in Japan and northwards.

407: Sea aster, Aster tripolium, *brightens up the coastline in summer below my house.*

This is a very hardy plant, not really surprisingly given its range and its extreme environment. It is able to withstand rapid changes in temperature as the tide ebbs and flows. Although I haven't constructed a saline bed in my garden yet, I have successfully cultivated the plant both on a sand bed and in a bucket with fresh water, both with seaweed mulch. It has a reputation for being a short-lived perennial, although the first plant I planted survived for about eight years. It is a good candidate for the coastal permaculture garden.

In a Dutch book on gourmet heirloom vegetables (Van der Muelen, 1998) there is a section on this plant. We can read that the revival in interest had started some twenty years previously. Before this time it was unknown as a vegetable apart from being foraged locally. It had been considered to be poor man's food as with other halophytes such as marsh samphire (*Salicornia*) and sea kale (*Crambe maritima*). Most local greengrocers and markets in Zeeland started selling it and it was also sold to Belgian restaurants. Because demand was in excess of supply, experiments aimed at growing *lamsoor* in areas inside the Dutch dykes started as long ago as 1991. Particularly for farmers that suffer from saline seepage onto their land, growing this plant gave new opportunities.

The plants transplant easily and can be easily divided. They are also easy to propagate by seed. Cold stratifying outside is the preferred germination method. Only one UK nursery is, however, offering it at present, so a visit to the coast may be required.

Aster tripolium exhibits a large natural genetic diversity so that the development of cultivars with desirable characteristics is possible. Varieties have already been selected in the Netherlands for increased leaf yield and resistance to fungal disease. At the moment, I am only aware of two varieties that are available in the horticultural trade, a white flowered form and a rayless variant, both of which turn up in the wild.

The young leaves can reportedly be harvested from the plants up to six times in the course of a season. From the Netherlands, it's reported that the leaves are cooked for about eight minutes without salt and then fried in butter with nutmeg. They are also used in mixed salads.

Barbarea vulgaris

FAMILY: Brassicaceae
ENGLISH: Commom Wintercress, Yellow Rocket, Garden Yellowrocket, Yellow Rocketcress
FRENCH: *La Barbarée Commune*, *Herbe de Sainte-Barbe*
GERMAN: *Echte Winterkresse*, *Barbarakraut*
ITALIAN: *L' Erba di Santa Barbara Commune*
NORWEGIAN: *Vinterkarse*

From spring to mid-summer, the colour yellow dominates on my daily cycle ride into my day job in Trondheim, starting with coltsfoot (*Tussilago farfara*) and followed in succession by dandelions (*Taraxacum*) and, finally, wintercress (*Barbarea vulgaris*). All are found growing in profusion in disturbed places such as roadside verges, wasteland as well as more natural habitats that are damp in winter. I remember being encouraged to try wintercress by Roger Phillips' description in *Wild Food* (1983): 'I find it makes a super vegetable lightly boiled'. I followed Phillips' lightly boiled recommendation, but I found that the taste was still rather bitter and it was many years later having learnt how to disguise bitter tasting greens that it became an important spring vegetable for me (see page 42).

This is a native plant of Europe and West Asia from Portugal in the west to central

408: Barbarea vulgaris growing en masse on waste land soon to be built on.

Russia and the western Himalayas in the east. It was introduced and is still spreading quickly in Scandinavia. It has otherwise been widely introduced in many areas of the world, including east and South Africa, Australasia and North America where it is a declared noxious weed in some states. Of the approximately 20 species in the genus *Barbarea*, this is the species you are most likely to encounter in the wild.

409: My favourite vegetables from wintercress are the flower buds and terminal leaves which are reminiscent of small broccoli heads.

In recent years I've learnt in particular to enjoy eating the milder flower buds and terminal leaves. Due to our hard winters, the leaves are not available in winter, often quoted by authors in milder climates to be the best time to harvest, as the taste is milder in the shorter days of winter. It takes quite a long time for the flowers to fully emerge, allowing quite a long harvest period. *Barbarea vulgaris* is a very variable species (Rich, 1987) and milder forms of the plant could no doubt be selected for a novel, attractive and nutritious crop. Although it is claimed that wintercress is either biennial or a short-lived perennial, my oldest plant is now about 20 years old. This particular plant is also sterile. It has been suggested (Lid and Lid, 2005) that these sterile individuals occur often where the common (in Norway) varieties of *B. vulgaris* var. *arcuata* and var. *vulgaris* grow side by side, so that these sterile plants are in fact hybrids. In Oregon in the US, Kallas (2010) has found wintercress to be a short-lived perennial (about three years).

410: Barbarea vulgaris variegata, the variegated form of wintercress.

Nowadays, annual cousin *Barbarea verna* (American land cress or Belle Isle cress) from southwest Europe is much more commonly grown in gardens, sometimes as a watercress substitute, and occasionally commercially. However, this hasn't always been the case. In *Sturtevant's Edible Plants of the World*, we can read that *B. vulgaris* '...has been cultivated in gardens in England for a long time as an early salad and also in Scotland, where the bitter leaves are eaten...' (Johnson, 1862). Vilmorin-Andrieux (1920) also refers to it being cultivated in English gardens, although it suggests that it was grown in the same way as land cress as a hardy annual, sown in the autumn for spring harvest.

Forager Steve Brill (1994) in New York says that the leaves are good in cold weather from late autumn to early spring, but horribly bitter at other times. The best account I have read is by John Kallas in Oregon (2010) who devotes 14 pages to this 'great springtime food'. His experience from an area with relatively cold winters is that the leaves are only slightly less bitter in early spring. He agrees that the bitters in the greens are particularly strong and leave a bitter aftertaste when eaten raw. However, he says that heat evaporates the unpleasant bitters, leaving behind superb tasting bitter flavours. In salads, he advises that the leaves should make up less than a quarter of the salad and that the leaves should also be cut up small so that the bitterness is well mixed into the other greens. You will have to try yourself, as different people perceive bitterness to different degrees, some people not sensing the bitter of wintercress at all. Kallas considers the wintercress broccolis to have the same strength as the spring leaves. Here, my experience differs, as does that of Steve Brill who, although noting the leaves to be too bitter to eat, says that the flower buds look and taste like broccoli.

In North America, various Native American tribes used different *Barbarea* species. The Cherokee used *B. vulgaris* and *B. verna* (the leaves either boiled and fried, or parboiled and seasoned with grease and salt and cooked until tender, effectively removing/disguising the bitter substances). In Alaska, another biennial/perennial species, *Barbarea orthoceras* (American yellow rocket) was used. It was cooked as a green vegetable or served in a mixed salad. In Nepal, another biennial/short-lived perennial species is used, *Barbarea intermedia* (intermediate wintercress), originally native to southern Europe, north and east Africa. The Maori of New Zealand also learned to use introduced *Barbarea* species as a vegetable, known as *toi* (Crowe, 1990).

Common wintercress is an easy plant to grow. The seeds can be sown at any time, the plants enjoying both open and somewhat shady sites, but soil shouldn't be allowed to dry out in winter. A variegated form of wintercress, 'Variegata' (aka 'Winter Cream') is relatively common in seed catalogues and is a valuable plant for your edible landscaping, coming true from seed. Impress your friends with variegated mini broccolis!

In the 19th century, a double-flowered form of wintercress was much sought after. It was known as double yellow rocket, *Barbarea vulgaris* var. *plena*. This cultivar was reliably perennial and was propagated vegetatively. I haven't managed to trace it later than 1943 (in Quebec). An article in the *American Florist* from 1910 mentions that the plant had completely died out of popularity.

Brassicas are difficult vegetables to cultivate organically without artificial barriers. It is therefore interesting that *Barbarea vulgaris* is resistant to larvae of butterflies and moths and, in my experience, is also not badly attacked by slugs. In fact, this species is planted deliberately for so-called dead-end trap cropping. Diamond back moths (a bad pest of *Brassica*, also in my garden) are attracted by the wintercress, but the larvae die, therefore decreasing the attack on the main crop. For this and other reasons, I now wouldn't be without wintercress in my garden.

Polygonum viviparum
(syn. *Persicaria vivipara* or *Bistorta vivipara*)

FAMILY: Polygonaceae

CHINESE: *Zhu Ya Quan Shen*

ENGLISH: Alpine Bistort,
Viviparous Knotweed

FINNISH: *Nurmitatar*

FRENCH: *Renouée Vivipare*

GERMAN: *Knöllchen-Knöterich*

ICELANDIC: *Kornsúra*

NEPALASE: *Khalti*

NORWEGIAN: *Harerug*

SIKKIM: *Maslun*

SWEDISH: *Ormrot*

When my kids were small they would enjoy nibbling the seeds, actually bulbils, of alpine bistort on our mountain hikes. It turns out that Norwegian children had for generations in the past enjoyed these bulbils. They would either just strip them off the flower stalks and eat them raw (they have a pleasant nutty flavour) or collect them and then eat them cooked up in milk. However, more than just a children's snack, knowledge of this plant has meant life or death to people in country areas when food was short. In the famine years from 1740-1742, it is known that the inhabitants of Oppdal, a Norwegian mountain village that is nowadays a ski resort, survived thanks to knowledge of this plant. Both the roots and bulbils are rich in carbohydrates and were either cooked in milk (called *råpesoll*) or ground into flour. The bulbil flour was also used in flatbread (see also page 253) instead of rye.

As with mountain sorrel (*Oxyria digyna*), this plant is circumpolar, including northern Britain. In Norway, it is a very common plant, particularly in the mountains and it is probably only in these highland areas that it grows in such quantities that it could sustain communities.

411 & 412: Alpine bistort is a very common plant in Norway, here in my garden (right). This plant's tubers (above) have in the past saved people from starvation, but it is the red or brown bulbils (which look like seeds in the pictures) which I find most useful in the garden.

413 (above left): The two colour morphs of Polygonum viviparum together with a so-far unidentified untested larger viviparous Polygonum species of garden origin (possibly Chinese Polygonum suffultoides).

414 (above right): The two colour phases of the bulbils are rather attractive when freshly picked (from my garden) and can either be used fresh or can be dried first, easily done on a sunny windowsill.

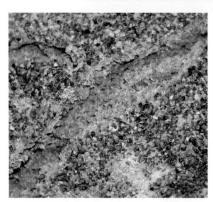

415 (left): Alpine bistort bulbils are excellent as a nutty finishing touch to baked dishes including bread.

It is not a very large plant and can be anything from 5 to 30cm tall, but almost the whole plant can be used for food. The bulbils form below the usually sterile white or pink flowers. It often has two forms growing side-by-side, with attractive reddish purple and light brown bulbils. The bulbils often develop green sprouts whilst still on the plant. Falling to the ground they can root immediately, making plants which are genetically identical to the parent. The plant produces sizeable rhizomes, in good conditions 1-2cm long, but I assume it takes several years for such monsters (relative to the size of the plant) to develop. This is true of another small plant with out-of-proportion large tubers, pignut, *Conopodium majus*.

This is a common wild plant here that I have in the past harvested from the wild, but when circumstances dictated less time to forage, I introduced it to my garden where it thrives and provides me with all I need.

Indigenous people throughout the high Arctic circumpolar region used this plant's rhizomes as a staple food. It was also considered to be a delicacy and fresh roots would be eaten as a snack as people nowadays would perhaps eat peanuts. In the

Aleutian Islands, the Unangan people used to eat the roots with dried salmon eggs. From Siberia and Alaska comes an interesting harvesting strategy. The local mice would store tubers, rhizomes and bulbs of this and other species in special caches for later use during the long hard winter. People would raid these mice stores, usually leaving a few tubers or a fish so that at least some mice would survive. Use of the bulbils raw has also been recorded in the Italian Alps (Dreon and Paoletti, 2009). Sundriyal et al (2004) have also recorded this plant being used for food in Sikkim in the Himalayas.

I mostly use the bulbils sprinkled on bread and other savoury dishes like quiche. I believe that with some selection effort, *Polygonum viviparum* could become a nutritious minor crop for marginal agricultural areas. This is a highly variable species, and a larger form, which I haven't managed to source (ssp. *macounii*), is recognised, a robust plant with larger leaves. Selection work should look for forms with delayed sprouting (as the young leaves are difficult to separate from the dried bulbils) and larger bulbils that are persistent on the plant. If you have access to enough plants, by all means try the rhizomes too. They have a pleasant nutty flavour raw, and are not at all astringent like their cousin bistort (see *Persicaria bistorta* at the end of this chapter).

At present the RHS online Plant Finder lists two nurseries in the UK supplying plants by mail order. I have not seen it offered in other countries. The bulbils being effectively young plants shouldn't be treated like seed and need to be stored cold and damp before dispatch. Plants do not require any depth of soil (there is no more than 5cm depth of soil over rock where my plants are growing) and they also tolerate dry conditions. This is a perfect plant for the edible rock garden, in full sun or part shade. As you harvest the bulbils, some will inevitably fall to the ground. You will end up with a ground cover of alpine bistort plants. Being such a small plant it is not very competitive in a garden bed and you should keep it weeded.

Rheum x rhabarbarum

FAMILY: Polygonaceae
CHINESE: *Bo Ye Da Huang*
ENGLISH: Rhubarb
FINNISH: *Raparperi,*
Tarharaparperi
FRENCH: *Rhubarbe des Jardins*
GERMAN: *Rhabarber*
NORWEGIAN: *Hagerabarbra*
POLISH: *Rabarbar Kędzierzawy*
SWEDISH: *Rabarber*

Rhubarb is one of the half-dozen well-known (in the West) perennial vegetables although most think of it as a fruit. However, vegetable it most definitely is, just unusual in that it is almost always sweetened. It has been used in this way since the early 1800s when sugar began to be affordable, and some people even sweeten it nowadays with homegrown stevia (*Stevia rebaudiana*), a tender perennial. Rhubarb became popular as a fruit for some of the same reasons that I was attracted to perennial vegetables. In particular, the fact that it is harvested at a time of year when traditional homegrown fruit is unavailable, thus prolonging the fresh fruit season in to springtime. Once established, rhubarb is a robust creature and I believe it is one of the truly permanent vegetables in my garden. It will probably long outlive me. I inherited about five or six plants when I moved here over 30 years ago. It grows under birch and spruce trees in shady but quite dry conditions. I've never divided the plants to renew them as is often recommended. I have never fed them either, although they probably got a good start as I suspect that the contents of the outside loo were dumped here originally. Elsewhere, I often see this plant neglected but still growing strongly beside old derelict farm buildings in organically charged soil. This is a very hardy plant and grows well even above the tree line in Norway. It is often planted next to mountain cabins, particularly in the network used by walkers, to supply the kitchen. The Norwegian dessert, *rabarbragrøt*, is standard fare at these cabins, meaning literally rhubarb-porridge, describing the consistency of the cooked and sweetened rhubarb, thickened with potato flour and often served with locally produced mountain sour cream (*seterrømme*).

There are many varieties of rhubarb representing selections with various characteristics including size of the petioles (leaf stalks), colour, stringlessness, flavour, oxalic acid content, earliness, hardiness etc. The collection at RHS Wisley just outside of

416 & 417: Rheum palmatum *(Chinese rhubarb) in my garden (left), one of the ancestors of garden rhubarb and long cultivated medicinally in Asia, growing in a sea of ground elder;* Rheum australe *is a smaller plant and flower stalks can be seen in front.* Rheum palmatum *(below) is also grown as an ornamental, here with ostrich fern and* udo *(*Aralia cordata*) in the background.*

London contains over 150 varieties. It is recognised that our cultivated rhubarbs are mostly hybrids, probably deriving from *Rheum palmatum*, of which there are a number of garden-worthy cultivars grown as ornamentals, with *R. officinale* and/or *R. undulatum*.

Garden rhubarb and some of the other species could be used much more as real vegetables. However, please only use the leaf petioles (leaf stalks) as the leaves have higher levels of oxalic acid. *Rheums* are used by native people as vegetables across their wild range. In Nepal, the petioles of various species (*Rheum acuminatum*, *R. australe* and *R. nobile*), were preserved by pickling. The spectacular but endangered *R. nobile* was also eaten raw in Nepal and Sikkim (and is, reportedly, pleasantly acid, but you'll have to go to the Himalayas to try it as it's difficult to cultivate). Blanched *Rheum australe* is sold on markets in Afghanistan and eaten mixed with spinach (blanching is done by mounding gravel over the plants or covering with a large jar). *Rheum palmatum* was eaten fresh or preserved in Mongolia. In Iran it's used in *koresh* (a stew), usually with lamb. In Turkey, *Rheum ribes* petioles have been considered a delicacy since at least the 13th century and in Poland, rhubarb stalks are used cooked as a vegetable with potatoes and herbs. Finally, in Alaska during the Gold Rush, scurvy was a problem and the Russians apparently introduced rhubarb to alleviate the problem.

Even in the UK there are old references to rhubarb being used as a vegetable in Ray's *Historia Plantarum* from 1686. It refers to the acid stalks of rhubarb being 'more grateful than sorrel', so perhaps it was originally used to a limited extent in the UK as a vegetable. Interestingly, there is one traditional use of rhubarb as a vegetable that just possibly has survived from pre-sugar England as rhubarb is one of many possible ingredients in the northern England traditional dock pudding (see box on page 262).

I've also observed that children seem to enjoy the taste of raw rhubarb in the same way as they do with sorrel. My daughter with a friend would, without our encouragement, enjoy nibbling on raw rhubarb in the garden. Rhubarb chutney also finds its way onto the British dinner plate. This probably originates from the pickling of rhubarb practised in the Himalayan region mentioned above (the word chutney derives from the Indian Sanskrit word, *caṭnī*).

418: Even common garden rhubarb is, apart from its food value, an interesting ornamental if allowed to flower. The flowers of some varieties are reddish and others pure white, reflecting the different parentage. The cauliflower-like flower broccolis can be cooked in various ways, but don't overdo it as the oxalic acid content is unknown.

419: Rhubarb collection at RHS Wisley. Collections of rhubarb cultivars can also be seen at RHS Harlow Carr in Yorkshire, UK (just outside the so-called Yorkshire Rhubarb Triangle where 90% of the world's forced rhubarb was once grown and scene of an annual Rhubarb Festival) and RHS Rosemoor.

Facciola (1998) tells us, 'the young inflorescences resemble cauliflower and may be deep fried, or boiled and served au gratin with cream sauce', and excellent this is too. I find it a lot easier to grow rhubarb cheese than cauliflower cheese, as there are few if any pests of rhubarb flowers. You could also try rhubarb flower *tempura*. They have been used in wine making (as have, more commonly, the leaf stalks). I have however, been unable to find an analysis of the oxalic acid concentration of the flowers. By all means try, but don't convert to a rhubarb flower diet just in case! If you are cultivating your rhubarb in good conditions, you might find that the plants won't flower. Flowering seems to be triggered when the plants are stressed. I'm happy that my plants do bolt as I then get the best of both worlds. The tendency to bolt has probably also been selected out of the developed cultivars, and some varieties are less prone to bolting than others. 'Victoria' is incidentally one variety that does readily bolt if you are looking for that trait.

If you'd like to try experimenting with rhubarb as a vegetable, and are starting from scratch, consider purchasing varieties such as 'Glaskin's Perpetual', which is the lowest oxalic acid variety, or sweeter varieties such as 'Champagne' and 'Canada Red'. Blanching the plants in spring also gives a milder tasting vegetable. Use a large pot or, better, get your friendly local potter to make you a traditional forcing pot. These were originally based on sea kale forcing pots as blanching of the latter predated rhubarb. Plants are available from nurseries, garden centres and from friends. They are readily divided in winter and spring and, with plenty of water, division may also succeed at other times of the year. Seed of various rhubarb varieties is also available, but be aware that, being a hybrid the resulting plants will not be identical with the parent. It is better therefore to propagate vegetatively (see also *Fallopia* spp., used in the same way, Chapter 4).

Allium fistulosum

FAMILY: Amaryllidaceae
CHINESE: *Cong*
ENGLISH: Welsh Onion, Japanese
  Bunching Onion
FRENCH: *La Ciboule, Ail Fistuleux*
GERMAN: *Winterzwiebel*
ITALIAN: *La Cipolla d'Inverno*
JAPANESE: *Negi*
KOREAN: *Pa*
NORWEGIAN: *Pipeløk*

The Welsh onion has nothing to do with Wales, the origin of the name probably being from the old Germanic word *welsch* used originally to refer to Romans or foreigners in general. It doesn't come from Rome either. This perennial, and extremely hardy, onion has been cultivated for at least 1,800 years, the first records coming from China. It was introduced to Japan around AD500 and possibly arrived in Europe in the early Middle Ages. When it did arrive in Britain it was as an onion from distant parts.

In William Turner's *The Names of Herbes* from 1548, it has the following popular names: Cromyon Schiston, Hole Leke and Wynteronyon (Britten, 1881).

In Norway, we don't know when it was introduced, but there is an interesting old variety found in the Gudbrandsdalen, an over 200km long mountain valley in southern Norway, which is also the main thoroughfare to the north. Traditionally, farm buildings almost always had turf or sod roofs, some few still surviving. It was an old custom to plant succulent plants on these roofs and in this area *Allium fistulosum* was often used. The Norwegian name is *pipeløk* (or pipe onion due to the hollow, pipe-like leaves), but locally it is known as *takløk* (roof onion) and the same name is also used for *Sempervivum tectorum* (house leek) and *Rhodiola rosea* (roseroot), two other species planted elsewhere on roofs.

In Ireland, cloves of ramsons (*Allium ursinum*) were sometimes planted in the thatch over the door on Irish cottages for good luck as were house leeks (Opie and Tatum, 1989).

In addition to superstitions and lightning protection, when we interview people in Norway about these onions it is clear that they were also harvested from the roofs for food, a place that was out of reach of grazing animals.

It's nice to think of these as the original vegetable roof gardens, now becoming popular in cities for urban food security and climate change mitigation. The Gudbrandsdal onion is recognised by some botanists as

420: *The vegetable roof gardens of Gudbrandsdalen were around long before roof gardening became fashionable. Old turf roofs covered in* Allium fistulosum *are still to be found in this relatively small area of Norway near to the town Otta. Some of these roofs are now protected by law, as are the onions themselves, but for some populations it is already too late.*

a distinct form or subspecies, developing through natural selection to the unique environmental pressures of its rooftop habitat. Interestingly, this onion only grows on the dry south-facing side of the roofs, as it is outcompeted by grasses on the damper north side.

Modern genetic analysis has shown that *Allium fistulosum*, which is not known from the wild, was domesticated from *Allium altaicum* (the Altai onion), found in the Altai republic in Russia, Mongolia, northern China and Siberia. The wild plant has undoubtedly been a popular foraged plant throughout its range for millennia. It is found even today in gardens in the Transbaikal region, but today it is a threatened species due to its value on the marketplace.

Allium fistulosum is like a very large version of the better-known chives (*Allium schoenoprasum*) with round, inflated, hollow leaves and indistinct bulbs. It is easy to start from seed, quickly divides into clumps, and the greeny-white flowers appear in the second year forming a compact, nearly spherical head. Plants reach normally about 70-80cm.

In the early 19th century in Europe and North America, *Allium fistulosum* was also used to produce spring onions, i.e. harvested young up to one year old. One can find references to the new *Allium cepa* cultivars being introduced as substitutes for Welsh onion varieties, which are nowadays in a minority.

However, there are a large number of *fistulosum* cultivars available particularly in the Far East where fistulosum remains the dominant species, including a number of F1 hybrids. There are both red and white-stemmed varieties. Single-stemmed varieties, which look more like leeks than Welsh onions, have also been developed where the tendency to divide has been bred out. I would recommend the reader interested in these new types, now also becoming available in Europe, to read Joy Larkcom's classic book, *Oriental Vegetables*. Despite their Siberian origins, my experience is that the new oriental cultivars are not as hardy. *Allium fistulosum* is clearly genetically diverse however, and more hardy varieties could certainly be developed, more suited to colder climates. In North America, Welsh onions are known as bunching onions and there are a number of varieties recognised, differing in the size, speed of multiplying and hardiness.

As some of the Asian varieties have limited hardiness or do not divide into bunches in the case of single-stem varieties, it is best to start with seed or plants of established perennial forms. Perennial plants are sometimes available in the herb section in garden centres. It is also easy to divide established clumps and this can be done more or less at any time of year. In my experience, seed germinates readily and cold treatment is not necessary even with the hardy perennial forms. Start with well-composted soil and the plants will be happy for many years. Deep soil is not

421 (right): Welsh onion is a productive perennial onion once it is established.

422 (far right): DNA analysis has shown that the Welsh onion originates from the wild species Allium altaicum which differs from Allium fistulosum through relatively small botanical differences in the flowers and the onion.

423: Welsh onion flower.

424: The Welsh onion produces masses of seed which can be sown for spring onions.

425: This single-stemmed leek-like variety (banno-ke-negi from Japan) did survive a cold winter here in Malvik.

necessary (it grows well on very shallow soil on turf roofs) and established plants will withstand drought. To maintain vigour, it is advisable to divide up the clumps every few years when the plants appear crowded. Each individual onion will then divide into a new clump.

I mostly harvest the leaves from my perennial clumps of Welsh onion along with other Alliums from early spring to mid-summer. The leaves can either be simply cut back to ground level, quickly regrowing, or one can thin a clump by just digging or pulling entire onions. Once the plant has flowered, the leaves do become coarser, although the young flowering stems are excellent. As with most perennial onions, the leaves and bulbs can be used in many dishes from quiches to stir-fries, pizza, salad etc. The inflated leaves can also be served stuffed with cottage cheese or other vegetarian mixes. It is easy to produce your own Welsh onion seed by letting some plants flower. Why not try sowing those seed straight away outside for a crop of spring onions the following year? They are not as succulent as some forms of *Allium fistulosum* bred for spring onions, but are still perfectly edible.

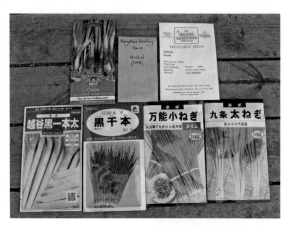

In one 19th century book I read, it was even recommended to plant Welsh onion as a perennial in the flower border and that 'Its quaintness of form is deserving of attention'. Vilmorin's (1920) perennial Welsh onion is actually a different species, *Allium lusitanicum* (see the description under *Allium senescens* in Chapter 3).

426: In Eastern Asia, there are a large number of cultivars of the 'annual' Allium fistulosum *(bottom row); a number of these new cultivars for spring onion production are now also becoming available in Europe (top row, left and right).*

Carum carvi

FAMILY: Apiaceae
ENGLISH: Caraway
FRENCH: *Carvi, Anis des Vosges*
GERMAN: *Kümmel*
ITALIAN: *Carvi, Cumino*
NORWEGIAN: *Karve*
RUSSIAN: *Tmin*

When I moved to Norway early in the 1980s, I soon discovered the newly started local group of the Norwegian Useful Plants Society (see page 210). That first spring, I joined the group's annual spring foraging excursion. This was where I was first introduced to *karve*, a common herb in coastal meadows, and second in popularity only to nettle (*Urtica dioica*) as a wild leafy green. *Karve* is none other than caraway (*Carum carvi*), the well-known herb which most of us associate with the aromatic seeds, used in various breads (particularly rye), sauerkraut (*surkål* in Norway), various European cheeses and various spirits, including the Norwegian national beverage, Aquavit. Use of the young spring greens is little known outside of Scandinavia. On our foraging trip, the tour leader Jan Erik Kofoed would demonstrate how to tell the young leaves of caraway apart from the main look-alikes, cow parsley (*Anthriscus sylvestris*) and yarrow (*Achillea millefolium*), difficult for novice foragers. Although rare in our area, young leaves could also potentially be confused with the leaves of the poisonous fool's parsley (*Aethusa cynapium*). So, please be absolutely sure of what you are picking.

In the UK, *Carum carvi* is probably not a native plant, but occurs as a garden escape. There's an amusing story of how caraway escaped into fields near one pub in England. The landlord had provided the seeds to drinkers wanting to disguise the smell of alcohol on their breath (Mabey, 1997). Caraway was also previously cultivated on a farm scale in England, particularly in Essex. It is today an uncommon plant in most of the UK apart from Shetland where it has naturalised (a Viking introduction perhaps?). On the other side of the North Sea, in Scandinavia and the Netherlands, this is a common wild plant, and in the Netherlands and Finland it is still grown commercially and small-scale caraway production has also recently started up again here in Norway, driven by interest in Slow Food Aquavit with locally sourced ingredients. In Norway, *karve* grows throughout the country, in the south

427: People often find caraway leaves (in the middle) difficult to tell apart from yarrow (on the left: leaves are softly downy) and cow parsley (right).

even being found in the mountains and, in the north, to the Arctic Ocean north of 70°N. Its range otherwise is throughout northern Europe including the Baltic states, most of Central Europe and east into Central Asia, Mongolia, Kamchatka, northern China and spread in the Himalayas. It is also found in Iceland and Greenland and has naturalised in many parts of North America. This is clearly a very hardy plant. Apart from coastal meadows, caraway is also found inland in dry meadows and roadsides.

Apart from the confusion between different wild umbellifers, the spice caraway is often confused in Scandinavia with cumin (*Cuminum cyminum*), also belonging to the same botanical family. However, caraway has a very different, sweeter taste than cumin. The confusion arises in that the Swedish name for caraway is *kummin* (*kümmel* in German).

The young spring shoots of caraway are ready for harvesting in early spring (April to early May). They have a mild parsley-like taste not at all like the seeds. They were traditionally used to make a soup (*karvekaalsuppe*). *Karvekaal* literally translates as caraway-cabbage or -greens. This soup is described in Norway's first cookery book by Hanna Winsnes in 1845. She recommends that the *karvekaal* should be cooked to soup either with meat or fish stock. Jens Holmboe, in his wartime Norwegian book

428: Caraway seed is commonly used in baking. The picture illustrates various wild and cultivated plants that can be used on bread; from top left and clockwise: Alpine bistort (Polygonum viviparum, see this chapter), caraway, sesame, opium poppy (Papaver somniferum), evening primrose (Oenothera biennis) and greater plantain (Plantago major).

429: Early spring leaf rosettes of caraway growing between rocks above the beach near where I live.

Free Food from Wild Plants (1941) wrote, 'There are many homes around the country in which the serving of the year's first fresh *karvekaalsuppe* brings on a real spring party atmosphere after the long hard winter'. I know exactly what he means.

Norwegian explorer Fridtjof Nansen describes having eaten *karvekaalsuppe* in 1888 at the beginning of the first crossing of Greenland where they pitched their tents on a grassy area: '...after a strenuous day, a fantastic warm *karvekaalsuppe*, which will be difficult to forget, was our reward for our efforts'.

I was taught to harvest the plants with a sharp knife, cutting through the uppermost part of the root. This allowed the root to re-sprout and seed still to be set in the same year, so that harvesting doesn't affect the local populations, a sound example of sustainable harvesting.

One old seed variety I've tried called 'Polaris' has leaves that are held upright in the spring, an advantage as the leaves are not so easily dirtied in heavy rain.

Although there are many Norwegian recipes for this soup on the internet, I found only one English page describing this prime slow food dish. See the box on the next page for a simple vegetarian recipe that I use. Norwegians will generally keep it simple and will normally use only caraway with water, stock cubes, butter and plain wheat flour. The soup will often be served decorated with hard-boiled eggs. Serve with real

The Genus *Carum*

Carum is a genus of some 20 species from temperate parts of the old world. The two best known species after caraway are the Indian curry spice plants *Carum roxburghianum* (*ajmud*) and *C. copticum* (*ajwain*). Again, it is the seeds which provide the main use, although the leaves of both species are also used raw or cooked.

430: Harvested **karvekaal** *in early spring; the top of the root is cut through with a sharp knife.*

Karvekaalsuppe

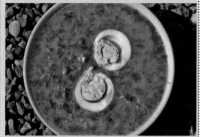

Karvekaalsuppe, *Norwegian caragreen (caraway greens) soup.*

Harvest your caraway greens and slice finely (the finer the better and to make it as authentic as possible no kitchen gadgets!). The greens should about half fill the volume of the final soup. Melt some butter in the saucepan or pressure cooker over a low heat. If harvesting from the wild, I might fry up some field garlic at this stage or some other perennial Allium from the garden and then add some barley, rye or oat flour, cooking gently whilst stirring. Gradually stir in water or your chosen stock (*miso* or *tamari* can also be used) and the greens. Cook for 10 minutes or so in a pressure cooker or about 20 minutes in a saucepan.

Norwegian flatbread[*] if you can get it. I also use the young leaves in spring mixed salads. It can also be used like parsley (at a time of year when there's no parsley available fresh), for example, cut up finely and sprinkled over potatoes.

In the UK, Lightfoot includes caraway in *Flora Scotica* (1789) and states that the young leaves are good and that the roots are delicate food. Later, in *Useful Plants of Great Britain*, C.P. Johnson (1862) notes that the young leaves form a good salad and large ones may be boiled as spinach. Through the efforts in many countries over only the last few years by ethnobotanists to document the old food traditions before they disappear, it seems that our *karvekaal* tradition was probably widespread (at least in times of scarcity) across the plant's range in the past. For example, the leaves of caraway are one of many herbs gathered in making the ritualistic spring dish *pistic* in northeast Italy (see Chapter 2). In Poland, the young plants were gathered together with other herbs and were boiled in a potherb dish called *warmuz*, served with potatoes and butter. As far east as Nepal, Tibet and northwest China, where caraway is also found in the wild, Manandhar's *Plants and People of Nepal* and Hu's *Food Plants of China* note that the tender leaves and shoots are used. Why not join me and introduce this wide-ranging tradition into your garden. The seeds will be a bonus.

Traditionally, in Norway, caraway seeds were often the only spice used in cookery

---

[*] As barley and oats were the main grains traditionally cultivated in Norway, grains not that suited to yeasted breads, flatbread was usually the bread of choice.

and the wild plant was so common that few found it necessary to cultivate. It wasn't just the leaves and seeds that were used however. Norwegian botanist Fredrik Christian Schübeler, who wrote a number of popular books on gardening in the mid-19th century, wrote in 1889 that in many places in the Austrian mountains, caraway roots were being grown in places where it wasn't possible to grow potatoes. He informs the reader that caraway roots are nutritious, easily digested and tasty. He also notes that the size of the roots can be improved by selection. Schübeler himself tells how he grew caraway as a root vegetable in the Botanical Gardens in Oslo in the 1850s and that he managed to develop roots as big as the Hamburg parsley (*Petroselinum crispum*). Today, as far as I am aware there are no cultivars of caraway bred for the roots. However, there are a number of high yielding cultivars developed for seed production. I agree with Schübeler that the roots have a pleasant, sweet taste. In fact, in *Sturtevant's Edible Plants of the World*, a reference is given to an article from 1904 in which the author states that the roots are considered better than parsnips! Starting with seed from wild plants in different parts of the country and an old cultivated variety, 'Polaris', I have now started to

431 (left): Starting with various wild accessions and an old cultivated variety of caraway, I started to select for larger roots. The picture shows the starting point for three of the varieties after one season. These long roots are already a useful size and the rejects were turned into an excellent soup.

432 & 433: Old Norwegian caraway variety 'Polaris' has an upright growth form (below left) whereas all the wild accessions I've tested, such as 'Lia i Vefsn' (below right), have ground-hugging leaves in the spring. An upright growth form is an advantage for a vegetable cultivar as the spring leaves are less likely to be soiled.

repeat Schübeler's experiment of selecting for larger roots.

After the first few years harvesting from the wild, I started growing a small patch in my own garden. Although caraway is a biennial, on a garden plot it self-sows readily and it can be treated as you would a perennial. Indeed, some people believe that it is perennial. (NB: I have recently received seed of a supposedly perennial form!) This is because some plants do not flower until the third year and there will always be some seed that falls to the ground when harvesting. Dropping its seed in late summer, the seed germinates the following spring. It can either be sown in autumn for the earliest germination the following spring or just sow the seed in early spring. The amount of work needed to grow caraway is minimal. Mulching with compost every couple of years or so and some weeding is all that is needed. The plant tolerates salt spray in the wild. If you have access to it, seaweed mulch can be used. Caraway is supposedly susceptible to carrot-root fly, but I have only noticed fairly minor damage to my plants (see photo 431 of the roots which were unprotected – carrots grown like this in my garden would have been badly damaged). This is one of many reasons that I believe that caraway has a real future as a root crop, particularly in colder climates like Norway.

If you live outside this plant's wild range, seed and plants are relatively easy to get hold of in Europe and North America, with 11 nurseries currently offering plants in the UK.

434: Caraway flowers from mid-summer attract a myriad of garden beneficial insects in my garden. It is a common plant in meadows near where I live and is most easily spotted when in flower.

Allium x proliferum (syn. *Allium cepa* var. *viviparum*)

FAMILY: Amaryllidaceae
ENGLISH: Egyptian Onion, Tree Onion
FRENCH: *Oignon d'Egypte*
GERMAN: *Ägyptische Zwiebel, Etagenzwiebel, Luftzwiebel*
NORWEGIAN: *Luftløk, Etasjeløk, Pensjonistløk*
USA: Walkabout, Topset Onion

Over the last five years I've been helping the Norwegian Genetic Resource Centre to find old heritage perennial vegetables. The most common traditional perennial vegetables here, all of which are discussed elsewhere in this book, are horseradish, rhubarb, Jerusalem artichoke, Scorzonera,

435: There are several varieties of Egyptian onion in cultivation. Unlike in North America, in Europe cultivar names are generally not used. From left to right: 'Catawissa Red', 'McCullar's White', and two varieties from Norwegian gardens.

asparagus, globe artichoke, Good King Henry, Caucasian spinach (*Hablitzia tamnoides*) and various perennial onions. The onion most commonly found is *luftløk* (literally, air onion). This is Egyptian onion or topset/walking onion depending on whether you are in the UK or North America respectively.

It is still popular due to a combination of its rather curious growth form, its hardiness, its food value and its ease of propagation (just take an aerial onion and press into the soil and you have a new plant). It is therefore easy to pass on to neighbours and friends. Most people aren't aware that there are actually a number of varieties in cultivation.

436: Some varieties send up several tiers of topsets, in this example one can harvest onions at three different levels.

The bulbils or topsets form in a group at the end of the 50-100cm stems, sometimes along with a few flowers that are sterile. I love the descriptive American name walking or walkabout onions due to their method of propagating themselves. The tall stems with onion sets atop fall sideways to the ground under their weight, planting themselves and in this way can move around, albeit rather slowly (see box on page 257). When I was first given this onion by a gardening friend many years ago, she called it by its alternative Norwegian name, *etasjeløk* (meaning storey onion), which is a particular variety that forms first one cluster of topsets from which a new stem grows up to the next storey and so on (as in photo 436 with three levels[*]). I call this variety the run-about onion as it

[*] If you manage to grow one with more than three storeys, I'd love to see a picture!

can move even faster than other varieties, as it is taller! It also has a third Norwegian name *pensjonistløk*, which I don't think I need to translate. It was given this name, as one doesn't have to bend down to harvest it…

A top candidate for Slow Food, perhaps? Walkabout Onion racing … any challengers? Slow Olympics?

The oldest accession of our old onion project may have been cultivated continuously for 120 years in Norway. It was most likely brought to Norway in the 1890s from the US. My informant, Ovin Udø, told me that the onion originally grew in his grandmother's kitchen garden that was on a small island, Udøy, off the south coast of Norway. He said he could be reasonably certain that they had been grown there since the early 1900s. Both the leaves and onions had been used in cooking. He could also tell me that it was the type that formed several tiers of topsets.

I had by this time also sourced a number of topset onions from the US via Seed Savers Exchange which every year lists several named varieties. These include 'Catawissa', 'Amish', 'McCullar's White', 'Heritage Sweet White', 'Moritz Egyptian', 'West Virginia Purple', 'Caudell Heirloom', 'Dawes Hill', 'Fleener', 'Minnesota Red' and 'Volga German'.

> ## Useless Fact
> ### *How fast does a Walkabout Onion actually walk?*
>
> Well, I have only one measurement so far: my calculation shows that a plant can move at the astonishing mean speed of 6 x10^{-6} mm/s or it takes 18 days to move a centimetre! However, its top speed is considerably faster than this…
>
>
>
> *After some patient stalking, I finally caught a walking onion walking.*

Topset onions were previously thought to be a mutation of the common onion, *Allium cepa* var. *proliferum*, but today it is known to be a hybrid between common onion (*Allium cepa*) and the Welsh onion (*Allium fistulosum*), *Allium* x *proliferum*. Such crosses have probably occurred in several places where the parent species have grown together, accounting for the number of varieties which can be found.

'Catawissa' is the most common walkabout onion in the US and its description fits our Norwegian *etasjeløk* having up to several tiers of topsets. More than that, its history seems to be well known. It is very likely that this variety was developed by a well-known English plant breeder, Frederick Merceron, who had moved to America as a 25-year-old. He was particularly interested in crossing species. Well-known American heirloom gardening author William Woys Weaver and a friend went to Merceron's former trial fields in the 1970s near to the town of Catawissa in Pennsylvania. Here they found this variety still growing and reintroduced it as 'Catawissa'.

437: Local historian Geir Neverdahl in Gudbrandsdalen, Norway, showing me his productive row of what looked like 'Catawissa' onions.

It can be dated from about 1885. It has subsequently become popular again. It is still common in gardens in Catawissa itself and can be traced back locally to at least around 1900.

Was there perhaps a link between the Norwegian island Udø and the US? I therefore asked my informant Ovin Udøy if he could shed any light on this and his response was that, well yes, his grandparents were actually in America for a couple of years around 1890!

Topset onions are only known for sure to have existed for about 200 years, with the first records from Germany in 1794 and Denmark in 1806.

Botanists recognise two groups of *Allium* x *proliferum* (Anon, 2002):

	Main cultivation area	Common name
Eurasian Group	North America, Europe and northeast Asia	Topset onion
East Asian Group	China, Japan and southeast Asia	Wakegi onion

I've never seen Wakegi onions, which are a cross between shallots (*Allium cepa* var. *aggregatum*) and Welsh onions. It has never been very popular in Asia and is today even less used (Hanelt, 2001). Dr. Reinhard Fritsch at IPK Gatersleben in Germany told me that they have one Wakegi onion in their Allium collection but that it '...grows very badly under our climate and has never flowered. It has narrow leaves of 3-5mm diameter (like a coarse type of chives) and is frost-tender'.

Topsetting onions are more popular in North America than in Europe and the numerous local varieties have been kept going for generations in families. There are various characteristics that separate them, including colour and size of the topsets, hardiness (there are local varieties from Florida to Canada), whether one cultivates the variety mainly for the topsets or for the onions at ground level, and also how quickly the ground onions divide. Egyptian onions only have one tier of topsets.

Another topsetting onion exists, *Allium* x *cornutum*. It is more slender with pinkish flowers, multiplying quicker than *Allium* x *proliferum* and is cultivated locally from Tibet through Europe to North America. *Allium cepa* is one parent, but the other is not known for sure. I've grown a couple of types but don't find them as useful as *A.* x *proliferum* due to their smaller stature.

Topset onions have similar demands to Welsh onions, but are easier to start and multiply, just press the bottom end of the topset firmly into the soil and it will quickly sprout. The bulbils can also be autumn planted and the scallions grow quickly and can be harvested the following spring to summer. Plant them maybe 5-8cm deep and you will get a tender long white shaft. I also plant them in the autumn in large pots and force them inside in a cool room for early spring onions.

Some varieties like 'Catawissa' and 'Egyptian' are very hardy and have been found growing comfortably in gardens up to the tree limit in southern Norway. Plants should be replanted after a few years to maintain vigour and size of topsets as they will get congested by the ground onions dividing and the topsets falling to the ground. They are relatively easy to source from garden centres and nurseries if you don't have a friendly neighbour growing them. Named varieties are not yet readily available in Europe. Be aware that Egyptian onions in the UK and elsewhere in Europe are often actually 'Catawissa' onions.

438: My oldest variety is shown and is probably identical with the 'Catawissa' topset onion.

One can use the leaves in the same way as Welsh onions. In dry warm summer climates, the plants have a rest during the warmest period. The ground onions are also a usable size in some varieties. Many people think that the small topset onions are too fiddly to bother with. However, it's easy and quick if you know how. To peel, simply slice the topsets in two with a sharp knife and squeeze and push the skin off. They come off even easier by soaking the topsets in tepid water first. The peeled topsets are used in all sorts of dishes. They can also be used for pickling. One can stimulate larger ground onions by cutting off the topset stalk, the subsequent spring shoots then also giving improved harvest.

439: Allium x proliferum 'Amish spreading topset' is a tasty and vigorous variety from the US similar to 'Catawissa', here picked in my garden at the end of May, together with stinging nettles (Urtica dioica) and buckler-leaved sorrel (Rumex scutatus).

Persicaria bistorta
(syn. *Bistorta officinalis, Polygonum bistorta*)

FAMILY: Asteraceae
CHINESE: *Quan Shen*
ENGLISH: Common Bistort, Snake Weed, Snake Root, Adder-Wort
FRENCH: *La Renouée Bistorte*
GERMAN: *Der Schlangen-Knöterich*
ITALIAN: *Poligono Bistorta*
NORWEGIAN: *Ormerot*

Norwegian explorer Roald Amundsen first navigated the Northwest Passage linking the Atlantic and Pacific oceans from 1903 to 1906 in his boat Gjøa. What has this to do with Bistort? Well, during winter 1905-1906 Amundsen and his crew overwintered for the third time during the trip and this was near Herschel Island in the Yukon not far from the Alaskan border. They here purchased sacks of 'Eskimo potatoes'. According to Amundsen it was rhizomes of *Persicaria bistorta* that helped them through the winter: 'We here obtained the first vegetables in these parts, so-called *kagmallik* potatoes as the whalers called them. It was the root of *Polygonum bistorta*; it tasted good both raw and cooked. The Eskimos called them *masku*'. However, some think that Amundsen may have been mistaken and that his Eskimo Potatoes were either *Hedysarum alpinum* (Alpine *sweetvetch*, also known as Alaskan carrots) or *Claytonia tuberosa* (tuberous spring beauty), both of which have also been used as Eskimo potatoes. All three are incidentally excellent garden edimentals.

There are various other perennials which have been used traditionally as important survival food in the high Arctic and many of these plants are also grown in our gardens as ornamentals, notably *Fritillaria camschatcensis* (Kamchatka lily), *Lilium martagon* (Martagon lily), *Allium victorialis* (victory onion, see this chapter) and *Erythronium dens-canis* (dog-toothed violet).

According to Johnson (1862) large quantities of bistort roots were gathered in Siberia. The roots are astringent in their raw state (I can vouch for that), but soaking and roasting made them edible. Others have reported that the Eskimoes cooked the roots and fried them in seal oil (Hedrick, 1919). The Dena'ina eskimoes in South Central Alaska are also reported to have dug the roots, cutting off the thick end of the root and replanting so as not to kill the plant. The Siberian foraging site[*] reports that the roots lose their bitterness when soaked and can be ground and mixed with flour in bread. The young leaves are also reported used in cheese, boiled, dried and pickled. I have also found that the flower shoots make a good vegetable later in the season.

Outside of the Arctic there is little evidence for the use of this plant as food and it is only in England that I find evidence of this today despite its extensive range! For the

---

[*] www.sibrast.ru

440 & 441: Hedysarum alpinum *(above left) and* Claytonia tuberosa *both have edible roots which were formerly used as Eskimo potatoes. Closely related* Claytonia virginica *(above right) also has small edible tubers and is an excellent edimental for the woodland garden.*

442 & 443: Erythronium dens-canis *(right) and* Fritillaria camschatcensis *(far right) are two other Arctic survival plants that are often seen in gardens grown as ornamentals.*

centre of bistort's culinary universe is a small village in Yorkshire in north England, Mytholmroyd, thanks to some ahead-of-their-time Slow Food enthusiasts. They placed an advert in *The Times* newspaper early in 1971 titled '*Polygonum bistorta*: How is your Dock Pudding?' It was an invite to the first World Championship Dock Pudding Contest (Mabey, 1972). The dock in question is *Persicaria bistorta* (bistort) which grows wild in this part of Yorkshire.

I first read of Dock or Easter Ledge Pudding in Roger Phillips' excellent *Wild Food* from 1983. The first competition was held on 13th April 1971 in Hebden Bridge and it attracted 50 entries. The dish was traditionally prepared during Lent and at Easter, usually on Palm Sunday. Richard Mabey (1997) found that although it is best known as a Yorkshire dish as a result of the competition, it is in Cumbria and the Lake District that the tradition has mostly survived.

Although bistort has to be one of the ingredients, there are many other wild-gathered and cultivated vegetables which are included such as stinging nettle (*Urtica dioica*), dandelion (*Taraxacum* spp.), lady's mantle (*Alchemilla* spp.), curled dock (*Rumex*

444: Bistort habitat in a Pyrenean alpine meadow (Andorra) with **Veratrum album** *(White False Helleborine)* in the foreground.

crispus), broad-leaved dock (*Rumex obtusifolius*), rhubarb (*Rheum*), redshank (*Persicaria maculosa*), cabbage, kale, spring shoots of Brussels sprouts, leek, onion, chives, parsley as well as blackcurrant or gooseberry leaves. There are no rules apart from the use of bistort, so just use what you have available, and most of the 80 plants in this book could be used.

There follows a traditional recipe adapted from *Mrs. Grieve's Modern Herbal* (1931), in which the greens are rather cooked to death (see box below).

Dock pudding is traditionally also fried as patties in bacon fat and served with bacon and egg for breakfast. It is also served with lamb on Easter Sunday. Nowadays, people don't cook the greens with the grains as in the traditional recipe and the lightly cooked vegetables are just mixed with the cooked barley and egg.

Traditional Easter Ledge Pudding

700g bistort

400g nettles

Chives (a bunch)

A few leaves of blackcurrant, sorrel and parsley leaves

Barley (a teacup)

Oatmeal (½ teacup)

Salt

Pepper

Easter Ledge pudding ingredients: Blanched dandelion, sorrel, nettle, bistort, lady's mantle, field garlic (Allium oleraceum), blanched rhubarb and cooked barley.

Finely chop the greens and place in a bowl with the barley (washed and soaked), oatmeal, and salt and pepper and mix in the chives. Boil the whole in a muslin bag for about 2.5 hours, to allow the barley to get thoroughly cooked. The bag should be tied firmly, for while the greens shrink, the barley swells. Turn out into a very hot bowl, add a lump of butter and a beaten egg: the heat of the turned-out pudding is sufficient to cook the egg.

445 (far left): Bistort has spread vegetatively over quite a large area in the author's garden from the original single plant; here shown at the best time to harvest.

446 & 447: The commonest cultivar is Persicaria bistorta 'Superba' (below) and the ssp. carnea, meaning 'flesh-coloured' (left), is also available through the trade.

The bistort leaves should be harvested as early as possible, the ideal size being shown in the photo 445 as they become too fibrous later on. The harvesting period is short here, about two weeks. 2011 was the 30th anniversary of the competition that has in recent years moved from Hebden Bridge to the neighbouring village, Mytholmroyd. On the village website,[*] Peter Crossland relates how his aunt sent him Dock Pudding each year from

1942 to 1961 whilst he served in the armed forces. His wife hated Dock Pudding, but Peter loved it. During the Second World War, the German propagandist William Joyce, better known as 'Lord Haw Haw', apparently announced on German radio that food rationing was so bad in Yorkshire that people had resorted to eating grass, unaware that Dock Pudding was actually a local delicacy. Evidence that eating wild bistort is probably an old tradition can be traced back to at least the 18th century when the young leaves were reported by Lightfoot (1789) to have been boiled and eaten.

Bistort (*Persicaria bistorta*) is a species in the knotweed family (*Polygonaceae*) along with the true docks (*Rumex*). It is circumpolar, ranging from the Iberian Peninsula and the UK in the west, through the Pyrenees and Alps, in Central Europe, Turkey, the Caucasus, Russia and east to northern China, Japan as well as in Alaska and the Yukon in North America. Wherever it thrives, in damp meadows, along rivers and in open woodlands, bistort often forms large stands. It spreads vegetatively through its rhizomes.

Bistort can today often be found in old gardens where it was grown as an ornamental, including the large flowered showier cultivar 'Superba'. 'Hohe Tatra'

[*] www.mytholmroyd.net

(from the High Tatra mountains of Slovakia) is another cultivar that is reputedly less vigorous, but it certainly spreads in my garden. The subspecies *Persicaria bistorta* ssp. *carnea* from the Caucasus is a daintier plant with attractive flesh-coloured flowers. All of these are readily available in the trade. It is a simple matter to vegetatively propagate bistort by division (just divide off a piece of rhizome). White flowered variants also occur in the wild, but such plants do not seem at present to be in cultivation. Bistort was originally cultivated from at least the Middle Ages in herb gardens as a medicinal.

Bistort has a bit of a reputation for being invasive and is therefore less often planted nowadays. However, there has been a bit of a revival thanks to the BBC. In a 2005 report from the Chelsea Flower Show in London, it was said that: 'A more subtle, understated star (of the show) is *bistort* which was woven into the planting of *many* of the small (show) gardens and was also used as a prominent plant for a moist or shady spot in the gardens'. This was part of the trend to more naturalistic garden design with a greater use of native British plants.

448: Persicaria bistorta 'Hohe Tatra' combines well with Hosta (Chapter 4). Your edimental garden could look like this one at the RHS Wisley Garden, UK. I have enjoyed visiting botanical and ornamental gardens while researching this book and spotting good but usually accidental edimental combinations.

There probably isn't a more fitting plant to end with and at the same time take us back to the start of our journey in London with a picture from Wisley Gardens of an accidental edimental combination. Bistort is found growing wild more or less throughout my journey. I hope you've enjoyed the trip exploring the temperate world of edible perennial plants and that it will not only inspire you to try them yourself, but to seek out other great perennial vegetables as many are certainly still undiscovered.

PLANT TABLE

Species	Form	Habitat	Main Harvest	Edimental? (scale 1 to 5)	Forest Garden	Page no.
Aegopodium podograria	Perennial	Woodland to sunny	Spring to early summer	3 (var. *variegata*)	Y	231
Allium 'Norrland Onion'	Perennial	Sunny to open woodland	Leaves: spring to summer (cut-and-come-again) Flowers: late summer	4		125
Allium ampeloprasum	Perennial	Sunny to open woodland	Leaves, shoots: spring to autumn Bulbs: autumn to winter	4	Y	34
Allium cernuum	Perennial	Sunny to open woodland; tolerates summer drought	Leaves: spring Flowers: summer Whole plant: winter	5		191
Allium fistulosum	Perennial	Sunny	All year, most useful in spring and in mild winters	3		247
Allium nutans	Perennial	Sunny to open woodland	Leaves: spring to summer (cut-and-come-again) Flowers: late summer Whole plant: winter	3 - 4		122
Allium obliquum	Perennial	Open woodland to sunny	Leaves: spring Bulbs: autumn	3		118
Allium oleraceum	Perennial	Open woodland to sunny	Leaves: spring Bulbs: autumn	1	Y	214
Allium ramosum	Perennial	Sunny to open woodland	Leaves: spring Flowers: early summer	2		130
Allium sativum	Perennial	Sunny	Leaves: spring Bulbs: autumn Bulbil shoots: forced in winter	3		114
Allium schoenoprasum sibiricum	Perennial	Sunny to lightly shaded	Leaves: spring and later (cut-and-come-again) Flowers: summer	3		226

Species	Form	Habitat	Main Harvest	Edimental? (scale 1 to 5)	Forest Garden	Page no.
Allium scorodoprasum	Perennial	Open woodland to sunny	Leaves: spring Bulbs: autumn Topset/bulbil sprouts: winter	2		215
Allium senescens	Perennial	Sunny to open woodland	Leaves: spring to summer (cut-and-come-again) Flowers: late summer Whole plant: winter	3		122
Allium triquetrum	Perennial	Open woodland to sunny	Leaves: spring Flowers: late spring Bulbs: autumn	4		90
Allium tuberosum	Perennial	Sunny to open woodland	Leaves: spring Flowers: late summer	4		130
Allium ursinum	Perennial	Open woodland; prefers damp soil	Leaves: spring Flowers: early summer	4	Y	50
Allium validum	Perennial	Sunny to open woodland; damp conditions, but needs good drainage in areas with milder winters	Leaves: spring Flowers: summer	3		179
Allium victorialis	Perennial	Sunny to open woodland; prefers damp soil	Leaves: spring	4	Y	218
Allium wallichii	Perennial	Sunny to open woodland	Leaves: late spring Flowers: late summer	4		119
Allium x proliferum	Perennial	Sunny	Leaves: spring Topsets: late summer to autumn Topset sprouts: winter	3		255
Angelica archangelica	Biennial under good conditions but usually 3 years, removing flower stems early prolongs life	Open woodland to sunny; prefers damp soil	Leaves, shoots: spring Stems: summer Seeds as spice	3		210
Apium nodiflorum	Perennial	Semi-aquatic to damp soils in sunny and shady locations	Leaves: winter and spring Seed: autumn	2		82
Aralia cordata	Perennial	Open woodland to sunny, but doesn't like dry conditions	Shoots: spring Flower broccolis: summer	4	Y	135

Species	Form	Habitat	Main Harvest	Edimental? (scale 1 to 5)	Forest Garden	Page no.
Aralia elata	Perennial	Open woodland to sunny, but doesn't like dry conditions	Shoots: spring	3	Y	133
Armoracia rusticana	Perennial	Open woodland to sunny	Shoots: spring or forced in winter Roots: autumn	3		53
Asparagus spp.	Perennial	Sunny; tolerates saline soil	Shoots: spring	3		94
Aster scaber	Perennial	Open woodland to sunny	Leaves, shoots: spring	5		139
Aster tripolium	Perennial	Sunny; tolerates saline soil	Leaves: spring to autumn (cut-and-come-again)	3		234
Barbarea vulgaris	Biennial to Perennial	Sunny; prefers damp soil	Leaves: winter to spring Flower broccolis: late spring	3		238
Beta vulgaris ssp. *maritima*	Perennial	Sunny, rich soil	Leaves: spring to autumn	2		23
Brassica oleracea	Perennial	Sunny, rich soil	Leaves: spring to autumn	2-4 (Daubenton variegated)		14
Bunias orientalis	Perennial	Open woodland to sunny	Leaves, shoots: spring Flower broccolis: summer Roots: winter	3		99
Campanula latifolia	Perennial	Woodland to sunny	Leaves, shoots: spring Flowers: summer Roots: autumn	5	Y	229
Campanula trachelium	Perennial	Woodland to sunny	Leaves, shoots: spring Flowers: summer	4	Y	81
Carum carvi	Biennial but self-seeds	Sunny to open woodland; edible lawn	Leaves: spring Seed: autumn Roots: winter	2		250
Chenopodium bonus-henricus	Perennial	Sunny to open woodland; tolerates dry conditions	Leaves and flower spikes: from spring (cut-and-come-again) Seeds: harvested 2-3 times in summer	2		91
Cicerbita alpina	Perennial	Open woodland to sunny; prefers damp rich soils	Leaves, shoots: spring	5	Y	227

Species	Form	Habitat	Main Harvest	Edimental? (scale 1 to 5)	Forest Garden	Page no.
Cichorium intybus	Perennial to biennial	Sunny; tolerates dry conditions	Leaves: spring Flowers: late summer Roots: winter, forced roots in winter (chicons)	4		88
Cirsium oleraceum	Perennial	Open woodland to sunny; prefers damp rich soil	Leaves, shoots: spring	3		55
Crambe cordifolia	Perennial	Open woodland to sunny	Shoots: spring Flower broccolis: late spring	5		110
Crambe maritima	Perennial	Sunny rich soil; tolerates saline soil	Leaves, shoots: spring Flower broccolis: late spring	4		5
Crithmum maritimum	Perennial	Sunny, good drainage; tolerates saline soil	Leaves: from spring (cut-and-come-again)	2		2
Cryptotaenia japonica	Perennial	Sunny to open woodland	Leaves: spring to late summer	4		146
Cynara cardunculus	Perennial	Sunny; prefers dampish soil in winter, but needs good drainage in colder climates	Leaf petioles: late winter in south to late summer; force in winter Flower receptacles: summer	4		66
Diplotaxis tenuifolia	Short-lived perennial	Sunny; tolerates dry conditions	Leaves: spring to autumn Flowers: summer	2		86
Fallopia sp.	Perennial	Open woodland to sunny	Shoots: spring	3	Y	150
Gunnera tinctoria	Perennial	Open to woodland; dislikes dry conditions	Leaf petioles: spring	4	Y	177
Hablitzia tamnoides	Perennial	Woodland to open woodland; sensitive to sunny, dry conditions in summer	Shoots: late winter to spring Leaves and shoot tips: summer	3	Y	102
Hemerocallis altissima	Perennial	Sunny to open woodland	Flower buds, flowers and wilted flowers: late summer	5		153
Hemerocallis citrina	Perennial	Sunny to open woodland	Flower buds, flowers and wilted flowers: late summer	5		153

Species	Form	Habitat	Main Harvest	Edimental? (scale 1 to 5)	Forest Garden	Page no.
Hemerocallis fulva	Perennial	Sunny to open woodland	Flower buds, flowers and wilted flowers: early summer	5		153
Hemerocallis lilioasphodelus	Perennial	Sunny to open woodland	Flower buds, flowers and wilted flowers: early summer	5		153
Heracleum spp.	Perennial	Open woodland to sunny; prefers damper locations	Shoots: spring Flower shoots: late spring Seeds as spice	3	Y	181
Hosta montana	Perennial	Woodland to sunny	Leaf shoots: spring Flowers: summer	5	Y	141
Hosta sieboldiana	Perennial	Woodland to sunny	Leaf shoots: spring Flowers: summer	5	Y	141
Humulus lupulus	Perennial	Woodland to sunny	Shoots: spring	3	Y	79
Hydrophyllum spp.	Perennial	Woodland to open woodland	Leaves: spring Flower stalks: late spring	3	Y	201
Laportea canadensis	Perennial	Woodland to open woodland; prefers damper conditions	Shoots and leaves: spring Plant tops before flowering: late spring/summer Seed: autumn	2	Y	188
Levisticum officinale	Perennial	Sunny to open woodland	Leaves, shoots: spring to summer	3		112
Maianthemum racemosum	Perennial	Woodland to open woodland; tolerates dry conditions in summer	Leaf shoots: spring	5	Y	186
Malva alcea	Perennial	Sunny to open woodland	Leaves: spring to autumn Flowers: summer to autumn Immature seed pods: summer to autumn	4		157
Malva moschata	Perennial	Sunny to open woodland	Leaves: spring to autumn Flowers: summer to autumn Immature seed pods: summer to autumn	4		157

Species	Form	Habitat	Main Harvest	Edimental? (scale 1 to 5)	Forest Garden	Page no.
Malva sylvestris	Short-lived Perennial	Sunny to open woodland	Leaves: spring to autumn Flowers: summer to autumn Immature seed pods: summer to autumn	4		157
Matteuccia struthiopteris	Perennial	Open woodland to sunny; prefers damp rich soils	Fiddleheads: spring	4	Y	196
Medicago sativa	Perennial	Open, sunny	Shoots: spring shoots Seeds: winter	2		162
Myrrhis odorata	Perennial	Open woodland to sunny; prefers damp rich soil	Leaves: spring Flowers and young seeds: summer	4		72
Nasturtium officinale	Perennial	Semi-aquatic to damp soils in sunny and shady locations	Leaves: all year Flowers: summer	2		11
Ornithogalum pyrenaicum	Perennial	Open woodland to sunny	Flower spikes: late spring	4	Y	26
Oxyria digyna	Perennial	Sunny to open woodland; prefers damp soil	Leaves: spring to summer (cut and come again)	3		225
Persicaria bistorta	Perennial	Open woodland to sunny; prefers damp soil	Young leaves: early spring Flower stems: summer	4	Y	260
Plantago coronopus	Annual to perennial	Sunny; tolerates saline soil, good drainage near its northern limit helps survival	Leaves, shoots: from spring (cut-and-come-again)	1		83
Polygonum viviparum	Perennial	Open woodland to sunny	Bulbils: summer Tubers: autumn	3		241
Ranunculus ficaria	Perennial	Sunny to woodland; tolerates dry summer conditions	Leaves: winter to spring before flowering	4	Y	74
Rheum x rhabarbarum	Perennial	Sunny to open woodland; prefers damp soil but will grow in quite dry soil	Stems: spring Emerging flower broccolis: summer	3		243
Rumex acetosa	Perennial	Open woodland to sunny; prefers damp soil but will grow in quite dry soil	Leaves: spring (all year for non-flowering cultivars)	1		221

Species	Form	Habitat	Main Harvest	Edimental? (scale 1 to 5)	Forest Garden	Page no.
Rumex scutatus	Perennial	Sunny	Leaves: most productive in spring but available from spring to autumn (cut-and-come-again)	2		85
Scorzonera hispanica	Perennial	Sunny	Leaves, shoots: spring Flower stems, buds and flowers: summer Roots: autumn to winter	3		63
Silene vulgaris	Perennial	Sunny to open woodland	Leaves, shoots: spring	3		77
Sium sisarum	Perennial	Open woodland to sunny; good drainage at its northern limit helps survival	Leaves, shoots: spring Roots: autumn	2		49
Sonchus spp.	Annual to Perennial	Open to half shade	Shoots: spring Leaves: summer	2		164
Taraxacum officinale	Perennial	Open woodland to sunny; edible lawn	Leaves and crowns: spring Flower stalks: early summer Flowers: summer Roots: autumn	3	Y	38
Tradescantia ohiensis	Perennial	Sunny to open woodland (*T. aspera* for deeper shade); tolerates drought	Leaves, shoots: spring Flowers: summer	5	Y (*T. aspera*)	193
Typha latifolia	Perennial	Sunny to somewhat shady conditions; in ponds, even in water depths of over 40cm	Leaf shoots: spring Flower spikes: summer Pollen: late summer Rhizomes: winter	4		203
Urtica dioica	Perennial	Open woodland to sunny; prefers damp rich soil	Leaves: spring to summer (cut-and-come-again)	1	Y	28
Wasabia japonica	Perennial	Woodland to open woodland; prefers cool running water	Leaves: spring Flowers: late spring Roots: autumn	3	Y	148

LIST OF *CALZONE* INGREDIENTS

see discussion on page 62

Allium ampeloprasum; Babington's leek
Allium moly; Golden garlic
Allium schoenoprasum; Chives
Allium sphaerocephalon; Round-headed leek
Allium vineale; Crow garlic
Apium nodiflorum; Fool's watercress
Armoracia rusticana; Horseradish
Asparagus officinalis; Asparagus
Balsamita major; Alecost
Bellis perennis; Daisy
Berberis vulgaris; Common wintercress
Beta vulgaris ssp. *maritima*; Sea beet
Campanula rapunculus; Rampion
Cardamine flexuosa; Wavy bittercress
Carum carvi; Caraway
Chenopodium bonus-henricus; Good King Henry
Cichorium intybus; Chicory
Cirsium oleraceum; Cabbage thistle
Clematis vitalba; Old man's beard
Cynara cardunculus; Cardoon
Filipendula vulgaris; Dropwort
Fragaria vesca; Wild strawberry
Hedysarum coronarium; French honeysuckle
Hypochaeris maculata; Spotted hawkweed
Lamium maculatum; Spotted nettle
Leontodon hispidus; Rough hawkbit
Leucanthemum vulgare; Ox-eye daisy
Lychnis flos-cuculi; Ragged Robin

Malva moschata; Musk mallow
Myrrhis odorata; Sweet cicely
Ornithogalum pyrenaicum; Bath asparagus
Oxalis acetosella; Wood sorrel
Phyteuma spicatum; Spiked rampion
Plantago coronopus; Buckler-leaved plantain
Plantago lanceolata; Ribwort plantain
Plantago major; Greater plantain
Persicaria bistorta; Bistort
Primula elatior; Oxlip
Primula vulgaris; Primrose
Rheum ribes
Rosa pimpinellifolia; Burnet rose
Rubus caesius; Dewberry
Rumex acetosa; Sorrel
Rumex acetosella; Sheep sorrel
Rumex alpinus; Alpine dock
Rumex patientia; Patience dock
Rumex scutatus; Buckler-leaved sorrel
Sanguisorba minor; Salad burnet
Scorzonera hispanica; Scorzonera
Silene dioica; Red campion
Silene vulgaris; Bladder campion
Taraxacum officinale; Dandelion
Trifolium pratense; Red clover
Urtica dioica; Stinging nettle
Valerianella locusta; Lamb's lettuce
Veronica beccabunga; Brookweed

BIBLIOGRAPHY AND REFERENCES

Ali-Shtayeh, MS et al (2008) 'Traditional knowledge of wild edible plants used in Palestine (northern West Bank): A comparative study' in *J. Ethnobiology and Ethnomedicine*. Vol 4, 13pp.

Amundsen, R (1907) *Nordvestpassasjen*. Kristiania, Norway.

Anon *Lökar På Bordet*. Botaniska trädgården Lunds Universitet. 38pp.

Anon RHS Plant Finder. apps.rhs.org.uk/rhsplantfinder

Anon (1976) *Ville Planter Til Mat Og Drikke (Nytevekstboka)*. Dreyers Forlag. Oslo.

Anon (1995) 'Neglected crops: 1492 from a different perspective' in *FAO Plant Production and Protection Series*.

Anon (2002) *Allium Crop Science: Recent Advances* (Rabinowitch, H.B. and L. Currah, eds.) CABI International.

Anon (2011) *Edible Wild Plants of Siberia* (in Russian), www.sibrast.ru.

Arenas, P and GA Scarpa (2003) 'The consumption of *Typha domingensis* Pers. (Typhaceae) Pollen among the ethnic groups of the Gran Chaco, South America' in *Econ. Bot.* Vol 57, No 2, pp181-188.

Baranov, AI (1967) 'Wild vegetables of the Chinese in Manchuria' in *Econ. Bot.* Vol 21, pp140-155.

Barstow, SF (2007) 'Caucasian spinach' in *Permaculture Magazine* No 52, pp46-47.

Barton, W. (1818) *Vegetable Materia Medica of the United States: Or, Medical Botany: Containing a Botanical, General, and Medical History, of Medicinal Plants Indigenous to the United States*, Vol. 2.

Baser, K (1997) 'Current knowledge on the wild food and non-food plants of Turkey' in *CIHEAM Options Méditer.* Vol. 23, pp129–159.

Bates, J (2008) 'Hablitzia: Climbing spinach, a new perennial for cold climates' in *Permaculture Activist*, No 68, pp17-18.

Berkutenko, AN and EG Virek (1995) *Lekarstvennye i Piscevye Rastenija Aljaski i Dal'nego Vostoka Rossii*. Vladivostok (*Medicinal and Edible Plants of Alaska and the Russian Far East*), Izdat, Dal'nevostocnogo Univ., 190pp.

Blekastad, H (1979) *Naturens Spiskammer*, Gyldendal.

Block, E (2009) *Garlic and Other Alliums: The Lore and the Science*, RSC Publishing, Cambridge, UK.

Bowles, EA (1914) *My Garden in Summer*, Dodge publishing 315pp.

Bretschneider, E *(1882) Botanicon Sinicum: Notes on Chinese Botany from Native and Western Sources*, Trubner & co, London.

Brill, S (1994) *Identifying and Harvesting Edible and Medicinal Plants*, Harper Collins, New York.

Brill, S (2002) *The Forager's Culinary Guide*, Harvard Common Press.

Britten, J (ed.) (1881) *The Names of Herbes A.D. 1548 by William Turner*, N. Trubner & Co., London.

Brøndegaard, VJ (1978-80) *Folk og Flora. I-IV*, Rosenkilde and Bagger.

Brussell, DE (2004) 'Araliaceae species used for culinary and medicinal purposes in Niigata-ken, Japan' in *Econ. Bot.* Vol 58, pp736-739.

Burr, F (1865) *Field and Garden Vegetables of America*, Applewood Books.

Campbell, G and Hall, A (2006) 'The flora of Roman roads, towns and gardens' in *The Archaeologist* Vol 50, pp32-33.

Chia, Ssu-hsieh (5th Cent. AD) *Ch'i-minyao-shu*.

Clarke, CB (1977) *Edible and Useful Plants of California*, University of California Press.

Coitir, NM (2008) *Irish Wild Plants: Myths, Legends and Folklore*, The Collins Press, Cork.

Cook, J (1824) *The Three Voyages of Captain Cook Round the World: With a Map of the World*, J. Limbird, 637pp.

Coon, N (1974) *The Dictionary of Useful Plants*, Rodale Press.

Cooper, RC and RC Cambie (1991) *New Zealand's Economic Native Plants*, Oxford Univ. Press.

Couplan, F (1983) *Le Régal Végétal: Plantes Sauvages Comestibles*, Debard.

Crowe, A (1990) *Native Edible Plants of New Zealand*, Hodder and Stoughton, Auckland.

Davidson, A (1999) *The Oxford Companion to Food*, Oxford University Press.

Davies, D (1992) *Alliums: The Ornamental Onions*, B.T. Batsford, London.

Della, A, D Paraskeva-Hadjichambi and ACh Hadjichambis (2006) 'An ethnobotanical survey of wild edible plants of Paphos and Larnaca countryside of Cyprus' in *J. of Ethnobiology and Ethnomedicine*, Vol 2, pp34-43.

Deppe, C (2000) *Breed Your Own Vegetable Varieties*, Green Books.

Dias, JS (2012) 'Portuguese perennial kale: A relic leafy vegetable crop' in (Notes on neglected and underutilized crops) *Genet. Resour. Crop Evol.* Vol 59, pp1201-1206.

Diaz-Bettencourt, M et al (1999) 'Weeds as a source for human consumption; A comparison between tropical and temperate Latin America' in *Revista de Biologia Tropical* Vol 47.

Dixon, ES (1855) *The Kitchen Garden; Or, The Culture in the Open Ground of Roots, Vegetables, Herbs and Fruits*, Routledge, Warne and Routledge, London.

Dixon, GR (2006) *Vegetable Brassicas and Related Crucifers*. Crop Production Science in Horticulture, No14, CABI publishing.

Dogan, Y, S Baslar, G Ay and HH Mert (2004) 'The use of wild edible plants in western and central Anatolia (Turkey)' in *Econ. Bot.* Vol 58, pp684-690.

Dreon, AL and MG Paoletti (2009) 'The wild food (plants and insects) in western Friuli local knowledge (Friuli-Venezia Giulia, northeastern Italy)' in *Contrib. Nat. Hist.* Vol 12, pp461–488.

Dunfjeld, S (2011) 'Nyttevekster i samisk tradisjon (II)' (Useful plants in Sámi tradition) in *Sopp og Nyttevekster*, Vol 7, pp34-37.

Eidlitz, K (1969) *Food and Emergency Food in the Circumpolar Area*, PhD Thesis, University of Uppsala.

Elias, TS and PA Dykeman (1982) *Field Guide to North American Edible Wild Plants*, Outdoor Life Books, New York.

Ertug, F (2004) 'Wild Edible Plants of the Bodrum Area (Mugla, Turkey)' in *Turk J Bot.* Vol 28, pp161-174.

Evelyn, J (1699) *Acetaria: A Discourse of Sallets*.

Facciola, S (1998) *Cornucopia II: A Sourcebook of Edible Plants*, Kampong Publications, Vista, USA.

Fern, K (1997) *Plants For A Future: Edible and Useful Plants for a Healthier World*, Permanent Publications.

Fernald, ML and AC Kinsey (1958) *Edible Wild Plants of Eastern North America*, Harper, New York.

Forster, G (1786) *De Plantis Esculentis Insularum Oceani Australis Commentatio Botanica*, Haude & Spencer.

Fosså, O (2006) 'Angelica: From Norwegian mountains to the English trifle' in *Wild Food – Proceedings of the 2004 Oxford Symposium on Food and Cookery*, (Richard Hosking, ed.), Prospect Books, Totnes, pp131-142.

Gabrielian, E and O Fragman (2008) *Flowers of the Transcaucasus and Adjacent Areas: Including Armenia, Eastern Turkey, Southern Georgia, Azerbaijan and Northern Iran*, Gantner Verlag, 416pp.

Gail, P (1989) *The Delightful Delicious Daylily: Recipes and More*, Goosefoot Acres Press, Cleveland, Ohio.

Gail, P (1994) *The Dandelion Celebration: A Guide to Unexpected Cuisine*, Goosefoot Acres Press, Cleveland, Ohio.

Gaut JB (1871) 'La salade champêtre' in *Rev. Agric. Forest Provence*, pp52–60.

Gibbons, E (1962) *Stalking the Wild Asparagus*, Alan C. Hood & Co, Chambersberg.

Grieve, M (1931) *A Modern Herbal*, J. Cape (online at www.botanical.com/botanical/mgmh/mgmh.html).

Gronover, CS and D Prüfer (2010) 'Rubber doesn't (just) grow on trees' in *TCE Today*, May 2010.

Grossheim, A (1952) *Rastitelnie Botatstva Kavkasa*, Moskovovskoe Obtshestvo Islitatelei Prirodi, Moscow.

Guarrera, PM and LM Lucia (2007) 'Ethnobotanical remarks on central and southern Italy' in *J. Ethnobiology and Ethnomedicine* Vol 3, pp23-34.

Hadjichambis, ACh et al (2008) 'Wild and semi-domesticated food plant consumption in seven circum-Mediterranean areas' in *Intnl. J. Food Sci. and Nutr.* Vol 59, pp383-414.

Hanelt, P (2001) *Alliaceae*. In *Mansfeld's Encyclopedia of Agricultural and Horticultural Crops*, Vol. 4, Springer-Verlag. Vienna, pp 2250-2269. (on-line at mansfeld.ipk-gatersleben.de)

Hart, RA de J (1991) *Forest Gardening*, Green Books.

Hedrick, UP (1919) *Sturtevant's Edible Plants of the World*, Dover Publications, New York (online at www.swsbm.com/Ephemera/Sturtevants_Edible_Plants.pdf).

Prendergast, HDV and N Rumball (2000) 'Walking sticks as seed savers – The case of the Jersey kale' in *Econ. Bot.* Vol 54, pp141-143.

Hill, DJ and Price, B (2000) 'Ornithogalum pyrenaicum L.', in *J. Ecology* Vol 88, pp354-365.

Hoffberg, CF (1792) *Anwisning til Wäxt-Rikets Kännedom*, Stockholm.

Holmboe, J (1941) *Gratis Mat av Ville Planter* (*Free Food from Wild Plants*), Cappelens, Oslo.

Horace (ca 30 BC) in *Odes 31, ver 15*.

Hosking, R (1995) *A Dictionary of Japanese Food*, Tuttle Publishing, 240pp.

Hu, S-Y (2005) *Food Plants of China*, Chinese University Press.

Hu, Y (1640) *Nung Cheng Ts'uan Shu* (*Complete Treatise on Agriculture*). 60 volumes.

Høeg, OH (1976) *Planter og Tradisjon*, Universitetsforlaget.

Irving, M (2009) *The Forager Handbook: A Guide to the Edible Plants of Britain*, Ebury Press.

Israelsson, L (1996) *Köksträdgården: Det Gröna Arvet*, Wahlström & Widstrand, Stockholm.

Israelsson, L (1998) *Din Orientalske Køkkenhave*, Christian Ejlers' Forlag, Copenhagen.

Israelsson, L (2002) *Jordens Täppor. Köksträdgårdar i Hela Världen*, Wahlström & Widstrand, Stockholm.

Johansson, L (1947) 'Frostviklapparnas födoämnen och maträtter fördomsdag' in *Jämten*, pp69-95.

Johnson, CP (1862) *Useful Plants of Great Britain: A Treatise Upon the Principle Native Vegetables Capable of Application as Food, Medicine, or in the Arts and Manufactures*, William Kent & Co, London.

Josselyn, J (1674) *An Account of Two Voyages to New-England*. Giles Widdows, London.

Källman, S (1997) *Vilda Växter Som Mat Och Medicin* (*Wild Plants as Food and Medicine*), ICA publishers, Sweden.

Khasbagan, H-Y Huai and S-J Pei (2000) 'Wild plants in the diet of the Arhorchin Mongol herdsmen in inner Mongolia' in *Econ. Bot.* Vol 54, pp528-536.

Kuhnlein, HV and NJ Turner (1986) 'Cow-parsnip (*Heracleum maximum Michx.*): An indigenous vegetable of native people of northwestern North America' in *J. Ethnobiology* Vol 6, pp309-324.

Ladio, AH (2001) 'The maintenance of wild edible plant gathering in a Mapuche community of Patagonia' in *Econ. Bot.* Vol 55, pp243-254.

Laghetti, G (2002) 'Collecting of landraces and wild relatives of cultivated plants in Ponziane Islands and Tuscan archipelago, Italy' in *PGR Newsletter*, No 131, pp55-62.

Larkcom, J (1989) *The Salad Garden*, Penguin Books.

Larkcom, J (1991) *Oriental Vegetables*, Frances Lincoln Publishers.

Larkcom, L and R Phillips (2003) *The Organic Salad Garden*, Frances Lincoln Publishers.

Lawrence, WR (1884) *The Valley of Kashmir*, Henry Frowde, London.

Leonti, M, S Nebel, D Rivera and M Heinrich (2006) 'Wild gathered food plants in the European Mediterranean: A comparative analysis' in *Econ. Bot.* Vol 60, pp130-142.

Li, S, P Smith and GA Stuart (2003) *Chinese Medicinal Herbs: A Modern Edition of a Classic Sixteenth-Century Manual*, Courier Dover Publications.

von Linné, C (ed.) (1760) *Grönsakstorget (Macellum Olitorium)*, Uppsala, Sweden.

Lentini, F and F Venza (2007) 'Wild food plants of popular use in Sicily' in J. *Ethnobiology and Ethnomedicine* Vol 3, pp15-27.

Li, H-L (1969) 'The vegetables of ancient China' in *Econ. Bot.* Vol 23, pp253-260.

Lightfoot, J (1789) *Flora Scotica: Or, A Systematic Arrangement, in the Linnæan Method, of the Native Plants of Scotland and the Hebrides*, London.

Low, T (1988) *Wild Food Plants of Australia*, Angus & Robertson.

Low, T (1989) *Bush Tucker: Australia's Wild Food Harvest*, Angus & Robertson Pubs.

Luczaj, L and W Szymanski (2007) 'Wild vascular plants gathered for consumption in the Polish countryside: a review' in *J. Ethnobiology and Ethnomedicine* Vol 3, pp17-39.

Mabey, R (1972) *Food for Free*, Fontana/Collins, Glasgow.

Mabey, R (1997) *Flora Britannica*, Chatto & Windus, London.

Manandhar, NP (2002) *Plants and People of Nepal*, Timber Press, Portland.

Mansfeld, R (from 1988) *Mansfeld's World Database of Agricultural and Horticultural Crops*, mansfeld.ipk-gatersleben.de

Mason, R (1950) 'Wild Plants for Food and Medicine' in *Tararua* Vol 4, pp45-50.

McFadden, C (2007) 'Foliar Feeding' in *The Garden*, September 2007, pp604-607.

Mehus, H and B Vorren (1978) 'Viltvoksende, grønne matplanter i Nord-Norge' in *Ottar* Vol 16, pp106-107.

Messiaen, C-M and A Rouamba (2004) *Allium ampeloprasum L*, In Grubben, G.J.H. & Denton, O.A. (eds). PROTA 2: Vegetables/Légumes. [CD-Rom], PROTA, Wageningen, Netherlands.

Moerman, DE (1998) *Native American Ethnobotany*, Timber Press, Portland, Oregon.

Van der Muelen, H (1998) *Traditionele Streekproducten / Druk 1: Gastronomisch Erfgoed van Nederland (Traditional Local Products / Gastronomical Heritage of the Netherlands)*, Reed Business Information, 95pp.

von Mueller, F (1891) *Select Extra-Tropical Plants: Readily Eligible for Industrial Culture Or Naturalisation, With Indications of Their Native Countries and Some of Their Uses*, Government of Victoria, Melbourne.

Musselmann, LJ (1997) 'Notes on economic plants: Is Allium kurrat the leek of the Bible?' in *Econ. Bot.* Vol 51, pp399-400.

Mvere, B and M van der Werff (2004) '*Brassica oleracea L.* (leaf cabbage)' in Grubben, G.J.H. & Denton, O.A. (eds.), PROTA 2: Vegetables/Légumes [CD-Rom], PROTA, Wageningen, Netherlands.

Nash, M (1995) *Cooking North America's Finest Gourmet Fiddleheads*, J. Melvin Nash.

Nebel, S, A Pieroni and M Heinrich (2006) 'Ta chòrta: Wild edible greens used in the Graecanic area in Calabria, southern Italy' in *Appetite* Vol 47, pp333-342.

Niiberg, T and E Lauringson (2007) *Umbrohud Tüliks Ja Tuluks*, Maalehe Raamat.

Nilsson, A (1976) *Spiselige Vekster i Skog och Mark*, Cappelens Forlag, Oslo.

Nyman, CF (1868) *Utkast Till Svenska Växternas Naturhistoria II*.

Opie, I and M Tatum (ed.) (1989) *A Dictionary of Superstitions*, Oxford.

Paoletti, MG, AL Dreon and GG Lorenzoni (1995) 'Pistic. traditional food from western Friuli, N.E. Italy' in *Econ. Bot.* Vol 49, pp26-30.

Pardo-de-Santayana, M, J Tardío, E Blanco, AM Carvalho, JJ Lastra, E San Miguel and R Morales (2007) 'Traditional knowledge of wild edible plants used in the northwest of the Iberian Peninsula (Spain and Portugal): A comparative study' in *J. Ethnobiology and Ethnomedicine* Vol 3, pp27-38.

Paulli, S (1648) *Flora Danica*.

Pemberton, RW and NS Lee (1996) 'Wild food plants in South Korea: Market presence, new crops and export to the United States' in *Econ. Bot.* Vol 50, pp57-60.

Péron, JY (1989) 'Approche de la physiologie et de la phytotechnie du *Crambe maritima* (*Crambe maritima* L.), cultivé à partir de boutures et produit sur le modèle de la chicorée de Bruxelles' in *Acta Hortic.* Vol 242, pp249–258.

Péron, JY (1990) 'Seakale: A new vegetable produced as etiolated sprouts' in Janick, J and JE Simon (eds.), *Advances in New Crops*, Timber Press, Portland, OR, pp419-422.

Petzold GM, GC Catril and CD Duarte (2006) 'Physicochemical characterization of petioles of Pangue (*Gunnera tinctoria*)' in *Rev. Chil. Nutr.* Vol 33, pp539-543.

Phillips, R (1983) *Wild Food*, Pan Books, London.

Phillips, R and M Rix (1991) *Perennials, Vol. 2 Late Perennials*, Pan Books, London.

Phillips, R and M Rix (1993) *Vegetables*, Pan Books, London.

Pieroni, A (1999) 'Gathered wild food plants in the upper valley of the Serchio River (Garfagnana), Central Italy' in *Econ. Bot.* Vol 53, pp327-341.

Pieroni, A and ME Giusti (2009) 'Alpine ethnobotany in Italy: Traditional knowledge of gastronomic and medicinal plants among the Occitans of the upper Varaita valley, Piedmont' in *J. of Ethnobiology and Ethnomedicine* Vol 5, pp32-45.

Pieroni, A, S Nebel, C Quave, H Munz and M Heinrich (2002) 'Ethnopharmacology of liakra: Traditional weedy vegetables of the Arbereshe of the vulture area in southern Italy' in *Journal of Ethnopharmacology* Vol 81, pp165-185.

Pliny the Elder (23-29 AD) *Naturalis Historia*.

Pratt, K and R Rutt (1996) *Korea: A Historical and Cultural Dictionary*, Curzon Press.

Preuss, HG, D Clouatre, A Mohamadi and ST Jarrell (2001) 'Wild garlic has a greater effect than regular garlic on blood pressure and blood chemistries of rats' in *Int. Urol. Nephrol.* Vol 32, pp525-530.

Ray, J, GJ Camel and JP de Tournefort (1686) *Historia Plantarum*.

Retzius, AJ (1806) *Försök til en Flora Oeconomica Sveciæ*, Lund, Sweden.

Rivera, D, C Obón, M Heinrich, C Inocencio, A Verde and J Fajardo (2006) 'Gathered Mediterranean food plants – Ethnobotanical investigations and historical development' in *Local Mediterranean Food Plants and Nutraceuticals* (*Forum Nutr.*), Heinrich M, WE Müller and C Galli (eds.) Basel, Karger vol 59, pp18–74.

Sacherer, J (1979) 'The high altitude ethnobotany of the Rolwaling Sherpas' in *Contrib. Nepal Studies* Vol 6, pp45-64.

Schmid, WG (1991) *The Genus Hosta*, Portland, Timber Press.

de Serres, O (1651) *Le Jardinier Français, Le Cuisinier Français*.

Seymour, J (1978). *The Self-Sufficient Gardener*, Faber & Faber Ltd., London.

Shishkin, BK (1968) *Flora of the USSR. Vol. 16 Umbelliflorae.* (Israel Program for Scientific Translations. Jerusalem 1973.)

Small, E (1997) *Culinary Herbs*, National Research Council of Canada.

Sundriyal, M, RC Sunriyal and E Sharma (2004) 'Dietary use of wild plant resources in the Sikkim Himalaya, India' in *Econ. Bot.* Vol 58, pp626-638.

Sørensen, FT (1994) 'Skvalderkål' in *Fra Kvangård til Humlekule* Vol 24, pp63-68.

Tardio, J, M Pardo-de-Santayana and R Morales (2006) 'Ethnobotanical review of wild edible plants in Spain' in *Botanical J. Linnean Soc.* vol 152, pp27–71.

Thayer, S (2006) *The Forager's Harvest*, Forager's Harvest Publishing (www.foragersharvest.com)

Thayer, S (2010) *Nature's Garden*, Forager's Harvest Publishing (www.foragersharvest.com)

Thomson, B and I Shaw (2002) 'A comparison of risk and protective factors of colorectal cancer in the diet of the New Zealand Maori and non-Maori' in *Asian Pac. J. Cancer Prevent.* Vol 3, pp319-324.

Toensmeier, E (2007) *Perennial Vegetables*, Chelsea Green Publishing.

Trichopoulou, A et al (2000) 'Nutritional composition and flavonoid content of edible wild greens and green pies: A potential rich source of antioxidant nutrients in the Mediterranean diet' in *Food Chemistry* Vol 70, pp319-323.

Turner, NJ, LJ Lukasz, P Migliorini, A Pieroni, AL Dreon, LE Sacchetti, and MG Paoletti (2011) 'Edible and tended wild plants, traditional ecological knowledge and agroecology' in *Critical Reviews in Plant Sciences* Vol 30, pp198-225.

Van den Eyden, V, E Cueva, and O Cabrera (2003) 'Wild foods from southern Ecuador' in *Econ. Bot.* Vol 57, pp576-603.

van Wyck, B-E (2005) *Food Plants of the World,* Timber Press.

van Wyck, B-E and N Gericke (2000) *People's Plants*, Briza Publications.

Vilmorin-Andrieux & co (1856) *Description des Plantes Potagères*, Paris.

Vilmorin-Andrieux & co (1920) *The Vegetable Garden*, (English edition). E.P. Dutton & Co.

Vizgirdas, RS and EM Rey-Vizgirdas (2009) *Wild Plants of the Sierra Nevada*, University of Nevada Press, 384pp.

Weaver, WW (2000) *100 Vegetables and Where They Came From*, Algonquin Books, Chapel Hill.

West, J (2009) 'Food exploration in the Caucasus' in *Permaculture Activist*, p72.

Whitefield, P (1996) *How to Make a Forest Garden*, Permanent Publications.

Williams, JT and N Haq (2002) *Global Research on Underutilized Crops: An Assessment of Current Activities and Proposals for Enhanced Cooperation*, Bioversity International.

Worlidge, J (1682) *Systema Horticulturae, Or, The Art of Gardening*, London.

Wright, CA (2001) *Mediterranean Vegetables: A Cook's ABC of Vegetables and Their Preparation,* Harvard Common Press.

Zeven, AC, Suurs, LCJM and J Waninge (1996) 'Diversity for enzymes, flowering behaviour and purple plant colour of perennial kale (*Brassica oleracea L.* var. *ramosa DC*) in the Netherlands' in *Proc. Int. Symp. on Brassicas, Ninth Crucifer Genetics Workshop.* (Eds. J.S. Dias, I. Crute. A.A. Monteiro) ISHS Acta Hort., pp61-66.

Zeven AC, KJ Dehmer, T Gladis, K Hammer and H Lux (1998) 'Are the duplicates of perennial kale (*Brassica oleracea L.* var. *ramosa DC.*) true duplicates as determined by RAPD analysis?' in *Genet. Resour. Crop Evol.* Vol 45, pp105–111.

INDEX

Books to empower your head, heart and hands

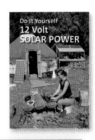

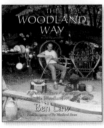

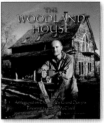

For our full range of titles, to purchase books
and to sign up to our enewsletter see:

www.permanentpublications.co.uk

Subscribe to
permaculture
practical solutions for self-reliance

Permaculture magazine offers tried and tested ways
of creating flexible, low cost approaches
to sustainable living

Print subscribers have FREE digital and app access
to over 20 years of back issues

To subscribe, check our daily updates
and to sign up to our eNewsletter see:

www.permaculture.co.uk